Baseball Roots

*The Fascinating Birth of America's Game
and the Amazing Players that were its Champions*

Compiled and Edited by
Ron McCulloch

Warwick Publishing
Toronto Los Angeles
www.warwickgp.com

We acknowledge the financial support of the Government of Canada
throught the Book Publishing Industry Development Program for our
publishing activities.

ISBN 1-894020-71-5

Published by Warwick Publishing Inc.
162 John Street, Toronto, ON M5V 2E5
www.warwickgp.com

Distributed by LPC Group
1436 West Randolph Street
Chicago, Illinois 60607
www.coolbooks.com

Photographs: courtesy Baseball Hall of Fame Library, Cooperstown, N.Y.

Design: Kimberley Young, mercer digital design

Copy Editor: Melinda Tate

Printed in Canada

Baseball Roots

*The Fascinating Birth of America's Game
and the Amazing Players that were its Champions*

Contents

Introduction

In 1904, Al Spalding, a former major league pitching ace who had gone on to become a baseball executive and wealthy manufacturer of sporting equipment, decided that it was demeaning that the great American pastime of baseball actually found its origins in the English children's game rounders. He assembled some like-minded friends, including two U.S. Senators, and established a commission to look into the origins of baseball. Their ultimate purpose was, if possible, to give baseball an American ancestry.

The commission, which was chaired by former National League president A.G. Mills, declared a deceased American Army General and Civil War hero by the name of Abner Doubleday to be the inventor of baseball. Their findings were based on a letter they had received from an elderly man by the name of Abner Graves who was a boyhood friend of Doubleday's.

Graves stated that, sometime around 1839, he had seen Doubleday directing some "20 to

50 boys" in a Cooperstown, N.Y., school yard while they played a game of Town Ball, a form of rounders. Because Doubleday had the boys form themselves into teams with eleven players on each side, and that four bases had been used in the game, Graves was convinced he had been witnessing the actual invention of baseball.

Unfortunately, the commission had no real evidence to support this conclusion. The game Graves described involved the practice of "soaking" runners, or throwing the ball at them to get an out, had been played in North America for at least 75 years prior to 1839, with definite sides of teams or sometimes with just one player against the whole school yard, using any number of bases. Furthermore, Doubleday, a voluminous letter writer, never mentioned the game, or was known by anyone who acquainted with him to have mentioned the game.

But these facts apparently made no difference to the commission. They accepted Graves' story and in 1907, declared Abner Doubleday as the inventor of baseball. Doubleday, the gallant Civil War hero, had turned out to be a convenient figurehead for the commission in their quest to give the game an all-American heritage.

From Elysian Fields to Cincinnati

Baseball's Origins

In the Beginning
There Was Rounders

Baseball took root on this continent in the mid 1700's when
English lads brought an offshoot of
the game of cricket to our shores.
This game, in which the fielders
put out a runner by belting him
with the ball as he ran from one
base to another, was called
"rounders" and it would evolve
over the next 150 years to become what we now know as baseball.

No one person invented baseball; many people contributed to the development of the game, and yes, there was one man who contributed more than
most, but it was nevertheless a constant refinement of rules and regulations
by many people over many years that gave us the game we have today.

Although the game of rounders took on many forms, it usually involved
a pitcher throwing a ball to a batter who would then hit it and run from base
to base while the ball was being fielded. In order to get him out, the fielders would try to "soak" or "plug" the runner with the ball — that is, hit him
with it — while he was off base.

Even though rules for rounders or rounders-type games were occasionally published in books in the 1700's and early 1800's, the game was usually played according to local custom, meaning the number of players on
a side, the number of bases (usually anywhere from two to five), the way

they were laid out and the distance between them, and other rules would vary from place to place.

Rounders was a pickup game played mostly by children, with the rules constantly subject to change and friendly dispute. For bases they used rocks, stakes, posts, inverted milking stools or anything else that was handy. Bats could be ax handles, rake handles, wagon spokes or any piece of wood, either flat or round, that was available. Balls were usually constructed of a piece of cork or some shreds of India rubber wrapped in twine and covered with chamois or sheepskin.

In one variation of the game there were no competing sides; the batter simply faced a yard full of playmates. Another variation involved one player throwing the ball at a barn wall so that it would bounce off, and another player, who was stationed about 12 feet away, hitting it with a stick, then trying to run to the wall and back while the first player retrieved the ball and tried to belt the runner with it before he returned to his original position.

Rounders the game was also known as "round ball," "sting ball," "soak ball," "burn ball," "town ball," the "Massachusetts Game," and sometimes even "base ball."

Another form of the game was called "catapult ball" or "cat ball." In this game a flat bat would be laid seesaw fashion across a log or rock with the ball (or some type of projectile, often a piece of wood) set on the lower end. One player would catapult the projectile into the air for another player to hit with his hand or a stick. Runners would then go back and forth between bases while the projectile was being retrieved. Sometimes this game involved digging one or more holes in the ground; the batter would then have to stick the bat in a hole to attain safety from being put out. As a result, the game was sometimes called "one hole cat," "two hole cat," "three hole cat," etc. As with rounders, there were no set or "official" regulations for cat ball; the rules would vary from location to location.

Versions of rounders and cat ball were played in the 1700's and early 1800's on cow pastures, village greens and college campuses throughout New England and the northeastern states.

Fortunately for us, this chaotic profusion of primitive ball-and-bat-type games was about to come to an end, for the introduction of what would become a universal form of baseball was just around the corner.

Baseball Grows Up

It was in the city of New York, in the year 1845, that some of the most significant developments in the history of baseball took place. It was at this time that a young fellow by the name of Alexander Cartwright put down on paper a set of rules and regulations that would be the foundation of today's game.

If anyone could be called the father of baseball it is Alexander Joy Cartwright, Jr. This 25-year-old bank teller and volunteer fireman, who stood 6'2" and weighed 215 pounds (which made him a giant in those days), was the founder of the Knickerbocker Base Ball Club of New York, a group of young gentlemen who usually got together on Sunday afternoons in the summer in a vacant lot at Murray Hill, near the present corner of Lexington Avenue and 34th street, to play baseball according to Cartwright's rules and regulations. He'd show up each week with a new design for baseball and they'd play and experiment.

Alexander Cartwright Jr.

What Cartwright did was take some of the various elements that were being used in the different forms of early baseball being played at that time and integrate them into his game, adding a few wrinkles of his own along the way. In doing so, Alexander Cartwright virtually handed us the game of baseball on a silver platter.

Cartwright didn't care for the five-base layout commonly used in the New York City area at that time. Instead, he incorporated a diamond configuration then popular in the Philadelphia vicinity. But he was not satisfied with the distance between the bases — he thought they were too close together — so, after a bit of experimenting, he made them farther apart, specifying that the distance straight across from home to second base and from first to third base would be 42 paces.

Now if you were to measure around Cartwright's diamond, you'd find that the distance from home to first, and from first to second, and so on, works out to be very close to the 90-foot distance between the bases we still use today. Of Cartwright's many baseball innovations, this one measurement was probably his greatest achievement.

Cartwright's specification of 90 feet between the bases meant that on a cleanly handled ground ball, both the throw and the runner would arrive at first base at the same time, with the throw usually beating the runner by a split second. This added elements of precision, perfection, drama and excitement to the game, because the ball had to be perfectly fielded and accurately thrown to get the runner out by half a step. If Cartwright had made the distance a few feet less it would have given a tremendous advantage to the runner, and if he had made it a few feet more it would have given the infielders too much time to scoop up the ball and fire it to first. This measurement has stood the test of time, remaining a constant part of baseball since 1845

Other dimensions have changed over the years. The distance the pitcher tosses the ball to home plate started out at 45 feet in Cartwright's day when they still pitched underhand; then it was changed to 50 feet in 1881; two years later pitchers were allowed to throw overhand, and the pitching distance was finally changed to the present 60 feet 6 inches in 1893. Outfield wall distances and configurations have always varied from ballpark to ballpark and still do today, but the 90 feet between bases has been the same ever since Alexander Cartwright staked out his diamond in 1845.

But this wasn't Cartwright's only innovation. Among the other rules and regulations he incorporated into his game were these:

Cartwright preferred the diamond shape to the square five-base layout. He modified the size of the diamond to fit his specifications by walking off 42 paces from home to second, and 42 paces from first to third, thereby giving us the dimensions for the baseball diamond that we still use today.

90 feet

90 feet

90 feet

90 feet

42 paces

Tagging the Runner

Cartwright did away with the practice of "soaking" or "plugging" the runners, that is, throwing the ball at them to get an out. Cartwright replaced this with tagging the runner with the ball instead, or getting the ball to the base ahead of the runner.

Canvas Bases

Cartwright eliminated the practice of using rocks or posts for bases and replaced them with flat bases. On his first diamond the bases consisted of canvas bags filled with sand or sawdust, and he used an iron plate for home base.

The Shortstop

On his diamond, Cartwright stationed one player at each of the bases, and then decided there would be only one "short roving infielder" (there had been two up until then) and positioned him between second and third, thereby creating the position of shortstop. In those days the number of players stationed in the outfield usually varied from game to game, so Cartwright specified there would be three outfielders and eliminated one of the two catchers they used behind the plate at the time, thus giving us the same nine positions on the field that we have today.

Batting Order

Cartwright wrote that the players would bat in a regular order, which was to be decided upon before the game.

Three Outs

Cartwright decided there would be three outs per side per inning. Previously, the whole team would have to come to bat before they changed sides, making for some extremely long ball games.

Three Strikes

Cartwright's rules also specified that a batter would be out after three strikes.

The Foul Ball

The ball would be considered foul if knocked outside of the ninety-degree quadrant of the field.

The Third Strike Rule

Cartwright decided that a dropped third strike was to be considered a fair ball, thereby enabling the batter to make a run for first base (a rule that still exists today), and he decreed that a runner could take the next base when a balk was made by the pitcher. Cartwright also stipulated that a run scored before a third force-out did not count.

His rules stated that the game would last until the first team had scored 21 runs (or "aces" as they were called then), after an equal number of players on both sides had come to bat. (The concept of the nine inning game did not come along until 1857.)

Although some of Alexander Cartwright's innovations, such as the three strike rule and the actual diamond configuration itself, did not originate with him, what he had the good sense to do was to take both original concepts of his own and ideas he borrowed (and usually improved upon) from other forms of early baseball and blend them together to create a game of his own. It was a revolutionary new form of baseball and it caught on immediately.

When the Knickerbockers were formed on September 23, 1845, membership was offered to "those whose sedentary habits required recreation." To the Knickerbockers, being a good player wasn't as important as having "the reputation of a gentleman."

The first officers of the Knickerbockers were Duncan F. Curry, President; William R. Wheaton, Vice President, and William H. Tucker, Secretary and Treasurer.

The Original Rules of Baseball

(as set out by Alexander Cartwright, and adopted by the Knickerbocker Base Ball Club of New York on September 23, 1845; I have added explanations where necessary in square brackets)

- The bases shall be from "home" to second base, forty-two paces; from first to third base, forty-two paces, equidistant.
- The game to consist of twenty-one counts, or aces [runs]; but at the conclusion an equal number of hands [outs] must be played.
- The ball must be pitched [underhand], and not thrown [freehand], for the bat.
- A ball knocked out of the field, or outside of the range of first or third base, is foul. [Note: If it hit inside but rolled out it was considered to be fair.]
- Three balls being struck at and missed and the last one caught, is a hand [player] out; if not caught is considered fair, and the striker bound to run.
- If a ball be struck, or tipped, and caught, either flying or on the first bound, it is a hand out.
- A player running the bases shall be out, if the ball is in the hands of an adversary on the base, or the runner is touched with it before he makes his base; it being understood, however, that in no instance is a ball to be thrown at him.
- A player running who shall prevent an adversary from catching or getting the ball before making his base, is a hand out.
- If two hands are already out, a player running home at the time a ball is struck cannot make an ace if the striker is thrown out.
- Three hands out, all out.
- Players must take their strike in regular turn.
- All disputes and differences relative to the game, to be decided by the Umpire, from which there is no appeal.
- No ace or base can be made on a foul strike.
- A runner cannot be put out in making one base, when a balk is made by the pitcher.
- But one base allowed when a ball bounds out of the field when struck.

Cartwright Gave Baseball "Adultness"

Everyone loved this new game Cartwright had come up with. By introducing his rules and regulations he had taken what had been up until that time a simple children's amusement and turned it into a game that grown-ups could play.

As Cartwright biographer Harold Peterson so aptly puts it, Cartwright "introduced adultness and complexity to a directionless kiddie pastime," his improvements made baseball "a game so much different, so much more rational and interesting." Peterson came to the conclusion that this new game's appeal was largely due to its combination of complexity, logical reasoning and physical exhilaration.

Peterson also points out that "the standardized shape and dimensions of the playing field meant that teams could meet on equal terms wherever they played, as did the standardized rules."

This radical new game Alexander Cartwright and his friends played in 1845 had noticeable differences from today's game: They caught the ball barehanded; fortunately, the ball was a lot lighter (and slightly larger) than the one we use today, and contained a large core of India rubber, which made it very bouncy. There were no called balls or strikes; the batter could just stand at home plate and wait, all day if he had to, until he got a pitch he wanted to swing at. And a ball caught on the first bounce was considered an out.

It was called the "Knickerbocker game" or the "New York game," and yes, it differed in several respects from what we now know as baseball, but nevertheless it was definitely the basis for the game we play today.

In October of 1845, the Knickerbockers made a number of trips over to Elysian Fields in Hoboken, New Jersey, to play intramural matches among themselves. The first game was held there on a Monday afternoon, Oct. 6, 1845, with only enough members present to play seven a side. This was the lineup:

	Runs		Runs
Cartwright	1	Curry	2

Moncrief	1	Neibuhr	3
DeWitt	2	Maltby	1
Tucker	3	Dupignac	2
Smith		Turney	2
Birney		Clare	
Brodhead	1	Gourlie	1
Total	8	Total	11

The game only lasted three innings and, as you can see, Cartwright's side lost the first recorded game of baseball by a score of 11-8. They didn't bother to start playing to 21 "aces" until the following game (which Cartwright's side lost 33-26).

The Knickerbockers continued to travel over to Hoboken to play ball all through October and well into November (at least 14 games were recorded, the last on November 18), and this led up to a monumental event that took place the following summer.

The Day Baseball Was Born

On June 19, 1846, just across the river from Manhattan, at Elysian Fields in Hoboken, New Jersey, the first baseball game ever played between two organized teams took place.

Alexander Cartwright's Knickerbocker club took on the "New York Nine," a team made up of original members of the Knickerbockers who had found traveling to Hoboken inconvenient and had continued to play at the old Murray Hill location in Manhattan. They were not a formally organized club, and the name "New York Nine" was something that was used just for this particular occasion.

The game, which was played under Cartwright's rules, lasted four innings, and Cartwright's team lost by a score of 23 to 1 — with Cartwright umpiring the game! Many baseball historians point to this eventful day as "The Day Baseball Was Born." Young Alexander Cartwright and his Knickerbocker club brought about a whole new era in baseball. In the ensu-

This New York Knickerbocker game book from June 19, 1846, records the very first baseball game ever played between two organized teams under Alexander Cartwright's rules and regulations. The game was played at Elysian Fields in Hoboken, New Jersey.

ing two-and-a-half decades, "the New York Game" would eventually replace all other forms of baseball that were being played in North America.

But in the meantime, from 1846 to 1851, due to a lack of organized competition, the Knickerbockers played almost all of their matches amongst themselves, and the game continued to evolve. At the club's fourth annual meeting on April 1, 1848, the rule that stated "A player running the bases shall be out, if the ball is in the hands of an adversary on the base" (meaning a player running to a base was out whether he was forced or not), was changed to state that a player running to first base (or forced to a subsequent base) was out if the ball was in the hands of an adversary on the base. (Note: If a batter overran first base he could be tagged out.) In 1849, the Knickerbockers adopted a uniform consisting of blue woolen pantaloons, white flannel shirts and straw hats.

By this time Alexander Cartwright's association with the Knickerbockers was coming to an end. On March 1, 1849, he and a group of friends left New York City and set out for the California goldfields, eventually settling in Hawaii. But Cartwright continued to be an ambassador for baseball. He brought bats and balls with him on his long travels, and taught the game to others along the way.

The New Game Catches On

Following the summer of 1846, the Knickerbockers continued to play at Elysian Fields, as rampant urbanization had made it difficult for them to find a suitable playing field in Manhattan. Other groups of young men soon formed baseball clubs for both social camaraderie and to challenge the Knickerbockers at their own game. The growth of baseball proceeded apace over the next years.

In 1851 the Knickerbockers finally found some organized competition to play against. On June 3 of that year they met the Washington Club (which had been formed the previous year) at their home field in Harlem and beat them 21-11 in eight innings. Four players for the Washington Club — Trenchard, Davis, Winslow and Case — had played against the Knickerbockers in 1846 as members of the New York Nine.

Two weeks later, on June 17, the Knickerbocker and Washington clubs played a return match at Elysian Fields and the Knickerbockers won that contest 22-20 in ten innings. Afterwards both teams repaired to a nearby hotel by the name of McCarty's for an evening of food and liquid refreshment. Post-game fellowship and revelry was a very important part of early baseball. It is quite likely that the reason Cartwright introduced his three outs per side rule was to speed up the game and get it over with sooner, so that players could get out of the hot sun and take refuge in some nearby tavern. They would then spend the rest of the day and most of the evening eating, drinking and socializing.

In 1852 the Washington Club changed its name to the Gotham Base Ball Club. There is no record of games played that year. On July 5, 1853, the Knickerbockers and Gothams played a match game at Elysian Fields with the Knickerbockers winning 21-12. A return match was played in Harlem on October 14, and the Knickerbockers won that one 21-14. That fall the Eagle Club was formed.

In the summer of 1854 the Knickerbocker, Eagle and Gotham Clubs played several matches against each other. By the end of the year two other baseball clubs had been established: the Empire Club, based at

Elysian Fields, and the Jolly Young Bachelors Base Ball Club of Brooklyn, later called the Excelsior Base Ball Club.

In the summer of 1855 the Excelsiors played amongst themselves while the four other clubs played eight games against each other from June 1 to October 15. This is how you could summarize what might be considered baseball's first real season:

	W	L		W	L
Gotham	4	1	Eagle	1	4
Knickerbocker	3	1	Empire	0	2

The year 1855 saw a huge growth in the formation of new baseball clubs in and around New York City. The Putnam Club was organized with grounds at Williamsburgh, Brooklyn. Brooklyn also saw the founding of two clubs composed of working men: the legendary Atlantic Base Ball Club, playing at the Capitoline Grounds, and the Eckford Club, based in the Greenpoint section (the Eckfords played no matches until the following year). On July 17, 1855, the Union Base Ball Club of Morrisania, Westchester County, New York, was formed.

In the meantime, dozens of lesser, more casual baseball teams had come into existence as baseball mania began to sweep the New York area. Bakers, laborers, clerks, mechanics and men from all walks of life had caught baseball fever, and by the mid to late 1850's more than a hundred baseball clubs flourished in and around New York City, as it seemed like every male in the vicinity had started to play the game, and hundreds of spectators lined the foul lines to watch them. Many junior organizations, such as the Stars and Enterprise, were formed.

But it was in the following year of 1856 that the game really began to take off. *Porter's Spirit of the Times*, an early New York newspaper, stated that "every available plot of ground for ten miles around the metropolitan area" was being utilized for games.

At the end of the 1856 season the matches played between the most prominent clubs were summarized as follows:

	W	L	T
Gotham	2	0	1
Empire	2	1	3
Eagle	2	2	1
Knickerbocker	1	3	1
Atlantic	0	1	2

New York City and Beyond

By 1857 the baseball had travelled far beyond the confines of New York City and had emerged in a scattered pattern in various locations all over the continent, spread there with the help of America's new and ever-expanding railroad network and accounts of the game in such early newspapers as the *New York Clipper* and *Porter's Spirit of the Times*.

In New York State, places like Buffalo, Syracuse, Albany and Troy all had local teams in the mid to late 1850's and the New York Game soon slipped across the Canadian border, as both Toronto and Hamilton, Ontario, had baseball clubs as early as 1859.

In 1857, the Minerva Club was formed in Philadelphia to play the New York Game in that city. In the next few years they were joined by the Winona, United and Benedict clubs. Then, in 1860, a group of Philadelphia lawyers and merchants formed the Athletic Base Ball Club, which was the predecessor of the very same A's that now play for Oakland in the American League.

In Detroit, the Franklin Club was organized to play baseball in 1857, and that same year there were reports of baseball clubs springing up in Cleveland, Chicago and even in the Minnesota Territory.

On the west coast, a baseball club called the Eagles (named after the New York Eagles) was formed in San Francisco in 1859. Baseball had been introduced there by two migrants from New York: Alfred DeForest Cartwright (Alexander's brother) and Frank Turk, a former Knickerbocker. And baseball was even flourishing in Hawaii in the 1850's, brought there by the master himself, Alexander Cartwright.

In Washington, D.C., two baseball teams composed mainly of government clerks, the Potomac Club and the Nationals, practiced and played each other in the back yard of the White House in 1859. And that same year, there were reports of this new form of baseball being played as far south as New Orleans.

So, in the first 10 to 15 years after its inception, the Knickerbocker game had not only taken New York City by storm, but was also being played in scattered regions all over the country. In another 10 years saturation would be complete.

Take Me Out to an Early Ball Game

If you were to attend a baseball game in the 1850's you would find a crude but recognizable form of today's game.

There were no grandstands (and no admission fees); you would either stand and watch the game from along the sidelines or park your horse and carriage in the outfield and observe from there (there were no outfield walls). Sometimes a tent or pavilion would be erected for the ladies, to shield them from the hot sun.

The field was all grass except for worn paths between the bases and down the pitching alley. There was no pitcher's mound; instead, there would either be a plate or a white line located 45 feet from home plate from which the pitcher would deliver the ball. He threw underhanded and the "striker" or batter who was armed with a bat of unlimited length (but which could be no more than 2 ½" in diameter at its thickest part) could wait until just the right pitch before he swung, as there were no called balls or strikes.

None of the players wore gloves, the basemen seldom moved very far from their bases (and never covered a base other than their own) and the catcher, who wore no protective gear, was often positioned some 30 feet behind the plate in order to catch the ball on the first bounce; only when there were runners on base would he come up and position himself directly behind the plate.

There was no players' bench, dugout or bat rack. The team that was at bat usually stood or sprawled alongside the base lines with their collection of bats strewn about on the ground.

Technically there were three umpires at each contest, but only one was actually in charge of the game. He usually wore a frock coat and top hat and either stood or was seated on the first base side. The other two "umpires" were really not umpires at all, but advocates representing each team. They would sit next to each other along the sidelines, at a scorer's desk or table, and yell "Out" or "Not Out" on close plays, in an attempt to influence the real umpire. The uselessness of these two "umpires" soon became apparent and they were eliminated from the game in 1858.

The crowd was generally quiet and mannerly. Instead of cheering or boos, you would usually hear only polite applause and an occasional "Well done" when a particularly good play was made.

As for uniforms, the Knickerbockers had set the standard, and all the other teams copied the style. The Knickerbockers wore dapper-looking blue pantaloons, white flannel shirts and straw hats (later on they changed to mohair caps and added wide patent-leather belts to their garb). Note: At no time did the Knickerbockers wear knickers! That style of baseball uniform didn't appear until 1869 when the Cincinnati Red Stockings burst onto the scene.

The New York Knickerbockers (left) and the Brooklyn Excelsiors (right) pose for a portrait in 1858. The gentleman in the middle with the top hat was the umpire.

The Game Gets Organized

As baseball grew in popularity, there came a need to form some kind of organization to oversee the game and administrate the rules and regulations. Up until 1857, the Knickerbockers were the lords of baseball — they made up the rules and everyone else played by them. But in May of that year the Knickerbockers agreed to meet with representatives from other clubs to form a rules committee. Sixteen clubs attended the meeting: Knickerbocker, Empire, Eckford, Eagle, Gotham, Putnam, Union, Harlem, Atlantic, Continental, Excelsior, Baltic, Bedford, Nassau, Olympic and Harmony. The attendees decided that from then on nine innings would constitute a game instead of 21 runs.

On June 24, 1857, the Mutual Club was formed by members of New York City's Mutual Hook and Ladder Company Number One. They played very few games during their first season, but the club survived to become one of the original members of the National League when it was formed in 1876.

The 1857 season ran from June 8 to November 16. Here is a summary of games played by the principal clubs among themselves:

	W	L		W	L
Atlantic	5	0	Empire	3	4
Eagle	5	5	Excelsior	2	3
Gotham	2	2	Eckford	2	4
Knickerbocker	2	2	Putnam	1	2
Union	2	2			

The National Association of Base Ball Players

In early 1858 Knickerbocker president "Doc" Adams and the presidents of the Gotham, Eagle and Empire clubs put out a call for another meeting of baseball clubs. On March 10 of that year representatives of 26 clubs gathered and "The National Association of Base Ball Players" was formed to oversee the game and administrate the rules and regulations.

The first officers of this organization were W. H. Van Cott of Gotham, President; J. B. Jones of Excelsior, first vice-president; Thomas S. Dakin of Putnam, second vice-president; J. Ross Postley of Metropolitan, recording secretary; Theodore F. Jackson of Putnam, corresponding secretary; E.H. Brown of Metropolitan, treasurer.

At the convention it was decided that, later that summer, a series of all-star games would be held between the best players from the New York teams and the best players from the Brooklyn teams. The first game or "Great Base Ball Match" as it was billed was held on July 20, 1858, at the Fashion Race Course, near Flushing, Long Island. Some 4,000 spectators showed up to see New York defeat Brooklyn by the score of 22 to 18. (Harry Wright of the Knickerbockers played for the New York team.)

This page from an unnamed 1859 publication heralds the nationwide spread of the exciting new game called Base Ball.

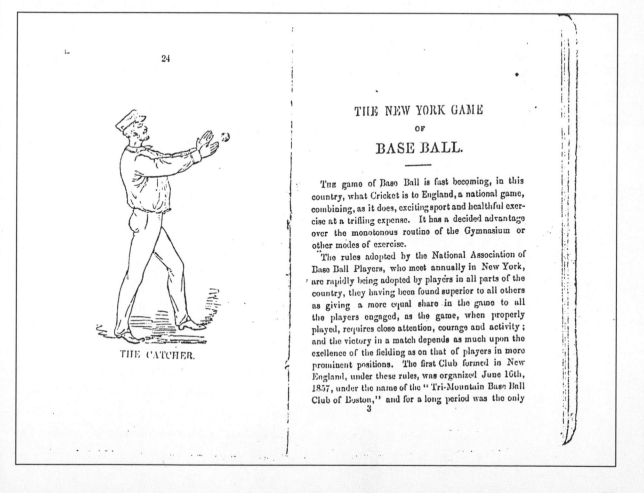

24

THE CATCHER.

THE NEW YORK GAME
OF
BASE BALL.

The game of Base Ball is fast becoming, in this country, what Cricket is to England, a national game, combining, as it does, exciting sport and healthful exercise at a trifling expense. It has a decided advantage over the monotonous routine of the Gymnasium or other modes of exercise.

The rules adopted by the National Association of Base Ball Players, who meet annually in New York, are rapidly being adopted by players in all parts of the country, they having been found superior to all others as giving a more equal share in the game to all the players engaged, as the game, when properly played, requires close attention, courage and activity; and the victory in a match depends as much upon the exellence of the fielding as on that of players in more prominent positions. The first Club formed in New England, under these rules, was organized June 16th, 1857, under the name of the "Tri-Mountain Base Ball Club of Boston," and for a long period was the only

3

An admission fee of 50 cents was charged to help recover the expenses of putting the grounds into shape for play. This is believed to be the first time admission was ever charged to a baseball game. (New York, by the way, went on to win the series two games to one).

The 1858 baseball season began on June 10 and ran to November 16. The first game ever played between the Knickerbocker and Excelsior clubs was held on July 8 at the Excelsior home grounds in the city of Brooklyn. The Excelsiors won the contest 31-13. A return match was held on August 20 at Elysian Fields and the Excelsiors also won this one by the score of 15-14.

After the game the Knickerbockers hosted a lavish dinner at the Odd Fellows Hall in Hoboken to honor the Excelsiors; over 200 gentlemen attended the event.

Also that year, modern baseball was played in New England for the first time when the Tri-Mountains defeated the Portland Club of Maine in a match held on the Boston Common.

Here's how the more prominent clubs racked up in games played against each other in 1858:

	W	L		W	L
Atlantic	5	1	Mutual	1	1
Empire	4	1	Gotham	2	6
Eckford	2	1	Eagle	1	3
Excelsior	6	4	Knickerbocker	0	3
Putnam	3	3	Union	0	1

When the National Association of Base Ball Players held its annual convention in New York City on March 9, 1859, 49 clubs were represented. Minor changes were made to the rules and regulations. That year young pitching ace James Creighton, along with shortstop George Flanley, left the Niagara Base Ball Club of Brooklyn to join the Star Club. At the end of the season they would both leave the Stars to join the exalted Excelsior Club for under-the-table "inducements."

When the top teams played against each other in 1859, these were the results:

	W	L		W	L
Atlantic	6	1	Union	2	3
Excelsior	7	2	Gotham	3	5
Star	2	1	Putnam	1	3
Eckford	5	3	Knickerbocker	1	3
Eagle	3	3	Mutual	0	5
Empire	3	4			

Strike!

A major turning point in the game of baseball took place in 1860: called strikes were introduced to the game. At the baseball convention of March 14, 1860, which was attended by 62 clubs, the following rule was adopted:

Sec. 37. Should a striker stand at the bat without striking at good balls repeatedly pitched to him, for the apparent purpose of delaying the game, or of giving advantage to a player, the umpire, after warning him, shall call one strike, and if he persists in such action, two and three strikes. When three strikes are called, he shall be subject to the same rules as if he had struck at three fair balls.

Thus, the era of pitcher-batter confrontations began, and it changed the whole character of the game. Up until 1860, the pitcher just lobbed the ball up to the plate with no attempt at deception — he was there to help the batter put the ball into play so the game could be decided by fielding. Now things were different: the pitcher could use speed and control of the ball to strike the batter out. The first great pitcher of this era was James Creighton of the Excelsior Club.

On Saturday, June 30, 1860, the Excelsiors boarded a train and embarked on the first great baseball tour. The first leg of their tour took them through New York State. On July 2 they defeated the Champion Club of Albany 24-6, on July 3 they beat the Victory Club of Troy 13-7,

The 1880 edition of *Dewitt's Base-Ball Guide* gave illustrated instructions on how to play the game.

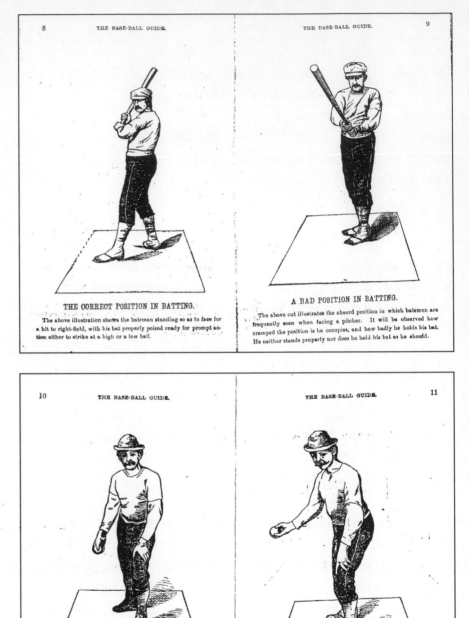

THE CORRECT POSITION IN BATTING.

The above illustration shows the batsman standing so as to face for a hit to right-field, with his bat properly poised ready for prompt action either to strike at a high or a low ball.

A BAD POSITION IN BATTING.

The above cut illustrates the absurd position in which batsmen are frequently seen when facing a pitcher. It will be observed how cramped the position is he occupies, and how badly he holds his bat. He neither stands properly nor does he hold his bat as he should.

A FAIR DELIVERY.

It will be seen by the above illustration what the rule means by the words, "with the arm swinging nearly perpendicular at the side of the body." This is the delivery of a pitch, a toss, a jerk, or an underhand throw, the ball in each case passing below the line of the hip as the hand holding it is swung forward in delivery.

AN ILLEGAL DELIVERY.

The rule governing the delivery of the ball requires that the ball shall be swung forward *below* the line of the hip. It will be seen that the pitcher in the above cut is delivering the ball on the line of the hip, instead of below that line, as the rule requires.

and on July 5 they walloped the Buffalo Niagaras 50-19 before 5,000 fans. Victories followed in Rochester and Newburgh.

The Excelsiors returned to Brooklyn on July 12 to prepare for the forthcoming "grand match" against the mighty Atlantic Club. On July 19 over 10,000 fans gathered at the Excelsior grounds for the first game of the great series between what were considered the two strongest baseball clubs in the country. No admission fee was charged. The Atlantics were considered to be the favorites. This is how it turned out:

ATLANTIC	Outs	Runs	EXCELSIOR	Outs	Runs
P. O'Brien, lf	4	0	Pearsall, 1b	5	2
Hamilton, rf	4	0	Reynolds, ss	5	1
Pearce, ss	2	1	J. Whiting, 3b	0	5
M. O'Brien, 3b	4	0	Holder, 2b	1	3
Price, p	3	1	Russell, lf	3	2
Smith, c	1	1	Brainard, rf	3	2
Joe Oliver, cf	2	1	Creighton, p	4	1
Oliver, 2b	3	0	Flanley, cf	3	3
F. Seinsoth, 1b	4	0	Legget, c	3	4
Totals	27	4	Totals	27	23

Atlantic   0 0 1 0 0 0 2 1 0 - 4
Excelsior   2 2 5 3 1 0 6 3 1 - 23

It was a great victory for the Excelsiors, who immediately left town and continued on their barnstorming tour. Three days later in Baltimore they defeated the Excelsior Club of Baltimore 51-6. They then went to Philadelphia and met a nine comprising players from the Olympic, Winona, Benedict, Equity, United and Athletic clubs. The Excelsiors won the game 15-4.

The Excelsiors returned to Brooklyn and played a second match against the Atlantics on August 9. The game took place before 12,000 spectators at the Atlantic grounds. The Atlantics won this contest 15-14. A third and deciding game was played between the two great clubs on August 23 at the grounds of the Putnam Club before an estimated 15,000 to 20,000 spectators. In the sixth inning the game was disrupted by unruly Atlantic supporters to such an extent that the Excelsiors (who were leading 8-6 at the time) walked off the field and refused to continue. The umpire, a Mr. Thorne of the Empire Club, declared the match a draw. No further games were ever played between the two clubs.

In 1860 the first game of New York-rules baseball was played on the west coast. The Eagle Club (which had been organized in November of 1859) met a club called the Red Rovers at Centre's Bridge, San Francisco on February 22, 1860. The Eagles won the game by default. With the score tied 33-33 at the end of nine innings, the Red Rovers complained that the pitching of Willock of the Eagles was "unfair" and refused to continue the contest. Umpire Matt McCloskey decided the complaint was unjustified and awarded the game to the Eagles.

The Knickerbockers played only one match in 1860, a "friendly" game with Excelsior; the score is not known. The National Association of Base Ball Players held its third annual convention on Wednesday, December 12, 1860.

Here is a summary of the games played by the top clubs among themselves in 1860:

	W	L		W	L
Excelsior	9	2	Eagle	2	3
Atlantic	8	2	Empire	2	4
Eckford	7	2	Independent	1	3
Gotham	3	1	Union	1	7
Charter Oak	2	1	Star	0	4
Putnam	2	3	Mutual	0	5

Baseball Goes To War

The Civil War, which began in 1861 and lasted until 1865, played a major role in the spread of baseball nationally. Union soldiers from the northeast often played baseball for recreation behind the lines. Other

Union soldiers and Confederate prisoners watched them and learned the game. And when the war was over they took baseball home with them and taught it to others. The game spread like wildfire and soon people in cities and towns and on farms in all parts of the country were playing baseball.

When the Civil War started in 1861 it had quite an effect on the New York baseball scene. Fewer matches were played than in the previous year. The Knickerbocker, Excelsior and Putnam Clubs played no games at all. A small number of matches were held between the more prominent clubs; this was the result:

This lithograph from the Civil War era shows Union prisoners playing baseball in a Confederate prison camp at Salisbury, North Carolina in 1862.

	W	L		W	L
Union	1	0	Eagle	2	3
Mutual	5	2	Eckford	1	2
Jefferson	2	1	Gotham	0	1
Atlantic	1	1	Empire	0	2

At the end of the season, Frank Queen of the *New York Clipper* newspaper put up the Silver Ball Trophy, to be presented to the winners of an all-star game between teams representing New York and Brooklyn. Some 15,000 fans showed up to witness the match, which was held at Elysian Fields in Hoboken on October 21, 1861. Several of baseball's great early players appeared in this match: Dickey Pearce, Jim Creighton and Al Reach played for Brooklyn; and Harry Wright played for New York. This is how it turned out:

NEW YORK	Out	Runs	BROOKLYN	Outs	Runs
Yates, 1b	2	2	Pearce, c	2	3
Brown, 2b	3	1	Creighton, p	4	2
McKeever, p	3	0	Beach, ss	2	3
McMahon, ss	3	1	Price, 3b	4	2
Cohen, c	4	0	Pearsall, 1b	2	2
A.B. Taylor, lf	4	0	Manolt, cf	2	2
H. Wright, 3b	1	1	Smith, 2b	2	2
Harris, cf	1	1	Flanley, lf	4	1
Culver, rf	3	0	Al Reach, rf	2	1
Totals	24	6	Totals	24	18

New York   2 2 0 0 2 0 0 0 x - 6
Brooklyn   2 0 0 0 7 1 0 8 x - 18
(The game was called at the end of eight innings, by mutual agreement.)

In 1862 the Mutual and Eckford clubs travelled to Philadelphia and Excelsior visited Boston. For the second year in a row the Knickerbockers played no matches. The Eckford and Atlantic clubs (both of Brooklyn) played a three-game series for the Silver Ball Trophy which was symbolic of the championship. In the first game, which was played on August 11, Eckford beat Atlantic 20-14. On August 18 Atlantic took the second game 39-5. Eckford won the third and deciding game on September 18, by the score of 8-3. Baseball lost one of its first stars when Excelsior pitcher James Creighton died at the age of 21 on October 18, 1862.

At the annual baseball convention, which was held on December 10, a new rule was proposed which allowed for the calling of balls as well as strikes, but it was not officially adopted until 1868. This is how the top clubs did in games played against each other in 1862:

	W	L		W	L
Eckford	7	1	Atlantic	2	3
Gotham	5	2	Union	2	3
Mutual	5	4	Harlem	1	6
Excelsior	1	1	Eagle	0	3
Jefferson	1	1			

In 1863 the Knickerbockers (who hadn't played any matches for the last two years) resumed playing on a limited basis. They only engaged in the occasional "friendly" match with clubs such as the Excelsiors. The Knickerbockers continued this practice until the club was disbanded sometime in the 1870's.

With the Civil War still raging, 1863 was another slow year for baseball. Only 28 clubs showed up at the annual baseball convention in December. A rule change eliminated an out on a fair ball caught on the first bound, as baseball adopted the "fly game," a concept which former Knickerbocker president Doc Adams had advocated for several years.

This is how the top nines did in games played against each other in 1863:

	W	L		W	L
Eckford	7	0	Union	1	2
Mutual	9	4	Empire	2	5
Atlantic	5	3	Eagle	1	3
Star	3	2	Athletics	1	3
Excelsior	2	3	Henry Eckford	1	5
Gotham	2	4			

The first international match ever recorded took place in September of 1864 when the Atlantic Club of Brooklyn took on the Young Canadian Club of Woodstock, Ontario, who were the champions of Canada, in a game played at Rochester, New York. The Atlantics beat the Young

Canadians 75-11, and then proceeded to demolish a club called Ontario of Rochester 54-5. Earlier, in August of that year, the Atlantics had travelled to Philadelphia where they defeated the Camden, Keystone, Olympic and Athletic clubs by large scores. The Atlantics played a total of 19 games in 1864, and won them all.

Harvard University formed its first baseball team in 1864 and Brooklyn Eckford second baseman Al Reach jumped to the Athletic Club of Philadelphia, having been offered $1,000 a year to captain the team.

This is a summary of games played among the leading clubs in 1864:

	W	L		W	L
Atlantic	8	0	Gotham	3	6
Mutual	13	2	Union	1	2
Excelsior	5	3	Eckford	1	3
Eureka-Newark	4	3	Empire	2	10
Active	4	4	Eagle	1	7
Newark	4	6			

Post–Civil War Baseball

The end of the Civil War in 1865 brought on a boom in baseball. Some 91 clubs were represented at the annual baseball convention, up from 30 the previous year. The year began with the Atlantics and Gothams playing a series in January — on ice skates! In the spring, the ball grounds at Elysian Fields were enlarged and improved, and several rows of seats were erected for the spectators. In June the Athletics of Philadelphia visited the New York area for the first time and defeated the Eureka, Eagle, Union and Resolute clubs.

The first "grand match for the championship of the United States" was played before a crowd of 20,000 at Elysian Fields on August 3. The Atlantic Club of Brooklyn took on the Mutual Club of New York. The game was called in the sixth inning due to a heavy rain storm, with the Atlantics, who were ahead 13-12 at the time, being declared the winners.

Later that month a second match was held between the two clubs and the Atlantics won that contest 40-28. Also in August, those mighty Athletics of Philadelphia visited Washington, Baltimore and Pittsburgh, and defeated all opposition.

The Atlantics travelled to Boston in September where they defeated Lowell, Tri-Mountain and Harvard by large scores. On the way home they beat the Charter Oak Club 37-11 in Hartford. In October the Excelsiors went to Washington and were defeated by the Nationals 36-30. They had better luck in Baltimore where they beat the Pastime Club 51-22.

In November the New England Association of Base Ball Players was formed, with 11 clubs represented. And in December the North-Western Association of Base Ball Players was organized in Chicago, with 15 clubs represented.

This is how the top clubs did in games played among themselves in 1865:

	W	L		W	L
Atlantic	17	0	Empire	6	9
Athletics	16	4	Keystone of Phila.	6	10
Excelsior	4	1	Camden, N.J.	3	7
Mutual	12	4	Gotham	3	9
Eureka of Newark	8	4	Newark, N.J.	1	7
Active	10	7	Resolute	0	6
Eckford	8	6	Enterprise	0	8
Union	9	10	Eagle	0	10
Star	3	4			

The Game Gets Rowdier

During the latter half of the 1860's, teams sprouted up everywhere, from the small towns to the big cities. It was along about this time that people began to see the commercial possibilities of the game. The concept of enclosing the field and then charging the spectators to enter the grounds, which had first begun on a regular basis at the Capitoline

Grounds in Brooklyn in 1862, was becoming more and more prevalent.

Baseball was no longer the gentleman's game that it was in Cartwright's day. A rowdier element had taken over baseball, and drinking and umpire baiting at games became commonplace. Open gambling, not only by the fans but by the players and even by the umpires, was common. In many places women were strongly advised to stay away from the ballparks.

The players were generally considered to be amateurs, but many were paid for their services, either under the table or by having fake jobs arranged for them. To be considered a professional baseball player was bad form in those days. Up until this time, there had been no such thing as professional sports; it was a concept that was totally foreign to society. The idea that someone could actually make a living by playing some sort of *game* was preposterous. You were supposed to be playing for the fun of it, or pretending to. One example of this early hypocrisy took place in 1867 when 16-year-old pitching ace Al Spalding was offered a "job" as a clerk with a Chicago grocery wholesaler for 40 dollars a week (which was about 10 times the average wage for this type of work). This was not really a job at all but an inducement to come to that city and pitch for Chicago's great Excelsior club. Meanwhile, in New York City, the infamous "Boss" Tweed, who was president of the New York Mutuals from 1860 to 1871, put all his players on the city payroll, where they were usually listed as "street sweepers."

In May of 1866 the Harvard University team visited Brooklyn and lost to the Atlantic and Excelsior clubs. When the mighty Atlantics lost the second game they played that year to a club representing Irvington, New Jersey, at Irvington, it was the first time they had been defeated since 1863. The final score was 23-17.

In June the Charter Oaks of Hartford defeated the Chesters of Norwalk for the championship of Connecticut. The Athletics of Philadelphia visited Morrisania, N.Y., where they defeated the Unions 33-20.

In July the Nationals of Washington journeyed to Philadelphia where they lost 22-6 to the Athletics before a crowd of 12,000 on July 2. They then went to Morrisania and lost to the Unions 22-8 on July 4. The following day the Excelsiors, behind the pitching of Asa Brainard, defeated

This Currier and Ives lithograph depicts the Grand Championship Match between the Philadelphia Athletics and the Brooklyn Atlantics, played on October 22, 1866, at the 15th and Columbia playing grounds in Philadelphia. Final score: Athletics 31, Atlantics 12.

the Nationals 46-33 in Brooklyn. Before heading home the Nationals played the Gothams, and lost that game as well. On September 13 the Atlantics defeated the Mutuals 17-15 before 15,000 at Elysian Fields. Meanwhile a crowd of 7,000, which included President Andrew Johnson, saw the Excelsiors defeat the Nationals 33-28 in Washington.

The first game of a three-game series between the Athletics and the Atlantics for the championship of the United States was to be played on October 1 at the 15th and Columbia playing grounds in Philadelphia. A crowd estimated at 30,000 paid anywhere from 25 cents to $5.00 to attend the first "Grand Match." Once the game was underway the gigantic crowd surged on the field in the bottom half of the first inning and made it impossible to continue the contest. The game was called and was replayed on October 15 at the Capitoline Grounds in Brooklyn, where a crowd of 18,000 showed up to see the Atlantics defeat the Athletics 27-17.

The second game was held in Philadelphia on October 22 before 20,000 spectators. The Atlantics also won that game, and the championship. The score was 31-12.

On December 12, 1866, some 402 clubs were represented at the annual baseball convention in New York.

Here is a summary of games played among the more prominent clubs in 1866:

	W	L		W	L
Union	14	3	Enterprise	4	5
Gotham	4	1	Eckford	5	8
Athletics	11	3	Eureka, Newark	4	7
Atlantic	10	3	National, Washington	2	5
Olympic, Patterson	4	2	Empire	2	5
Mutual	7	4	Eagle	1	6
Active	8	6	Star	1	6
Excelsior	6	6	Eclectic	0	6
Irvington, N.J.	5	5	Keystone, Phila.	0	7

The small village of Irvington, New Jersey, was a baseball hot-bed during the summer of 1867, as the local Irvington Base Ball Club took on, and usually defeated, the top clubs from the New York area. Thousands of spectators would show up at the Eureka grounds in Irvington, which was located some four miles west of Newark, for these matches.

In order to get to Irvington, baseball fans would have to take the ferry to Jersey City and then the New Jersey Railroad to Newark, from where they could either walk down the dusty road to Irvington or hop on their choice of various horse-drawn omnibuses, dilapidated hacks or mud-splattered farm wagons, all charging exorbitant prices.

As many as 7,000 spectators would show up to see Irvington, or "the country boys" as they were often referred to, take on such clubs as Eureka, the Unions of Morrisania, the Mutuals of New York and the Brooklyn Atlantics. The Irvington club was also a top draw on the road, attracting large crowds wherever they went.

Also in 1867, 20-year-old George Wright jumped from the Unions of Morrisania to the Nationals of Washington, as captain and shortstop. His occupation was listed as "government clerk." On July 11 the Nationals embarked on the first Western trip ever made by a ball club. Baseball writer Henry Chadwick accompanied the club on the journey, which covered five states and involved some 3,000 miles of travel.

The club easily beat teams in Columbus, Cincinnati, Louisville, Indianapolis and St. Louis. On July 25, before a large crowd at Dexter Park in Chicago, the famous visitors from the East met the Forest Citys of Rockford. The Forest Citys had 17-year-old Ross Barnes and 29-year-old Bob Addy in the infield, and a nervous 17-year-old by the name of Al Spalding in the pitchers box.

When Rockford won the game 29-23, local baseball fans were in shock. The next day, when the Nationals took on Chicago's famous Excelsior club, the locals bet heavily on the Excelsiors, who had beaten the Forest Citys in two recent matches. When the Nationals easily won the game 49-4 the *Chicago Tribune* accused them of having thrown the Forest City game "for the purpose of securing bets" and thus "thousands of bettors were cleaned out in Chicago." The Nationals demanded, and got, a retraction from the paper. The next day they beat the Chicago Atlantics 76-17, to bring their Western trip to an end.

On July 31 the mighty Atlantic Club of Brooklyn, champions of all baseball, lost to the Unions of Morrisania 32-19 in a game played in Melrose, N.Y. Five days later the Irvington Club beat them 34-32 before 4,000 spectators in Irvington. On August 12, the Atlantics finally won a game, when they defeated the Mutuals 18-13 before 6,000 fans at the Union grounds in Brooklyn

In late August the Mutuals travelled to Washington and met President Andrew Johnson at the White House. Johnson declared baseball to be "the National Game." On August 26, some 6,000 spectators, including President Johnson, were on hand when the Mutuals played the Nationals at their new grounds, and beat them 40-16.

On the trip home the Mutuals stopped off along the way to defeat the Philadelphia Athletics 23-21, and beat Irvington 19-15.

On September 16, the Brooklyn Atlantics met the Philadelphia Athletics in the first game of a home and home series for the championship of the United States. Fifteen thousand spectators packed the Union grounds in Brooklyn to see the Atlantics win 28-16. The second game was held before 16,000 at Philadelphia on September 23, and the Athletics evened the series by beating the Atlantics 28-8.

A third and deciding game was to be held in Brooklyn on September 30, but the Atlantics asked for a postponement, claiming they had several injured players. The Athletics showed up anyway, so the Atlantics agreed to let the game go on using their poorest or "muffin" players. This upset the Athletics, who refused to play this group and declared they would play no further games with the Atlantics that year. The series never was decided.

On October 3, at the Satellite grounds in Brooklyn, the Excelsiors of Philadelphia played the Uniques of Brooklyn for the "colored championship of the United States." The Excelsiors were declared winners when the game was called on account of darkness in the seventh inning, with the Philadelphia club ahead 42-17.

In October the Atlantics, who had held the championship for three years, finally lost their crown when they were swept in two straight games by the Unions of Morrisania.

Teams of fully paid professionals were now the custom in baseball, not only in the East, but as far West as Cincinnati and Chicago and as far South as New Orleans.

Called balls were introduced to the game. After a warning, the umpire could call three balls (effectively giving the batter four balls) before awarding the batter first base. The umpires were already calling three strikes after giving the batter a warning (thereby giving the batter four strikes).

The Philadelphia Athletics travelled west in June and defeated the newly created Cincinnati Red Stockings 20-13 before 5,000 fans. They then trounced the Unions of St. Louis 54-12. On June 18, in Chicago, they beat the Forest Citys of Rockford, and young Al Spalding, 94-13.

On the trip the Athletics record was 18-1. They scored a total of 860 runs to 232 for the opponents.

The Unions of Morrisania, "Champions of America," played their first game of the year on June 15, defeating a club called the Mohawks 34-11.

The once-mighty Atlantics lost to the Niagaras at Buffalo on June 16, by the score of 19-15. But they soon regained their old form when they went on a western tour and defeated clubs in Detroit, Chicago, Cleveland and Cincinnati by large scores. They came home with a 16-1 record, outscoring their opponents 836 to 229.

The long-standing rivalry between the Atlantics and the Athletics was renewed on August 31. Some 20,000 spectators showed up in Philadelphia to see the Athletics beat the Atlantics 18-9 in a game that was called after eight innings due to a rain storm. A second contest was held on September 7 at the Union grounds in Brooklyn and the Athletics also won that game. The score was 37-13.

But the Unions of Morrisania were still considered the champions of baseball. After they had opened their brand new Tremont Park by beating a club from Yale 19-9 they then embarked on a Western journey that eventually took them to Cincinnati where they split a pair of games with the Red Stockings.

Those very same Red Stockings were the first Western club to make an Eastern trip. That September they were defeated by the Olympics in Washington, the Athletics in Philadelphia, and the Atlantics at Brooklyn before finally edging the Mutuals of New York 29-28.

Meanwhile the Unions defended their crown against the club they had won it from, the Atlantics of Brooklyn. A best-of-three series was held. After the Unions lost the first game in Brooklyn, a second match was held at Tremont Park on October 6. Thousands of spectators showed up to see the Atlantics defeat the Unions 24-8 and thereby regain the "Championship of the United States." But they soon lost it again, this time to the Mutuals, who beat them twice later that October.

At their annual meeting in December, the National Association of Base Ball Players recognized professional players for the first time. They divided players into two distinct classes, professional and amateur. Although the professionals were now monopolizing baseball and truly amateur clubs had ceased to be of any national importance, the "professional" clubs still masqueraded as amateur organizations.

The First True Professionals

Harry Wright

All of this duplicity began to end in 1869 when a fellow by the name of Harry Wright who managed a baseball club in Cincinnati declared to the world that his team was indeed professional. The club, which wore bright red stockings made for them by a young lady named Margaret Truman, was called the Cincinnati Red Stockings. With a total annual payroll of $9,300, they were the first openly professional baseball team, and that year they barnstormed all over the country, taking on all comers.

The English-born Wright, a former professional cricket player and a jeweler by trade, had been hired by club president Aaron Champion to turn the Red Stockings into a top-caliber team. Harry Wright imported players from all over the country, including his brother George, who was an all-star shortstop in New Jersey; the only player that was actually from Cincinnati was Charlie Gould, the first baseman.

The great Red Stockings national tour of 1869 took the team to such cities as New York, Boston, Washington, Cleveland, Chicago and as far west as San Francisco. They played the best local teams they could find and annihilated them all, ending up with a record of 56 wins and one tie. (The tie resulted when the Troy Haymakers walked off the field in the sixth inning with the score tied 17-17 so that gamblers who had laid money on the Troy team could avoid paying off.)

The Red Stockings also revolutionized the way baseball players dressed; the spiffy knee-length flannel knickers and long stockings they wore soon became all the rage among ball clubs and replaced the traditional long trousers that dated back to the early days of the Knickerbocker Club.

When the Red Stockings got to New York in June, a crowd of 3,500 watched them narrowly defeat the Mutuals 4-2 at the Union grounds in a game played on June 15. Then, the following day, the Red Stockings walloped the Atlantics 32-10 before 10,000 onlookers at the Capitoline Grounds. The day after that they went back to the Union grounds and beat the Eckfords 24-5 before 8,000.

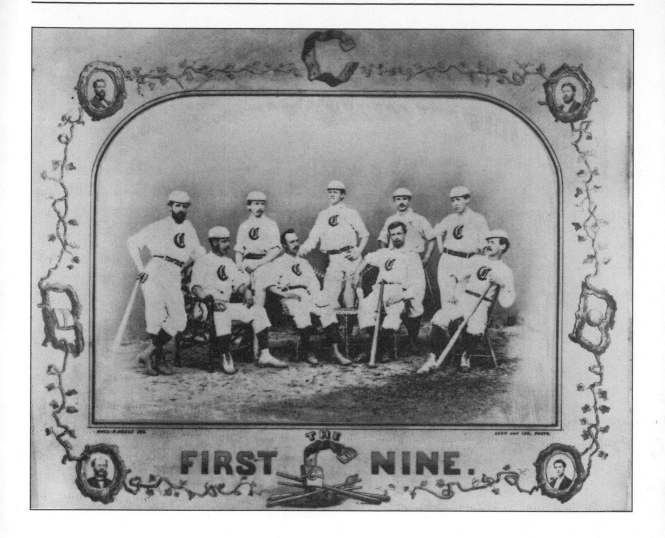

FIRST THE NINE.

On their way to Philadelphia the Red Stockings, who had several former Irvington, N.J., players in their lineup, stopped in at Irvington and defeated "the country boys" 20-4. In Philadelphia, 25,000 showed up at the 15th & Columbia grounds to see the Red Stockings defeat the Athletics 27-18.

In 1869 the normal admission fee to most professional baseball games was 25 cents, but the Red Stockings were such a draw on the road that they usually demanded, and got, a guarantee that a 50-cent entrance fee be charged.

By 1869 several "colored" clubs had sprung up in the east and middle

The 1869 Cincinnati Red Stockings were the first openly professional baseball team.

west. The first "mixed" match of note took place in Philadelphia on September 18 when the Pythians (colored) beat the City Items (white) 27-18. Two days later in Washington, in what the local press termed as "a unique contest," the Negro Alerts of Washington played the white Olympic Club. The Olympics won the game 55-4.

In mid-September the Red Stockings embarked on the West Coast part of their nationwide tour. They played against, and easily beat, all of the more prominent clubs in San Francisco, including the Pacific Coast-champion Eagle Club. On the way back they played games in Sacramento, Virginia City, Nevada, Nebraska City and Omaha.

On their 1869 nationwide tour, in which they defeated every prominent team in the country, the Red Stockings travelled nearly 12,000 miles and played before over 200,000 persons. Total gate receipts were $29,724.87; salaries and expenses, $29,726.26; net profit, $1.39.

The 1869 Cincinnati Red Stockings Roster and Payroll

Harry Wright	center field (and manager)	$1,200
George Wright	shortstop	1,400
Asa Brainard	pitcher	1,100
Fred Waterman	third base	1,000
Charles Sweasy	second base	800
Charles H. Gould	first base	800
Douglas Allison	catcher	800
Andrew J. Leonard	left field	800
Calvin A. McVey	right field	800
Richard Hurley	substitute	800
TOTAL		$9,300

The Cincinnati Red Stockings had become the acknowledged champions of the nation. By June of 1870, they had stretched their winning streak to 79 when they were finally defeated by the Brooklyn Atlantics, who edged them 8-7 in eleven innings on June 14. Several other defeats later on in the season caused interest in the team to drop off at home, and

this combined with the club's heavy travel expenses and mounting players' salaries caused the demise of the team.

So Harry Wright packed up those bright red stockings the team had
worn and moved to Boston where he formed the Boston Red Stockings.
He took several Cincinnati players with him. Once again Harry Wright
defied tradition and declared his new team to be professional; almost at
once the other great teams of the era cast off their amateur disguises, and
this brought about the era of the professional baseball league.

It was an era that would have a bumpy start though, for as we shall see
in the next section, the first pro baseball league was destined to fail

From the Reds to the Black Sox

The Age of Innocence

A New Era Begins

On Saint Patrick's Day, March 17, 1871, at Collier's Cafe on Broadway and Thirteenth Street in New York City, representatives from some of the best baseball clubs in the land gathered together to form the very first professional baseball league. They named their new creation the "National Association of Professional Baseball Players."

The league, which would begin play that summer, was composed of the Boston Red Stockings, the Chicago White Stockings, the New York Mutuals, the Philadelphia Athletics, the Troy Haymakers, two clubs from Washington, D.C. (the Nationals and the Olympics), two clubs with the same nicknames (the Cleveland Forest Citys and the Rockford Forest Citys), and the Fort Wayne Kekiongas. (The Kekiongas dropped out of the league in August and were replaced by the Brooklyn Eckfords.)

Unfortunately, the National Association turned out to be an embarrassment to all those associated with it. It was a loosely knit organization renowned for its rowdiness, erratic schedule, open gambling on games, liquor selling in parks, bribery and other forms of chicanery.

The league, which was in fact run by the players, lasted only five years. The N.A. was characterized by teams that would not honor their schedules late in the season when it meant travelling far from home, players who would jump from club to club (sometimes in mid-season), and a lack of control of the games by umpires, who were usually unpaid. There was a turnover of some twenty-five or so clubs in the five years of the league's existence.

Despite its many shortcomings, the National Association did much to

help popularize the game of baseball. Leading newspapers across the land printed accounts of the N.A. games and wrote about the players. And they had a lot to write about: in its first season there was an exciting three-way battle for first place among the Chicago White Stockings, the Philadelphia Athletics and the Boston Red Sox. The A's finally took the pennant, beating out the other two clubs by two games.

Chicago's home park burned down in early October in the great Chicago fire, and the White Stockings were forced to play out the rest of the schedule on the road. They then dropped out of the league until 1884.

The N.A. was sometimes referred to as "Harry Wright's League." His Boston Red Stockings, with such stars as pitcher Al Spalding, infielders Ross Barnes and George Wright, outfielder Jim O'Rourke and catcher Deacon White, came in first in four of the five seasons the league existed.

Among the N.A.'s top hitters were Long Levi Meyerle of the Athletics,

This 1873 drawing depicts baseball action in the early 1870's. It's reasonable to assume that this is a Philadelphia Athletics home game from the pennants that are flying above the grandstand, which would be in honor of Philadelphia's 1871 National Association championship.

Chicago and Philadelphia Whites, who led the league in batting average twice (.492 in 1871 and .403 in 1874), and Boston's Ross Barnes, who led the league with a .422 batting average in 1872 and then the following year led the N.A. in runs scored (125), hits (137), doubles (28), triples (10) as well as batting average (.425). The league's premier pitcher was Boston's Al Spalding, who led the league in wins each of its five years of life. He had a total of 207 wins and 56 losses during this period — an average of 41 wins per season.

"Hippodroming," or dumping games, was a common practice carried on by many teams, most notably the Troy Haymakers and the New York Mutuals. When the league folded in 1875 it was in such a state of disarray that nearly half of the 13 teams that were fielded that year failed to finish the schedule.

The N.L. Takes Over

The demise of the National Association was brought about by Chicago club president William Hulbert who led a movement to replace the floundering association with a new league, a league that decent folk would not be

William Hulbert

ashamed to bring their families to watch. His would be a tightly organized league where the play would be honest, a league that would keep to a firm schedule of games, a league that would be an organization not of baseball players, but of baseball clubs, with the final authority in the hands of management.

On February 2, 1876, at the Grand Central Hotel in New York City, William Hulbert and delegates from other clubs gathered together to form a new league, and thus the National Association was replaced by the National League of Professional Baseball Clubs.

The National League immediately banned open gambling and liquor sales at games, vowed to expel clubs that failed to stick to schedules and later on even prohibited the playing of league games on Sunday.

It was agreed that written contracts between clubs and players were to be respected, thereby ending the practice of teams pirating players away from each other. Only cities with populations of at least 75,000 would be eligible for franchises in this new venture. Umpires were to be paid (they got $5 per game). An admission fee of 50 cents to all league games was set.

Each club agreed to play each rival team 10 times during the season; failure to do so would result in expulsion from the league. Clubs agreed to pay $100 in annual dues. The first president of the N.L. was banker and insurance executive Morgan G. Bulkeley. Bulkeley would go on to become a U.S. senator and eventually serve on the Mills commission (which was responsible for cooking up the myth of Abner Doubleday as inventor of baseball).

**Morgan G.
Bulkeley**

The National League started out with eight clubs: the Philadelphia Athletics, Boston Red Caps, Hartford Dark Blues and New York Mutuals in the East; and the Cincinnati Red Stockings, Louisville Grays, St. Louis Brown Stockings and Chicago White Stockings in the West.

There is also a more cynical view of William Hulbert's motives for founding the new league. In 1875 Hulbert made a deal with Boston superstar pitcher Al Spalding to have Spalding jump to the Chicago club the following year, not only to pitch, but to act as captain and manager of the team as well. Hulbert then got Spalding to persuade fellow Boston teammates Cal McVey, Ross Barnes and Deacon White, who were the very heart of the Red Stockings lineup, to join him in his defection to the White Stockings. And if this wasn't enough, Hulbert and Spalding also made a deal with Adrian "Cap" Anson, the Philadelphia Athletics' young slugger, to jump ship to the Chicago club when the next season began.

It was the very first wholesale defection of baseball stars, and a number of baseball historians contend that Hulbert feared the National Association would expel the White Stockings for his act of gross piracy, so he avoided a confrontation by forming a new league.

No matter what Hulbert's true intentions were, in one fell swoop he did, in fact, clean up baseball and create a respectable new league that has remained in business for well over a hundred years.

The first National League game was played in Philadelphia on April 22, 1876, before 3,000 fans, with the Boston Red Caps defeating the Philadelphia Athletics by the score of 6 to 5. The winning pitcher was Joe Borden, who, a year earlier, had recorded the only no-hitter ever thrown in the National Association. At the end of the season Hulbert's Chicago White Stockings took the first N.L. pennant with a record of 52 wins and 14 losses.

In the winter following that first season of '76, William Hulbert took over presidency of the league. He was determined to run a tight ship, and the first thing he did was to throw both the New York and Philadelphia clubs out of the league for failing to make their final western road trips at the end of the season. (Neither city was admitted back into the league until 1883 — the N.L. went with only six clubs in 1877 and '78.)

In 1877 it was discovered that four Louisville players (Jim Devlin, George Hall, William Craver and Al Nichols) had conspired to throw the pennant to Boston. Hulbert banned the players from baseball for life.

At a National League meeting in Buffalo in 1879 an agreement was adopted whereby each club could "reserve" five players for the next season. Eventually this reserve clause was extended to cover all major league players, virtually binding a player to the same club for life. The reserve clause was a major bone of contention for the players when they revolted in 1890 to form their own league.

In 1880, Hulbert booted Cincinnati out of the league for selling beer at home games and leasing their park to teams that played on Sunday.

In the first few years of the N.L., the road was rather rocky. Almost all the clubs lost money; Hartford, St. Louis and Louisville dropped out before the start of the '78 season, to be replaced by Providence, Indianapolis and Milwaukee. The latter two clubs dropped out in '79 and four new teams — Cleveland, Buffalo, Troy and Syracuse — then joined. Franchises would come and go (in its first 25 years of existence some 21 cities were represented in the National League at one time or another), but yet the league survived due to stern, uncompromising management and the solid foundation that was laid down by Hulbert and the rest of the men who established the league.

The ballparks during the latter part of the '70's were quite small (usually holding anywhere from 1,500 to 4,000 spectators) and generally not

A baseball game underway at the New York Polo Grounds in 1878

constructed in a very durable fashion, as the owners had no reason to believe that the National League would stay in business for very long. According to Bill James in his *Historical Baseball Abstract*, the owners usually "bought some wood and threw up fences and primitive bleachers and maybe a clubhouse or a dugout; the players often assisted in the construction. In a couple of years the thing fell down or burned down or rotted out, or they just got tired of it and built another one." Clubs would sometimes switch home ballparks in mid season.

The First Golden Age: Baseball in the 1880's

Many historians refer to the 1880's as baseball's first golden age. A major stimulus for professional baseball's rapid expansion in the '80's was the nation's thriving economy and rapid urban growth.

The National League (N.L.) was just beginning to gain steady ground in the early 1880's, when suddenly it faced competition. In 1882, a rival league called the American Association was formed. This new league began with six clubs which were located in Cincinnati, Philadelphia, Pittsburgh, St. Louis, Louisville and Baltimore; the following year they would add New York and Columbus.

The American Association, which lasted for nine years and was also called "the beer ball league," started out by cutting ticket prices from 50 to 25 cents, scheduling games on Sundays and allowing beer to be sold in the stands.

After an initial skirmish, the N. L. decided to try and co-exist with the new league, and they worked out a document called the National Agreement which led to mutual protection over players' contracts and brought about the first post-season series between league champions in 1884. In this premiere edition of the World Series, the N.L.'s Providence Grays, led by the pitching of Charles "Old Hoss" Radbourn, defeated the A.A. champion New York Metropolitans in three straight games, in a best out of five series.

The 1880's was the decade when professional baseball truly captured the hearts and minds of the nation. Daily newspapers all across the land were now printing accounts of big-time baseball on a regular basis. and assigning reporters to cover the game full-time.

In the '80's the game itself went through several major changes: In 1881 the pitching distance was increased from 45 to 50 feet, and then two years later, in 1883, pitchers were allowed to throw overhand, giving them a tremendous advantage over the batters (as the pitching distance was still ten and a half feet closer to the plate than it is now). During this era, the average pitcher would win between 20 and 50 games a season depending on the quality of the team behind him.

"Old Hoss" Radbourn, using a cricket-style pitching motion that included a running start, won 60 out of the 73 games he pitched in for Providence in their world championship year of 1884. Also in '84, Guy Jackson Heckler, pitching for the American Association's Louisville Eclipse, finished the season with a record of 52 wins and 20 losses, and over in the National League, the Buffalo Bisons' James F. Galvin had a 1884 record of 46 wins and 21 losses (this followed a 44-29 record the previous year).

Gloves specifically designed for fielding purposes were introduced in the mid 1880's (gloves intended for the protection of the hands only had been worn as early as 1878); also masks and chest protectors for catchers were adopted during this era. The first fielding glove was invented in 1883 by Arthur Irwin, a shortstop for the Providence Grays. In order to continue playing after breaking the third and fourth fingers of his left hand, Irwin took a buckskin driving glove that was several sizes too large, filled it with padding and had the third and fourth fingers sewn together to accommodate his broken digits. He immediately discovered that his new contraption made the act of catching a baseball and then snapping a throw off a whole lot easier and faster. When New York pitcher John Montgomery Ward saw Irwin's invention he immediately ordered one. A sporting goods firm started manufacturing this type of glove and soon hundreds of orders came in. Within a year almost every player in the major leagues wore a glove.

Up until 1887, a batter had the right to request the pitcher to throw either a high or a low pitch. It took nine balls to get a batter to first at the start of the decade, seven in 1882, five in 1887, and finally four in 1889. In 1888 the three strike rule was finally adopted. (During the previous season, it took four strikes to get a batter out.)

It was the era when the bunt first became a major part of offensive strategy. Bats with one side flattened were usually employed for this purpose (and remained legal until 1893).

In the National League of the 1880's, the Chicago White Stockings were the pre-eminent team; they won the N.L. pennant five out of seven seasons between 1880 and 1886. On the field they were led by manager

In the mid 1880s catchers began wearing masks, chest protectors and padded gloves. Here's an early advertisement for baseball equipment.

SPALDING'S TRADE-MARKED CATCHER'S MASKS.—Continued.

No. 1-0. SPALDING'S REGULATION LEAGUE MASK, made of heavy wire, well-padded and faced with horsehide, warranted first-class in every respect...........................$3 00
No. 1. SPALDING'S BOYS' LEAGUE MASK, made of heavy wire, equally as heavy in proportion to size as the No. 2-0 mask. It is made to fit a boy's face and gives the same protection as the League Mask..............................2 50

AMATEUR MASKS.

To meet the demand for good masks at a low price, we have manufactured a line of amateur masks, which are superior to any mask in the market at the same price. We do not guarantee these masks, and believe that our Trade-Marked Masks are worth more than the difference in price.

No. A. AMATEUR MASK, made the same size and general style as the League Mask, but with lighter wire and faced with leather (we guarantee this mask to be superior to so-called League or professional masks sold by other manufacturers).........................$1 75
No. B. BOYS' AMATEUR MASK, similar to No. A Mask, only made smaller to fit a boy's face........................1 50

Amateur Mask.

Any of the above masks mailed post-paid on receipt of price.

SPALDING'S TRADE-MARKED CATCHER'S GLOVES.

After considerable expense and many experiments we have finally perfected a Catcher's Glove that meets with general favor from professional catchers.

The old style of open backed gloves introduced by us several years ago is still adhered to, but the quality of material and workmanship has been materially improved, until now we are justified in claiming the best line of catcher's gloves in the market. These gloves do not interfere with throwing, can be easily put on and taken off, and no player subject to sore hands should be without a pair. Our new patent seamless palm glove is admittedly the finest glove ever made, and is used by all professional catchers. We make them in ten different grades, as follows:

No. 4-O. SPALDING'S SPECIAL LEAGUE CATCHER'S GLOVE. Patented, full left hand. Made from choice soft buck-skin, padded and lined with kid. Soft leather tips on fingers of left glove. This is the finest fielder's glove ever produced. Each pair packed in separate box.
Per pair............$5 00

No. 4-O.

CHICAGO, A. G. SPALDING & BROS, NEW YORK.

and first baseman "Cap" Anson who accumulated over 3000 hits and 1700 RBIs in the 22 years he played major league baseball, a phenomenal feat when you consider that in his prime years the season schedule consisted of fewer than a hundred games.

But as great a player as he was, Anson was constantly being upstaged in the press by another Chicago player, flamboyant outfielder and catcher Mike "King" Kelly, who was baseball's first major superstar. Kelly had perfected the hook slide, and whenever the handsome, hard-playing, hard-drinking Kelly got on base he would be greeted by chants of "Slide Kelly Slide!" from the stands. A popular song of the day went:

> *Slide, Kelly, slide!*
> *Your running's a disgrace!*
> *Slide, Kelly, slide!*
> *Stay there, hold your base!*
> *If someone doesn't steal ya,*
> *And your batting doesn't fail ya,*
> *They'll take you to Australia!*
> *Slide, Kelly, slide!*

When the charismatic Kelly was sold to Boston after the '86 season for the then unheard-of sum of $10,000, the news totally shook the baseball world and the press dubbed him "The Ten Thousand Dollar Beauty." (Kelly himself was to receive $4,000 per year at Boston; he had been making $2,500 per year at Chicago in an age when the average major league ball player was paid about $1,600 per season.)

On the mound, the White Stockings were well represented by pitchers; Larry Corcoran, who pitched three no hitters in the early part of the decade, and John Clarkson, who won 53 games for Chicago in the 1885 championship season and then followed up with seasons of 35 and 38 wins. (A year after "King" Kelly was sold to Boston for $10,000, Clarkson was also sold to the same club for $10,000.)

Over in the American Association, the foremost team during this era was the St. Louis Browns, who won four straight Association championships between 1885 and 1888. They were owned by the flamboyant Chris Von der Ahe, a German immigrant who was the proprietor of a beer garden in St. Louis. He had originally gotten into baseball because he saw it as a great opportunity to sell beer (at the St. Louis ball park Von der Ahe's vendors prowled the stands at every game peddling steins of the golden liquid to the thirsty crowd).

Chris Von der Ahe

Von der Ahe, who was basically ignorant about baseball itself, was nevertheless constantly interfering with the running of the club, much to the chagrin of field manager Charles Commiskey.

Major league baseball has had a long history of colorful team owners, and Chris Von der Ahe was the very first. Such characters as George Steinbrenner, Marge Shott, Charles O. Finley, Bill Veeck and the like, have just been carrying on a tradition that was undoubtedly started by Von der Ahe.

In *Baseball, The Early Years*, Harold Seymour says that "Von der Ahe himself could have played in vaudeville. He was a heavy-set man whose face featured a great bulbous nose and a full mustache. He wore loud clothes, spent money liberally, and liked to exclaim 'Nothing is too goot for my poys!'" and when "Der Boss President" was at the ballpark he "made the players nervous, watching their every move with field glasses, running around the stands blowing a whistle at them, or storming into the dressing room swearing at players whose errors lost the game."

Seymour tells of an incident when Von der Ahe supposedly boasted to a delegation of visitors that he had the biggest baseball diamond in the world. When Commiskey took him aside and whispered that all diamonds were the same size, Von der Ahe promptly retreated and simply claimed that he owned the biggest infield!

Von der Ahe would ceremoniously take each day's game receipts to the bank in a wheelbarrow, flanked by armed guards, and once he allowed himself to be arrested at the ballpark after he defied a Missouri law which prohibited baseball on Sunday.

Probably his biggest fiasco took place after the 1887 season when Von der Ahe, after being inspired by Chicago's sale of "King" Kelly and John

Clarkson to Boston for the then astronomical amount of $10,000 each, decided to fatten his own purse, so he promptly decimated his team by selling his top two pitchers, Robert Lee Caruthers and Dave Foutz, along with his number-one catcher "Doc" Bushong to Brooklyn for $10,000, and then peddling star outfielder Curt Welch and his only shortstop Bill Gleason to Philadelphia for $5,000.

Unbelievably, Commiskey, starting from almost scratch, was able to recruit enough new players to put together a team for the following year that was good enough to win the pennant.

Charles Commiskey's exploits as Browns manager and first-baseman are legendary. He is generally credited for revolutionizing the way the position of first base was played. Until he came along, it was customary for all the basemen to stay very near their bases, so when Commiskey ventured out to short right field to catch a fly ball, or when he would gobble up a hot grounder while playing away from the bag, and then have the pitcher go over to first to cover the play, it changed baseball forever. He was also the first manager to shift his infield in or out, depending on the situation and stage of the game.

On the mound, before they were traded, the Browns were led by pitchers: Bob Caruthers who won 40 games in '85, and then followed up with seasons of 30 and 29 wins; and Dave Foutz who won 33 games in '85 and then followed up with seasons of 41 and 24 wins. The Browns offence was bolstered by outfielder Tip O'Neill who hit .435 in 1887 (He was originally credited with a .492 batting average, as walks were counted as hits for that one season).

Racism, unfortunately, became an official policy of professional baseball in the 1880's. In 1884, Moses Fleetwood Walker was the first black major league player. He, along with his brother Welday, played in the American Association for the Toledo Blue Stockings, but a stop was soon put to this by the men who ran the game, and no black player was again allowed to compete at a major league level until Jackie Robinson put on a Brooklyn Dodgers uniform in 1947.

In the 1880's, the quality and size of ballparks improved somewhat from the rinky dink structures that were prevalent in the '70's, as baseball attendance grew and major league baseball started to look like it would be around for a while. The finest ballpark in the land was Lakefront Stadium in Chicago, which seated 10,000 spectators, had 18 private boxes and featured a brass band that played between innings. Towards the end of the decade a 20,000-seat double-decker stadium was built in Philadelphia.

Moses Fleetwood Walker

In 1884, another major league, called the Union Association, was born. The U.A. was founded by Henry V. Lucas, a St. Louis real estate agent. The two established leagues raided enough of the new league's players to put it out of business in one year.

The next league to come along was the Players League in 1890. Billy Voltz, a minor league manager from Chattanooga, had founded the National Brotherhood of Professional Base Ball Players in 1885. It was baseball's first labor organization. The Brotherhood's first president was New York Giant pitcher John Montgomery Ward, who had obtained a law degree by studying at night at Columbia Law College. After a number of clashes with major league brass over the next several years, Ward led the Brotherhood in open revolution at the end of the 1889 season, and this resulted in the formation of the Players League in 1890.

The Players League was really a kind of a slaves' revolt, as it was composed of players from the two leagues who were frustrated with limited salaries, unjust fines and the reserve clause (which virtually bound a player to the same team for life). A lack of administrative leadership and heavy gate competition brought about this league's demise after a year.

In 1888 Ernest L. Thayer wrote his famous poem, "Casey at the Bat." When actor De Wolf Hopper recited Thayer's verse on a Chicago stage the following year, it became a sensation. Hopper would recite the piece some 10,000 more times during his career.

Casey at the Bat *by Ernest L. Thayer*

The outlook wasn't brilliant for the Mudville nine that day;
The score stood four to two, with but one inning more to play,
And then when Cooney died at first, and Barrows did the same,
A pall-like silence fell upon the patrons of the game.

A straggling few got up to go in deep despair. The rest
Clung to that hope which springs eternal in the human breast;
They thought, "If only Casey could but get a whack at that —
We'd put up even money now, with Casey at the bat."

But Flynn preceded Casey, as did also Jimmy Blake,
And the former was a hoodoo, while the latter was a cake;
So upon that stricken multitude grim melancholy sat;
For there seemed but little chance of Casey getting to the bat.

But Flynn let drive a single, to the wonderment of all,
And Blake, the much despised, tore the cover off the ball;
And when the dust had lifted, and men saw what had occurred,
There was Jimmy safe at second and Flynn a-hugging third.

Then from five thousand throats and more there rose a lusty yell;
It rumbled through the valley, it rattled in the dell;
It pounded through on the mountain and recoiled upon the flat,
For Casey, mighty Casey, was advancing to the bat.

There was ease in Casey's manner as he stepped into his place;
There was pride in Casey's bearing and a smile lit Casey's face.
And when, responding to the cheers, he lightly doffed his hat,
No stranger in the crowd could doubt 'twas Casey at the bat.

Ten thousand eyes were on him as he rubbed his hands with dirt.
Five thousand tongues applauded when he wiped them on his shirt.
Then while the writhing pitcher ground the ball into his hip,
Defiance flashed in Casey's eye, a sneer curled Casey's lip.

And now the leather-covered sphere came hurtling through the air,
And Casey stood a-watching it in haughty grandeur there.
Close by the sturdy batsman the ball unheeded sped —
"That ain't my style," said Casey. "Strike one!" the umpire said.

From the benches, black with people, there went up a muffled roar,
Like the beating of the storm-waves on a stern and distant shore;

"Kill him! Kill the umpire!" shouted some one on the stand;
And it's likely they'd have killed him had not Casey raised his hand.

With a smile of Christian charity great Casey's visage shone;
He stilled the rising tumult; he bade the game go on;
He signaled to the pitcher, and once more the dun sphere flew;
But Casey still ignored it, and the umpire said "Strike two!"

"Fraud!" cried the maddened thousands, and echo answered "Fraud!"
But one scornful look from Casey and the audience was awed.
They saw his face grow stern and cold, they saw his muscles strain,
And they knew that Casey wouldn't let that ball go by again.

The sneer has fled from Casey's lip, the teeth are clenched in hate;
He pounds with cruel violence his bat upon the plate.
And now the pitcher holds the ball, and now he lets it go,
And now the air is shattered by the force of Casey's blow.

Oh, somewhere in this favored land the sun is shining bright,
The band is playing somewhere, and somewhere hearts are light,
And somewhere men are laughing, and little children shout;
But there is no joy in Mudville — mighty Casey has struck out.

(First appearing in the San Francisco Examiner, *June 3, 1888)*

New York Metropolitans
1886 St. George Cricket Field

The game of baseball had spread so wide during the '80's that some 15 minor leagues were operating by 1889. Also in 1889, the A.A.'s Brooklyn Bridegrooms became the first club to attract over 300,000 spectators in a single season.

National League Monopoly: The 1890's

In 1891 the American Association folded leaving in its wake a legacy of Sunday games and league control of umpires. Four of its clubs were absorbed by the senior loop, and for the greater part of the 1890's a 12-team National League had a monopoly on major league baseball.

This 12-club N.L. consisted of Cincinnati, Cleveland, St. Louis, Louisville, Chicago and Pittsburgh in the west, and Philadelphia,

This photo shows the view from the Grand Pavilion of Boston's South End Grounds in the early 1890s. The stadium burned to the ground in 1894.

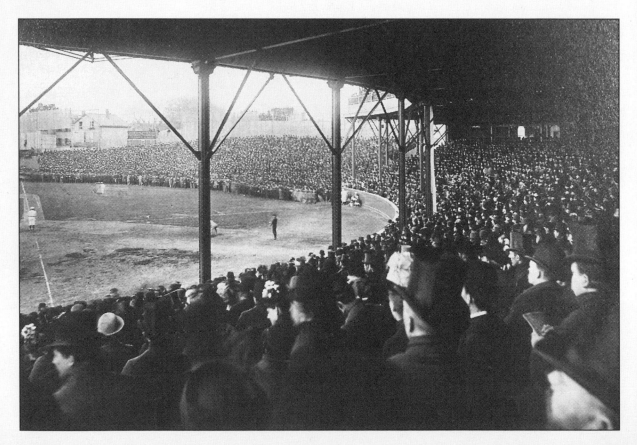

Brooklyn, Boston, New York, Baltimore and Washington in the east.

On the field, baseball took another major evolutionary step when, in 1893, the pitching distance was changed from 50 feet to the present 60 feet 6 inches (the extra 6 inches were the result of a mismeasurement). This put an end to the tremendous advantage the pitchers had enjoyed over the batters. In 1892 the collective batting average for the National League was .245; in '83, when the distance was increased, it jumped up to .280, and to .309 the following year.

New York Giant pitcher Amos Rusie was generally considered to be the main reason why the pitching distance was moved back to 60' 6". The "Hoosier Thunderbolt" not only threw a blazing fastball, he also tended to be a bit wild and it was deemed unfair, and just plain dangerous, for batters to have to face him from 50 feet. When the pitching distance was changed, the pitching box was replaced with a rubber slab on top of a mound.

Although the National League held a monopoly on major league baseball in the 1890's it did not do well financially. This was due to such factors as a chronic national economic recession, the 1898 Spanish-American War, and a competitive imbalance in the league (during this era Boston, Baltimore and Brooklyn won all the races, causing fan interest to drop off in the other cities).

During this period the N.L. owners played their own type of hard ball with the players by imposing a $2,400 salary ceiling and arbitrarily cutting players' salaries whenever they felt like it. The players, with no place else to go, had to grit their teeth and put up with it.

A post-season National League championship series began in 1894. William Temple, owner of the Pittsburgh Pirates, donated a trophy, and the first- and second-place teams played each other for the Temple Cup. The first Temple Cup was won by the New York Giants, who routed the Baltimore Orioles in four straight games.

Those very same Baltimore Orioles were probably the most famous team to come out of this era. The feisty Orioles made baseball into a real team sport, specializing in relays and cut-offs and pioneering the hit and run. Renowned for the "Old Oriole Spirit" which impelled men to ignore injuries and keep on playing, the gritty Orioles were managed by "Foxy"

Ned Hanlon and featured such players as John McGraw and Wee Willie "Hit 'em where they ain't" Keeler. They won three pennants in the 1890's and are known as baseball's first "greatest team of all time."

In 1898 the playing schedule was lengthened to 154 games, and it would stay that way until 1961. Rule changes in the 1890's allowed player substitutions, treated foul bunts as strikes and introduced the infield fly rule.

Though the Baltimore Orioles were the most famous team of the 1890's, the Boston Beaneaters won the most pennants, walking off with a total of five during the decade.

The New Century: A Challenge from the West

It was inevitable that someone else would come along to challenge the National League's supremacy, and that person was a former sportswriter by the name of Ban Johnson. Johnson was the president of the Western League, a minor league that operated in the midwest. He had dreams of someday transforming his circuit into another major league, and in 1900, after the National League dropped four of its twelve franchises, he felt the time was right. So, he changed the name of his circuit to the American League and placed clubs in several eastern cities. Then he snubbed the National Agreement, under which all of organized baseball now operated, and raided the National League for enough talent to give the American League major league status when the season started in 1901.

Bancroft Johnson

Johnson was assisted in his assault on the National League by his good friend and drinking companion Charles Commiskey. Commiskey, whose playing days were now over, had become the owner of the St. Paul Western League franchise, and in 1900 he wanted to move his team into Chicago. Al Spalding who then owned Chicago's N.L. club couldn't see anything wrong with a minor league club moving into town so he let Commiskey have an old decaying baseball facility by the

name of Brotherhood Park under one condition: Commiskey's team could not identify itself as a Chicago club! Commiskey agreed to this provision and then got around it by calling his new club the White Stockings. The National League team (which was then called the Orphans and would soon become the Cubs), had long since stopped calling itself the White Stockings, yet everyone knew it was a name that belonged to Chicago!

Once established in Chicago, Commiskey soon turned his club into a major league operation and eventually built a new ball park for them to play in. In 1904, Commiskey's team became officially known as the *Chicago* White Sox.

A war ensued between the American League and the N.L. for the 1901 and 1902 seasons, with many of the senior circuit's top stars jumping ship to the A.L.

In 1903 the National League decided enough was enough, and made peace with the upstart league. The two leagues signed a new National Agreement which gave them both equal status and that October the first modern-day World Series was held with the A.L.'s Boston Americans, led by the pitching of Cy Young and Bill Dinneen, defeating the N.L.'s Pittsburgh Pirates five games to three in a best of nine affair.

In 1904 the two leagues took to squabbling again and no World Series was held. But in 1905 they both kissed and made up and, with the exception of an unsuccessful challenge by the upstart Federal League in 1914 and '15, the two leagues have enjoyed a monopoly on major league baseball ever since.

1901-1919: The Dead Ball Era

The first two decades of this century were collectively called the "dead ball era," a period in baseball when pitching dominated the game. Rather than going for the long ball, batters of the day would try to squeeze out runs by bunting, stealing and punching out base hits. On the

The first modern-day World Series was played in 1903 between the Boston Americans and the Pittsburgh Pirates. At the first game, which was played at Boston's Huntington Avenue Base Ball Grounds, the crowd floods the field. This was a common occurrence at baseball games played during this era.

mound, the spitball and other trick pitches were often employed and ERA's of 3.00 or less were quite normal.

Large concrete and steel ballparks, which often held crowds of 30,000 or more, were built to replace the old wooden structures; as the game got more and more popular (and profitable), annual attendance rose from 4.7 million in 1903 to over 10 million in 1911. Players' salaries also got fatter, but not as fat as the owners' bank accounts. In 1910 the average big league baseball player made $2,500 per year, with a few stars getting as much as $12,000.

In the A.L. the leading offensive star of the dead ball era was Ty Cobb, who stole 765 bases from 1905 to 1919 while capturing 10 batting titles and hitting .364. His counterpart in the N.L. was Honus Wagner, who won eight batting titles and stole 639 bases from 1900 to 1917. Other great offensive stars of the day were Tris Speaker, Nap Lajoie, Eddie Collins, Sam Crawford and Shoeless Joe Jackson.

Among the great pitchers of this era were such immortals as Cy Young, Walter Johnson, Christy Mathewson, Grover Cleveland Alexander, Eddie Plank and spitball artist Ed Walsh.

During the first two decades of the twentieth century the top National League clubs were John McGraw's New York Giants, who bagged six pennants, and the Chicago Cubs, who won seven. In the American League, Connie Mack's Philadelphia Athletics walked off with seven pennants, the Boston Red Sox won five, and Ty Cobb and the Detroit Tigers took home three.

Baseball attendance in the A.L. and N.L. dropped to around 5 million per year in 1914 and 1915 when the well financed Federal League burst onto the scene. After the demise of the F.L., the two leagues had almost gotten back on their feet when World War I came along. Many players went into the service, resulting in depleted rosters and a shortened playing schedule in 1918 and 1919. Attendance hit a low of 3 million in 1918, but rebounded to 6.5 million in 1919.

In 1918 the Boston Red Sox unwittingly helped to create a baseball legend. In order to help fill the holes in their lineup which had been caused by the war, Boston manager Ed Barrow was forced to put pitching ace Babe Ruth in the outfield between starts, and it changed baseball forever. That year he hit .300 and had 66 RBI (third best in the A.L.), the following year he belted a record 29 homers and his career as a pitcher was over.

After the 1919 season, Boston owner Harry Frazee sold Ruth to the Yankees for $100,000 and a $300,000 mortgage on Fenway Park, and the rest is history. Who knows what would have happened if circumstances hadn't necessitated sticking Ruth in the outfield that fateful summer. He might have remained just what he was — one of the best pitchers in the American League.

The era ended with the game's biggest disgrace: the Black Sox Scandal. In 1919 the Chicago White Sox were the hottest thing in baseball. They won the American League pennant that year with a 88-52 record and were 5-1 favorites to beat the Cincinnati Reds in the World Series.

But even before the Series began there were rumors swirling about that a "fix" was in. And when Cincinnati took the best of nine series five games to three, it didn't sit well with a lot of baseball fans. One year later, a Chicago Grand Jury blew the whole thing wide open, naming eight Chicago players as having conspired with gamblers to throw the series.

Kenesaw Mountain Landis

As it turned out, Chicago's poorly paid players (owner Charles Commiskey was one of the stingiest men in baseball) were easy pickings for the gamblers who had offered the eight teammates $100,000 (but actually only paid $10,000) to lose the series.

The most famous conspirator was outfielder "Shoeless Joe" Jackson, an illiterate farm boy from South Carolina, whose lifetime batting average of .356 and outstanding running and fielding abilities would have eventually put him in the Hall of Fame, if it hadn't been for this tragedy.

Rocked by the scandal, major league baseball appointed its first commissioner, a stern, no-nonsense federal judge by the name of Kenesaw Mountain Landis, to try and restore the game's reputation for integrity.

Landis ruled baseball with an iron fist, and even though the eight players were acquitted in a conspiracy trial (after some of the transcripts of their testimony mysteriously disappeared from court files), Landis nevertheless banned them all from baseball for life.

By 1920 the game of baseball had certainly come a long way since the days when Alexander Cartwright and his friends formulated the first rules and regulations some 75 years earlier. So far, the game had seen nation-wide growth and acceptance, gambling and the birth of professionalism, the formation of the first leagues, the first superstar players, and the game's first major scandal. Yet baseball still had a long way to go.

In 1920, after a livelier ball was introduced to the game, Babe Ruth would hit a record-breaking 54 home runs for the New York Yankees in his first season with the club, and the era of the slugger would begin. It would also be the beginning of The Golden Age of Baseball, which would see major-league attendance records soar, large stadiums built to accommodate new fans, Sunday games legalized in most places, and the first big revenues for both owners and players.

Ah, but that's another era (and another book); for now let us focus our attention on baseball during its infancy and adolescence. Let's examine the "National Pastime" during its formative years, as we look at the years 1845 through 1919 — from Cartwright to Shoeless Joe.

Baseball Biographies

Charles Adams

Pitcher (Charles Benjamin "Babe" Adams)
Born: May 18, 1882, Tipton, Indiana
Died: July 27, 1968, Silver Spring, Maryland

After pitching a single game for the Cardinals in 1906 and appearing in four games for Pittsburgh in 1907, Babe Adams came back to the Pirates in 1909 for what would be his official rookie season ... and what a year it was for the 27-year-old righthander. He finished the regular season with a 12-3 record and a ERA of 1.11 and then went on to face Ty Cobb and the Detroit Tigers in the World Series. He won the first game (4-1), the fifth game (8-4) and, on two days rest, the final game (8-0) to become the first pitcher to win three games in a seven-game series.

He was a mainstay of the Pirates pitching staff for the next 16 years, winning 20 games twice and finishing his career with a lifetime ERA of 2.76. His control was so good that in 1920 he walked only 18 men in 263 innings and allowed only 430 bases on balls in his 19-year career.

Adams, Charles Benjamin
BL/TR, 5'11.5", 185 lbs. Deb: 4/18/06

YEAR	TM/L	W	L	PCT	G	IP	H	HR	BB	SO	ERA
1906	StL-NL	0	1	.000	1	4	9	0	2	0	13.50
1907	Pit-NL	0	2	.000	4	22	40	1	3	11	6.95
1909	Pit-NL	12	3	.800	25	130	88	0	23	65	1.11
1910	Pit-NL	18	9	.667	34	245	217	4	60	101	2.24
1911	Pit-NL	22	12	.647	40	293.1	253	5	42	133	2.33
1912	Pit-NL	11	8	.579	28	170.1	169	4	35	63	2.91
1913	Pit-NL	21	10	.677	43	313.2	271	8	49	144	2.15
1914	Pit-NL	13	16	.448	40	283	253	5	39	91	2.51
1915	Pit-NL	14	14	.500	40	245	229	6	34	62	2.87
1916	Pit-NL	2	9	.182	16	72.1	91	2	12	22	5.72
1918	Pit-NL	1	1	.500	3	22.2	15	0	4	6	1.19
1919	Pit-NL	17	10	.630	34	263.1	213	1	23	92	1.98
1920	Pit-NL	17	13	.567	35	263	240	6	18	84	2.16
1921	Pit-NL	14	5	.737	25	160	155	4	18	55	2.64
1922	Pit-NL	8	11	.421	27	171.1	191	1	15	39	3.57
1923	Pit-NL	13	7	.650	26	158.2	196	8	25	38	4.42
1924	Pit-NL	3	1	.750	9	39.2	31	1	3	5	1.13
1925	Pit-NL	6	5	.545	33	101.1	129	7	17	18	5.42
1926	Pit-NL	2	3	.400	19	36.2	51	5	8	7	6.14
Total	19	194	140	.581	482	2,995.1	2841	68	430	1,036	2.76

Daniel "Doc" Adams

Baseball Pioneer (Daniel Lucas Adams)
Born: November 1, 1814
Died: January 3, 1899

"Doc" Adams was an original member of the New York Knickerbockers when they were formed in 1845. He also served as the club's president from 1847 to 1862. Adams (who was a medical doctor) actually made the first balls the Knickerbockers and other early teams played with, and supervised the manufacture of the bats. He is believed to be the first person to play the position of shortstop.

Adams, as head of the oldest baseball club in the land, became presiding officer at the first convention of baseball players in 1857. It was this convention that established nine innings (rather than 21 runs) as the length of a game.

In March of the following year, when baseball's first governing body, The National Association of Base Ball Players, was formed, Adams was appointed chairman of the rules committee. The committee fixed a firm distance of 30 yards between the bases (instead of the rather vague 42 paces from home to second and from first to third that had been in effect) and set a definite pitching distance of 45 feet. Adams also advocated changing the rules so that only balls caught on the fly, rather than on the first bounce, were considered an out. This rule was finally adopted in 1864, shortly after Adams left the committee.

Franklin P. Adams

Baseball Writer
Born: 1861
Died: 1960

On July 10, 1908, while on his way to a Giants-Cubs game at the Polo Grounds, this New York columnist scribbled down one of baseball's most famous poems. It was called "Baseball's Sad Lexicon" and its popularity ultimately helped the Cubs double play combination of Joe Tinker, Johnny Evers and Frank Chance to get elected to the Hall of Fame. This is what he wrote:

These are the saddest of possible words —
Tinker to Evers to Chance
Trio of bear cubs and fleeter than birds —
Tinker to Evers to Chance
Thoughtlessly pricking our gonfalon bubble,
Making a Giant hit into a double,
Words that are weighty with nothing but trouble —
Tinker to Evers to Chance.

Bob Addy

Outfielder - Manager (Robert Edward Addy)
Born: February, 1845, Rochester, New York
Died: April 9, 1910, Pocatello, Idaho

Bob Addy is generally credited with being the first player to slide into a base. He apparently developed the technique in the 1860's when he played for the Forest City Club of Rockford, Illinois, and brought it along with him when the club joined the National Association in 1871. Later he played for, and briefly managed, Chicago in the National league.

Addy, Robert Edward "Magnet"
BL/TL, 5'8", 160 lbs. Deb: 5/6/1871

YEAR	TM/L	G	AB	R	H	2B	3B	HR	RBI	BB	SO	AVG
1871	Rok-NA	25	118	30	32	6	0	0	13	4	0	.271
1873	Phi-NA	10	51	12	16	1	0	0	9	2	0	.314
	Bos-NA	31	152	37	54	6	2	1	36	1	0	.355
	Yr	41	203	49	70	7	2	1	45	3	0	.345
1874	Har-NA	50	211	25	50	9	2	0	2	—	—	.237
1875	Phi-NA	69	311	60	79	11	4	0	0	—	—	.254
Total	4 N	185	843	164	231	33	8	1	105	INC	INC	.274
1876	Chi-NL	32	142	36	40	4	1	0	16	5	0	.282
1877	Cin-NL	57	245	27	68	2	3	0	31	6	5	.278
Total	2	89	387	63	108	6	4	0	47	11	5	.279

Eddie Ainsmith

Catcher (Edward Wilbur "Dorf" Ainsmith)
Born: January 4, 1892, Cambridge, Massachusetts
Died: September 6, 1981, Fort Lauderdale, Florida

A steady catcher for 15 years, known mostly for his defensive skills, Ainsmith's career was highlighted in 1918 when he appealed against being drafted into the military in World War I on the grounds that since baseball was the national pastime, then he, as a professional baseball player, was therefore engaged in a patriotic endeavor.

Secretary of War Newton D. Baker didn't buy it though, and subsequently declared baseball an unessential amusement with all its players and personnel subject to the draft.

Ainsmith, Edward Wilbur "Dorf"
BR/TR, 5'11", 180 lbs. Deb: 8/9/10

YEAR	TM/L	G	AB	R	H	2B	3B	HR	RBI	BB	SO	AVG
1910	Was-AL	33	104	4	20	1	2	0	9	6	—	.192
1911	Was-AL	61	149	12	33	2	3	0	14	10	—	.221
1912	Was-AL	61	186	22	42	7	2	0	22	14	—	.226
1913	Was-AL	84	229	26	49	4	4	2	20	12	41	.214
1914	Was-AL	62	151	11	34	7	0	0	13	9	28	.225
1915	Was-AL	47	120	13	24	4	2	0	6	10	18	.200
1916	Was-AL	51	100	11	17	4	0	0	8	8	14	.170
1917	Was-AL	125	350	38	67	17	4	0	42	40	48	.191
1918	Was-AL	96	292	22	62	10	9	0	20	29	44	.212
1919	Det-AL	114	364	42	99	17	12	3	32	45	30	.272
1920	Det-AL	69	186	19	43	5	3	1	19	14	19	.231
1921	Det-AL	35	98	6	27	5	2	0	12	13	7	.276
	StL-NL	27	62	5	18	0	1	0	5	3	4	.290
1922	StL-NL	119	379	46	111	14	4	13	59	28	43	.293
1923	StL-NL	82	263	22	56	11	6	3	34	22	19	.213
	Bro-NL	2	10	0	2	0	0	0	2	0	0	.200
	Yr	84	273	22	58	11	6	3	36	22	19	.212
1924	NY-NL	10	5	0	3	0	0	0	0	0	0	.600
Total	15	1078	3048	299	707	108	54	22	317	263	INC	.232

YEAR	TM/L	W	L	PCT	G	IP	H	HR	BB	SO	ERA
1913	Was-AL	0	0	—	1	0.1	2	0	0	0	54.00

Grover Cleveland Alexander

Pitcher (Grover Cleveland Alexander "Pete")
Born: February 26, 1887, Elba, Nebraska
Died: November 4, 1950, St. Paul, Nebraska

Though plagued with alcoholism for most of his career, Alexander was nevertheless one of baseball's all-time greatest pitchers. This 6'1", 185 lb. farm boy from Nebraska, who was one of 13 children, began his professional career at the age of 22 for Galesburg, IL, of the Central Association in 1909. He had a record of 15-8 with 198 strikeouts and 42 walks for Galesburg, when, one fateful day, while trying to break up a double play he took the shortstop's throw directly in the head and was knocked unconscious for 56 hours. He woke up with double vision and Galesburg, in a rather underhanded deal, sold his contract to Indianapolis, where on his first pitch he broke three of the manager's ribs.

Over the winter Indianapolis peddled his contract to Syracuse of the New York State League. But before the 1910 season started Alexander's double vision cleared up and he went on to lead the league with a 29-14 record in only 43 games. This earned him a promotion to the big leagues when Philadelphia drafted him at the end of the season.

In his rookie season for the Phillies he led the National League with 28 victories, including seven shutouts (four were consecutive). Both his 367 innings and 31 complete games were highest in the league.

He spent 19 more years in the National League and during his remarkable career he led the league in wins six times, ERA five times, strikeouts six times, complete games six times, shutouts seven times (including a record 16 in 1916) and he won more than 20 games nine times (including three seasons in a row of more than 30 wins).

In 1915 he finished the season with an ERA of 1.22. This was a National League record that stood until 1969 when the Cardinals' Bob Gibson bettered it. Although he never pitched a no-hitter in the big leagues, the four one hitters he pitched in 1915 is a record for a single season.

While serving in France in World War I he lost the hearing in one ear due to shelling and developed a form of epilepsy.

The highlight of his later career was in 1926 when he won two complete games for St. Louis against the Yankees in the World Series and then made a dramatic relief appearance in the seventh inning of the final game to strike out Tony Lazzeri with the bases loaded, thereby preserving the Cardinals 3-2 win.

Grover Cleveland Alexander was inducted into the National Baseball Hall of Fame in 1938.

Alexander, Grover Cleveland
BR/TR, 6'1", 185 lbs. Deb: 4/15/11

YEAR	TM/L	W	L	PCT	G	IP	H	HR	BB	SO	ERA
1911	Phi-NL	28	13	.683	48	367	285	5	129	227	2.57
1912	Phi-NL	19	17	.528	46	310.1	289	11	105	195	2.81
1913	Phi-NL	22	8	.733	47	306.1	288	9	75	159	2.79
1914	Phi-NL	27	15	.643	46	355	327	8	76	214	2.38
1915	Phi-NL	31	10	.756	49	376.1	253	3	64	241	1.22
1916	Phi-NL	33	12	.733	48	389	323	6	50	167	1.55
1917	Phi-NL	30	13	.698	45	388	336	4	56	200	1.83
1918	Chi-NL	2	1	.667	3	26	19	0	3	15	1.73
1919	Chi-NL	16	11	.593	30	235	180	3	38	121	1.72
1920	Chi-NL	27	14	.659	46	363.1	335	8	69	173	1.91
1921	Chi-NL	15	13	.536	31	252	286	10	33	77	3.39
1922	Chi-NL	16	13	.552	33	245.2	283	8	34	48	3.63
1923	Chi-NL	22	12	.647	39	305	308	17	30	72	3.19
1924	Chi-NL	12	5	.706	21	169.1	183	9	25	33	3.03
1925	Chi-NL	15	11	.577	32	236	270	14	29	63	3.39
1926	Chi-NL	3	3	.500	7	52	55	0	7	12	3.46
	StL-NL	9	7	.563	23	148.1	136	8	24	35	2.91
	Yr	12	10	.545	30	200.1	191	8	31	47	3.05
1927	StL-NL	21	10	.677	37	268	261	11	38	48	2.52
1928	StL-NL	16	9	.640	34	243.2	262	15	37	59	3.36
1929	StL-NL	9	8	.529	22	132	149	10	23	33	3.89
1930	Phi-NL	0	3	.000	9	21.2	40	5	6	6	9.14
Total	20	373	208	.642	696	5,190	4,868	164	951	2,198	2.56

Nick Altrock

Pitcher - Coach - Clown
Born: September 15, 1876, Cincinnati, Ohio
Died: January 20, 1965, Washington, D.C.

Southpaw Nick Altrock won 19 games for the White Sox in 1904 and then followed that with two 20-win seasons in '05 and '06. The following year his arm gave out and he was eventually traded to Washington in 1909. His pitching appearances with that club were minimal but he stayed with them until 1953 as a coach. He is probably best remembered as one of baseball's first clowns. He worked up a pantomime act with Al Schacht which they would perform before games and between ends of doubleheaders.

Altrock, Nicholas
BB/TL, 5'10", 197 lbs. Deb: 7/14/1898

YEAR	TM/L	W	L	PCT	G	IP	H	HR	BB	SO	ERA
1898	Lou-NL	3	3	.500	11	70	89	2	21	13	4.50
1902	Bos-AL	0	2	.000	3	18	19	0	7	5	2.00
1903	Bos-AL	0	1	.000	1	8	13	0	4	3	9.00
	Chi-AL	4	3	.571	12	71	59	4	19	19	2.15
	Yr	4	4	.500	13	79	72	4	23	22	2.85
1904	Chi-AL	19	14	.576	38	307	274	2	48	87	2.96
1905	Chi-AL	22	12	.647	38	315.2	274	3	63	97	1.88
1906	Chi-AL	20	13	.606	38	287.2	269	0	42	99	2.06
1907	Chi-AL	7	13	.350	30	213.2	210	3	31	61	2.57
1908	Chi-AL	5	7	.417	23	136	127	2	18	21	2.71
1909	Chi-AL	0	1	.000	1	9	16	0	1	2	5.00
	Was-AL	1	3	.250	9	38	55	0	5	9	5.45
	Yr	1	4	.200	10	47	71	0	6	11	5.36
1912	Was-AL	0	1	.000	1	1	1	0	2	0	18.00
1913	Was-AL	0	0	—	4	9	7	0	4	2	5.00
1914	Was-AL	0	0	—	1	1	3	0	0	0	0.00
1915	Was-AL	0	0	—	1	3	7	0	1	2	9.00
1918	Was-AL	1	2	.333	5	24	24	1	6	5	3.00
1919	Was-AL	0	0	—	1	0	4	0	0	0	\
1924	Was-AL	0	0	—	1	2	4	0	0	0	0.00
Total	16	82	75	.522	218	1,514	1,455	17	272	425	2.67

Cap Anson

Infielder - Manager (Adrian Constantine Anson)
Born: April 11, 1852, Marshalltown, Iowa
Died: April 14, 1922, Chicago, Illinois

Cap Anson was one of baseball's most prominent figures of the 1880's. Counting his five years in the National Association, he spent 27 years playing major league baseball. Anson accumulated over 3,000 hits and 1,700 RBI in this time, a phenomenal feat when you consider that in his prime years the season schedule was fewer than one hundred games. Only three times in his 27 seasons did he bat less than .300 and he led the N.L. in batting average twice (his personal best was a blistering .399 in 1881), he also led the league in RBI eight times.

He was the manager and first baseman for the Chicago White Stockings when they won five National League pennants in the 1880's. As a manager he was one of the first to employ the hit-and-run play and the practice of having fielders back up other fielders on throws. He also originated platoon baseball and was one of the first to use signals on the field.

Anson was also a well known racist. In one famous incident in 1883, when Chicago played an exhibition game against the American Association's Toledo Blue Stockings, Anson refused to take the field because Toledo had a black catcher (Moses Fleetwood Walker, the first black to play major league ball). Anson changed his mind though, when told he wouldn't get paid unless he played. This incident apparently lead to baseball's adoption of the infamous "color bar" which kept any more blacks from playing in the major leagues until Jackie Robinson put on a Dodger uniform in 1947.

Anson became part owner of the White Stockings in 1888. When he launched a youth movement in 1890 the club's nickname was changed to the "Colts," and his image was so linked with the team that when he left after the 1897 season they became known as the "Orphans" (they became the "Cubs" in 1902).

Cap Anson was inducted into the Baseball Hall of Fame in 1939.

Anson, Adrian Constantine
BR/TR, 6', 227 lbs. Deb: 5/6/1871

YEAR	TM/L	W	L	PCT	G	IP	H	HR	BB	SO	ERA
1883	Chi-NL	0	0	—	2	3	1	0	1	0	0.00
1884	Chi-NL	0	1	.000	1	1	3	2	1	1	18.00
Total	2	0	1	.000	3	4	4	2	2	1	4.50

Frank "Home Run" Baker

Infielder (John Franklin Baker)
Born: March 13, 1886, Trappe, Maryland
Died: June, 28, 1963, Trappe, Maryland

Although he never hit more than 12 home runs in a single season, back in the era of the dead ball Frank "Home Run" Baker led the A.L. in homers four consecutive years from 1911 to 1914 and also led the league twice in RBI and once in triples.

"Home Run" earned his nickname when he hit the game-winning home run in the second game of the 1911 World Series and the game-tying home run in the following game, helping Connie Mack's Philadelphia Athletics defeat John McGraw's New York Giants four games to two.

This left handed third baseman was part of the A's fabled "$100,000 infield" (along with first baseman Stuffy McInnis, second baseman Eddie Collins and shortstop Jack Barry). He hit .375 in the 1911 series and went on to play in the American League for 13 years, finishing with a lifetime batting average of .307.

At the end of the 1914 season he threatened to jump to the Federal League if Philadelphia owner Mack didn't match the kind of money the Feds were offering. When Mack refused, Baker sat out the 1915 season in protest. Mack sold him to the Yankees in 1916 for $35,000.

Baker spent another year out of baseball in 1920 when he left the game to care for his terminally ill wife. In 1921 he came back as a part-time player for the Yankees and appeared in the club's first two World Series in '21 and '22.

Baker was inducted into the Baseball Hall of Fame in 1955.

Baker, John Franklin "Home Run"
BL/TR, 5'11", 173 lbs. Deb: 9/21/08

YEAR	TM/L	G	AB	R	H	2B	3B	HR	RBI	BB	SO	AVG
1908	Phi-AL	9	31	5	9	3	0	0	2	0	—	.290
1909	Phi-AL	148	541	73	165	27	19	4	85	26	—	.305
1910	Phi-AL	146	561	83	159	25	15	2	74	34	—	.283
1911	Phi-AL	148	592	96	198	42	14	11	115	40	—	.334
1912	Phi-AL	149	577	116	200	40	21	10	130	50	—	.347
1913	Phi-AL	149	564	116	190	34	9	12	117	63	31	.337
1914	Phi-AL	150	570	84	182	23	10	9	89	53	37	.319
1916	NY-AL	100	360	46	97	23	2	10	52	36	30	.269
1917	NY-AL	146	553	57	156	24	2	6	71	48	27	.282
1918	NY-AL	126	504	65	154	24	5	6	62	38	13	.306
1919	NY-AL	141	567	70	166	22	1	10	83	44	18	.293
1921	NY-AL	94	330	46	97	16	2	9	71	26	12	.294
1922	NY-AL	69	234	30	65	12	3	7	36	15	14	.278
Total	13	1,575	5,984	887	1,838	315	103	96	987	473	INC	.307

Lady Baldwin

Pitcher (Charles Busted Baldwin)
Born: April 8, 1859, Oramel, New York
Died March 7, 1937, Hastings, Michigan

Lady Baldwin's one outstanding major league season was in 1886 when he won 42 games for the Detroit Wolverines, an all-time record for a left-hander. His teammates gave him his strange nickname because he didn't smoke, swear or drink.

Baldwin, Charles Busted
BL/TL, 5'11", 160 lbs. Deb: 9/30/1884

YEAR	TM/L	W	L	PCT	G	IP	H	HR	BB	SO	ERA
1884	Mil-UA	1	1	.500	2	17	7	0	1	21	2.65
1885	Det-NL	11	9	.550	21	179.1	137	2	28	135	1.86
1886	Det-NL	42	13	.764	56	487	371	11	100	323	2.24
1887	Det-NL	13	10	.565	24	211	225	8	61	60	3.84
1888	Det-NL	3	3	.500	6	53	76	5	15	26	5.43
1890	Bro-NL	1	0	1.000	2	7.2	15	0	4	4	7.04
	Buf-PL	2	5	.286	7	62	90	5	24	13	4.50
Total	6	73	41	.640	118	1,017	921	31	233	582	2.85

YEAR	TM/L	G	AB	R	H	2B	3B	HR	RBI	BB	SO	AVG
1884	Mil-UA	7	27	6	6	3	0	0	—	0	—	.222
1885	Det-NL	31	124	12	30	6	3	0	18	6	22	.242
1886	Det-NL	57	204	25	41	6	3	0	25	18	44	.201
1887	Det-NL	24	85	15	23	0	1	0	7	10	6	.271
1888	Det-NL	6	23	5	6	0	0	0	3	3	3	.261
1890	Bro-NL	2	3	1	0	0	0	0	0	1	1	.000
	Buf-PL	7	28	4	8	1	0	0	2	2	1	.286
Total	6	134	494	68	114	16	7	0	INC	40	INC	.231

Frank Bancroft

Manager (Franklin Carter Bancroft)
Born: 1846
Died: 1921

Bancroft managed six major league clubs in the 1880's. In 1884 his Providence Grays won the National League pennant and then went on to defeat the New York Metropolitans in the very first World Series. Later, he spent 29 years as business manager of the Cincinnati Reds. He is also credited with introducing baseball to Latin America when he took a touring team to Cuba in 1879.

Ross Barnes

Infielder (Roscoe Charles Barnes)
Born: May 8, 1850, Mount Morris, Illinois
Died: February 5, 1915, Chicago, Illinois

Barnes won the National League's first batting crown with a .429 average in 1876. Previously he had won two batting championships in the National Association (in '72 and '73). He specialized in the "fair-foul" hit — bunts that would start out in fair territory then roll foul, but were considered fair under rules in effect at the time. When the rule was changed in 1877 his batting average dropped drastically.

Barnes, Roscoe Charles
BR/TR, 5'8.5", 145 lbs. Deb: 5/5/1871

YEAR	TM/L	G	AB	R	H	2B	3B	HR	RBI	BB	SO	AVG
1871	Bos-NA	31	157	66	63	10	9	0	34	13	1	.401
1872	Bos-NA	45	230	81	97	28	2	1	44	9	4	.422
1873	Bos-NA	60	322	125	137	28	10	3	61	18	2	.425
1874	Bos-NA	51	259	72	89	12	4	0	—	8	—	.344
1875	Bos-NA	78	393	114	142	22	6	1	—	7	—	.361
Total	5 n	265	1361	458	528	100	31	5	INC	55	?7	.388
1876	Chi-NL	66	322	126	138	21	14	1	59	20	8	.429
1877	Chi-NL	22	92	16	25	1	0	0	5	7	4	.272
1879	Cin-NL	77	323	55	86	9	2	1	30	16	25	.266
1881	Bos-NL	69	295	42	80	14	1	0	17	16	16	.271
Total	4	234	1,032	239	329	45	17	2	111	59	53	.319

YEAR	TM/L	W	L	PCT	G	IP	H	HR	BB	SO	ERA
1876	Chi-NL	0	0	—	1	1.1	7	0	0	0	20.25

Jake Beckly

Infielder (Jacob Peter Beckly)
Born: August 4, 1867, Hannibal, Missouri
Died: June 25, 1918, Kansas City, Missouri

"Eagle Eye" Beckly held the all-time record for games played at first base (2368) until Eddie Murray surpassed him in 1994. The left-handed first baseman hit better than .300 thirteen times in his 20-year career. When he stepped up to the plate he would attempt to rattle the pitcher with his cry of "Chickazoola."

As a fielder, though he had no problem with hits or balls thrown to first, he was known to have a rather wild throwing arm and runners always took the extra base on him. Beckly was also famous for his hidden-ball trick, where he would hide the ball under one corner of the base and then pull it out and tag out an unsuspecting runner.

Jake Beckly was inducted into the National Baseball Hall of Fame in 1971.

Beckly, Jacob Peter "Eagle Eye"
BL/TL, 5'10", 200 lbs. Deb: 6/20/1888

YEAR	TM/L	W	L	PCT	G	IP	H	HR	BB	SO	ERA
1902	Cin-NL	0	1	.000	1	4	9	0	1	2	6.75

YEAR	TM/L	G	AB	R	H	2B	3B	HR	RBI	BB	SO	AVG
1888	Pit-NL	71	283	35	97	15	3	0	27	7	22	.343
1889	Pit-NL	123	522	91	157	24	10	9	97	29	29	.301
1890	Pit-PL	121	516	109	167	38	22	9	120	42	32	.324
1891	Pit-NL	133	554	94	162	20	19	4	73	44	46	.292
1892	Pit-NL	151	614	102	145	21	19	10	96	31	44	.236
1893	Pit-NL	131	542	108	164	32	19	5	106	54	26	.303
1894	Pit-NL	131	533	121	183	36	18	7	120	43	16	.343
1895	Pit-NL	129	530	104	174	31	19	5	110	24	20	.328
1896	Pit-NL	59	217	44	55	7	5	3	32	22	28	.253
	NY-NL	46	182	37	55	8	4	5	38	9	7	.302
	Yr	105	399	81	110	15	9	8	70	31	35	.276
1897	NY-NL	17	68	8	17	2	3	1	11	2	—	.250
	Cin-NL	97	365	76	126	17	9	7	76	18	—	.345
	Yr	114	433	84	143	19	12	8	87	20	—	.330
1898	Cin-NL	118	459	86	135	20	12	4	72	28	—	.294
1899	Cin-NL	134	513	87	171	27	16	3	99	40	—	.333
1900	Cin-NL	141	558	98	190	26	10	2	94	40	—	.341
1901	Cin-NL	140	580	78	178	36	13	3	79	28	—	.307
1902	Cin-NL	129	531	82	175	23	7	5	69	34	—	.330
1903	Cin-NL	120	459	85	150	29	10	2	81	42	—	.327
1904	StL-NL	142	551	72	179	22	9	1	67	35	—	.325
1905	StL-NL	134	514	48	147	20	10	1	57	30	—	.286
1906	StL-NL	87	320	29	79	16	6	0	44	13	—	.247
1907	StL-NL	32	115	6	24	3	0	0	7	1	—	.209
Total	20	2,386	9,526	1,600	2,930	473	243	86	1,575	616	INC	.308

Chief Bender

Pitcher (Charles Albert Bender)
Born: May 5, 1884, Crow Wing County, Minnesota
Died: May 22, 1954, Philadelphia, Pennsylvania

Chief Bender was the first American Indian elected into the Hall of Fame. The 6'2", 185 lb. righthander was a pitching mainstay for the Philadelphia Athletics in the early 1900's. He had a good fastball and an overhand curve and delivered his pitches with a high leg kick. In his 16-year career he led the league in saves twice and in winning percentage three times.

On May 12, 1910, he threw the only no-hitter of his career, a 4-1 win over the Cleveland Indians. Only a walk to Terry Turner kept it from becoming a perfect game.

Bender appeared in five different World Series for the A's. His two wins in the 1913 Series (when the A's beat the Giants four games to one) made him the first six-game winner in Series history.

Bender, Charles Albert
BR/TR, 6'2", 185 lbs. Deb: 4/20/03

YEAR	TM/L	W	L	PCT	G	IP	H	HR	BB	SO	ERA
1903	Phi-AL	17	14	.548	36	270	239	6	65	127	3.07
1904	Phi-AL	10	11	.476	29	203.2	167	1	59	149	2.87
1905	Phi-AL	16	11	.615	35	229	193	5	90	142	2.83
1906	Phi-AL	15	10	.600	36	238.1	208	5	48	159	2.53
1907	Phi-AL	16	8	.667	33	219.1	185	1	34	112	2.05
1908	Phi-AL	8	9	.471	18	138.2	121	1	21	85	1.75
1909	Phi-AL	18	8	.692	34	250	196	1	45	161	1.66
1910	Phi-AL	23	5	.821	30	250	182	1	47	155	1.58
1911	Phi-AL	17	5	.773	31	216.1	198	2	58	114	2.16
1912	Phi-AL	13	8	.619	27	171	169	1	33	90	2.74
1913	Phi-AL	21	10	.677	48	236.2	208	2	59	135	2.21
1914	Phi-AL	17	3	.850	28	179	159	4	55	107	2.26
1915	Bal-F	4	16	.200	26	178.1	198	5	37	89	3.99
1916	Phi-NL	7	7	.500	27	122.2	137	3	34	43	3.74
1917	Phi-NL	8	2	.800	20	113	84	1	26	43	1.67
1925	Chi-AL	0	0	—	1	1	1	1	1	0	18.00
Total	16	210	127	.6253	459	3,017	2,645	40	712	1,711	2.46

Bill Bergen

Catcher (William Aloysius Bergen)
Born: June 13, 1878, North Brookfield, Massachusetts
Died: December 19, 1943, Worcester, Massachusetts

BERGEN BROOKLYN

Bill Bergen is the worst hitter ever to play regularly in the major leagues. His .170 lifetime batting average (in 3,028 appearances) is 42 points below any other batter with 2,500 or more at-bats. Obviously it was his defensive skills that made him a first-string receiver for Cincinnati and Brooklyn from 1901 to 1911.

Bergen, William Aloysius
BR/TR, 6', 184 lbs. Deb: 5/6/01

YEAR	TM/L	G	AB	R	H	2B	3B	HR	RBI	BB	SO	AVG
1901	Cin-NL	87	308	15	55	6	4	1	17	8	—	.179
1902	Cin-NL	89	322	19	58	8	3	0	36	14	—	.180
1903	Cin-NL	58	207	21	47	4	2	0	19	7	—	.227
1904	Bro-NL	96	329	17	60	4	2	0	12	9	—	.182
1905	Bro-NL	79	247	12	47	3	2	0	22	7	—	.190
1906	Bro-NL	103	353	9	56	3	3	0	19	7	—	.159
1907	Bro-NL	51	138	2	22	3	0	0	14	1	—	.159
1908	Bro-NL	99	302	8	53	8	2	0	15	5	—	.175
1909	Bro-NL	112	346	16	48	1	1	1	15	10	—	.139
1910	Bro-NL	89	249	11	40	2	1	0	14	6	39	.161
1911	Bro-NL	84	227	8	30	3	1	0	10	14	42	.132
Total	11	947	3,028	138	516	45	21	2	193	88	INC	.170

George Bradley

Pitcher (George Washington Bradley)
Born: July 13, 1852, Reading, Pennsylvania
Died: October 2, 1931, Philadelphia, Pennsylvania

On July 15, 1876, George Bradley threw the first no-hitter in National League history as his St. Louis Brown Stockings defeated the Hartford Dark Blues 2-0. It was the league's first season. That year his 1.23 ERA was best in the league and his 16 shutouts is a major league record that was tied only by Grover Cleveland Alexander in 1916.

Bradley, George Washington "Grin"
BR/TR, 5'10.5", 175 lbs. Deb: 5/4/1875

YEAR	TM/L	W	L	PCT	G	IP	H	HR	BB	SO	ERA
1876	StL-NL	45	19	.703	64	573	470	3	38	103	1.23
1877	Chi-NL	18	23	.439	50	394	452	4	39	59	3.31
1879	Tro-NL	13	40	.245	54	487	590	12	26	133	2.85
1880	Pro-NL	12	9	.571	28	196	158	2	6	54	1.38
1881	Cle-NL	2	4	.333	6	51	70	2	3	6	3.88
1882	Cle-NL	6	9	.400	18	147	164	5	22	32	3.73
1883	Phi-AA	16	7	.696	26	214.1	215	7	22	56	3.15
1884	Cin-UA	25	15	.625	41	342	350	7	23	168	2.71
Total	8	137	127	.519	287	2,404.1	2,469	42	179	611	2.5

Asa Brainard

Pitcher
Born: 1841, Albany, New York
Died: December 29, 1888, Denver, Colorado

In 1869 Brainard was the pitcher for the Cincinnati Red Stockings, baseball's first professional team. He was paid $1,100 for the season. The Red Stockings barnstormed all over the country that year, taking on all comers. By June of 1870 they had run up a 79-game winning streak when they were finally defeated by the Brooklyn Atlantics.

Brainard played in baseball's first professional league, the National Association from 1871 to '74, pitching for the Washington Olympics, Middletown Mansfields and the Lord Baltimores, but was never able to duplicate his successful years with the Red Stockings.

Brainard, Asa "Count"
TR, 5'8.5", 150 lbs. Deb: 5/5/1871

YEAR	TM/L	G	AB	R	H	2B	3B	HR	RBI	BB	SO	AVG
1871	Oly-NA	30	134	24	30	4	0	0	21	7	2	.224
1872	Oly-NA	9	41	8	16	3	0	0	6	0	0	.390
	Man-NA	6	25	2	5	0	0	0	0	1	0	.200
	Yr	15	66	10	21	3	0	0	6	1	0	.318
1873	Bal-NA	16	69	18	18	2	0	0	8	0	2	.261
1874	Bal-NA	46	198	19	50	5	0	0	—	2	—	.253
Total	4 n	107	467	71	119	14	0	0	INC	10	INC	.255

YEAR	TM/L	W	L	PCT	G	IP	H	HR	BB	SO	ERA
1871	Oly-NA	12	15	.444	30	264	361	4	37	—	.288
1872	Oly-NA	2	7	.222	9	79	147	0	5	—	.332
	Man-NA	0	2	.000	2	8	14	1	0	—	—
	Yr	2	9	.182	11	87	161	1	5	—	—
1873	Bal-NA	5	7	.417	14	108.2	182	0	9	—	.323
1874	Bal-NA	5	22	.185	29	239	403	1	27	—	.326
Total	4 n	24	53	.312	84	698.2	1,107	6	78	—	.312

Roger Bresnahan

Catcher - Manager (Roger Philip Bresnahan)
Born: June 11, 1879, Toledo, Ohio
Died: December 4, 1944, Toledo, Ohio

During the early 1900's the fiery, pugnacious Bresnahan was probably best known as Christy Mathewson's catcher. He was behind the plate for Mathewson's record-setting three shutouts in the 1905 World Series when the Giants beat the A's four games to one. His lifetime .280 batting average and his speed on the base path made him one of the few catchers ever used in the leadoff spot.

In 1907 he wore a crude form of batting helmet (after being beaned earlier that year) and devised shin guards for catchers. He gave up on the batting helmet idea at the end of the season but catchers have been wearing shin guards ever since.

In 1909 he became player-manager for the St. Louis Cardinals, but was fired as manager after a sixth-place finish in 1912. After he finished his playing career in 1916 he became owner-manager of his hometown minor league Toledo Mud Hens and then coached for the Giants and Tigers in the late '20's and early '30's.

Roger Bresnahan was inducted into the National Baseball Hall of Fame in 1945.

ROGER BRESNAHAN
St. Louis National League

Bresnahan, Roger Philip "The Duke Of Tralee"
BR/TR, 5'9", 200 lbs. Deb: 8/27/1897

YEAR	TM/L	G	AB	R	H	2B	3B	HR	RBI	BB	SO	AVG
1897	Was-NL	6	16	1	6	0	0	0	3	1	—	.375
1900	Chi-NL	2	2	0	0	0	0	0	0	0	—	.000
1901	Bal-AL	86	295	40	79	9	9	1	32	23	—	.268
1902	Bal-AL	65	235	30	64	8	6	4	34	21	—	.272
	NY-NL	51	178	16	51	9	3	1	22	16	—	.287
1903	NY-NL	113	406	87	142	30	8	4	55	61	—	.350
1904	NY-NL	109	402	81	114	22	7	5	33	58	—	.284
1905	NY-NL	104	331	58	100	18	3	0	46	50	—	.302
1906	NY-NL	124	405	69	114	22	4	0	43	81	—	.281
1907	NY-NL	110	328	57	83	9	7	4	38	61	—	.253
1908	NY-NL	140	449	70	127	25	3	1	54	83	—	.283
1909	StL-NL	72	234	27	57	4	1	0	23	46	—	.244
1910	StL-NL	88	234	35	65	15	3	0	27	55	17	.278
1911	StL-NL	81	227	22	63	17	8	3	41	45	19	.278
1912	StL-NL	48	108	8	36	7	2	1	15	14	9	.333
1913	Chi-NL	69	162	20	37	5	2	1	21	21	11	.228
1914	Chi-NL	101	248	42	69	10	4	0	24	49	20	.278
1915	Chi-NL	77	221	19	45	8	1	1	19	29	23	.204
Total	17	1,446	4,481	682	1,252	218	71	26	530	714	INC	.279

YEAR	TM/L	W	L	PCT	G	IP	H	HR	BB	SO	ERA
1897	Was-NL	4	0	1.000	6	41	52	1	10	12	3.95
1901	Bal-AL	0	1	.000	2	6	10	0	4	3	6.00
1910	StL-NL	0	0	—	1	3.1	6	0	1	0	0.00
Total	3	4	1	.800	9	50.1	68	1	15	15	3.93

Dan Brouthers

Infielder (Dennis Joseph Brouthers)
Born: May 8, 1858, Sylvan Lake, New York
Died: August 2, 1932, East Orange, New Jersey

In the 1800's Big Dan Brouthers was one of baseball's first genuine superstars. This 6'2", 200 lb. lefthander won five batting championships in his 19-year career. His .342 lifetime batting average is the highest for a first baseman in the history of the game (and ninth highest overall).

Brothers sprang to prominence with the N.L.'s Buffalo Bisons in the early 1880's when he teamed up with outfielders Hardie Richardson and Deacon White, and catcher Jack Rowe to form the "big four of the National League." With Buffalo, he won his first two batting titles in '82 and '83. He was traded to Detroit in 1886 and while with that club he hit some of the longest home runs of the era.

Dan Brouthers was inducted into the National Baseball Hall of Fame in 1945.

Brouthers, Dennis Joseph "Big Dan"
BL/TL, 6'2", 207 lbs. Deb: 6/23/1879

YEAR	TM/L	G	AB	R	H	2B	3B	HR	RBI	BB	SO	AVG
1879	Tro-NL	39	168	17	46	12	1	4	17	1	18	.274
1880	Tro-NL	3	12	0	2	0	0	0	1	1	0	.167
1881	Buf-NL	65	270	60	86	18	9	8	45	18	22	.319
1882	Buf-NL	84	351	71	129	23	11	6	63	21	7	.368
1883	Buf-NL	98	425	85	159	41	17	3	97	16	17	.374
1884	Buf-NL	94	398	82	130	22	15	14	79	33	20	.327
1885	Buf-NL	98	407	87	146	32	11	7	59	34	10	.359
1886	Det-NL	121	489	139	181	40	15	11	72	66	16	.370
1887	Det-NL	123	500	153	169	36	20	12	101	71	9	.338
1888	Det-NL	129	522	118	160	33	11	9	66	68	13	.307
1889	Bos-NL	126	485	105	181	26	9	7	118	66	6	.373
1890	Bos-PL	123	460	117	152	36	9	1	97	99	17	.330
1891	Bos-AA	130	486	117	170	26	19	5	109	87	20	.350
1892	Bro-NL	152	588	121	197	30	20	5	124	84	30	.335
1893	Bro-NL	77	282	57	95	21	11	2	59	52	10	.337
1894	Bal-NL	123	525	137	182	39	23	9	128	67	9	.347
1895	Bal-NL	5	23	2	6	2	0	0	5	1	1	.261
	Lou-NL	24	97	13	30	10	1	2	15	11	2	.309
	Yr	29	120	15	36	12	1	2	20	12	3	.300
1896	Phi-NL	57	218	42	75	13	3	1	41	44	11	.344
1904	NY-NL	2	5	0	0	0	0	0	0	0	—	.000
Total	19	1,673	6,711	1,523	2,296	460	205	106	1,296	840	—	.342

YEAR	TM/L	W	L	PCT	G	IP	H	HR	BB	SO	ERA
1879	Tro-NL	0	2	.000	3	21	35	0	8	6	5.57
1883	Buf-NL	0	0	—	1	2	9	0	3	2	31.50
Total	2	0	2	.000	4	23	44	0	11	8	7.83

Three Finger Brown

Pitcher (Mordecai Peter Centennial Brown)
Born: October 19,1876, Nyesville, Indiana
Died: February 14, 1948, Terre Haute, Indiana

Mordecai "Three Finger" Brown spent 14 years pitching in the big leagues starting in 1903. His pitching hand had been mangled in a farm accident when he was a child and when he threw the ball he was able to put a wicked spin on it by releasing it off of his stubbed forefinger.

Brown was the pitching ace of the legendary Tinker-to-Evers-to-Chance Chicago Cub team that won four pennants and two World Series from 1906 to 1910. In 1906 this righthander led the N.L. with a 1.04 ERA and began a six-year streak of 20 or more wins per season. In 1909 he led the league with 27 wins.

Three Finger Brown was inducted into the Baseball Hall of Fame in 1949.

Brown, Mordecai Peter Centennial "Three Finger" or "Miner"
BB/TR, 5'10", 175 lbs. Deb: 4/19/03

YEAR	TM/L	W	L	PCT	G	IP	H	HR	BB	SO	ERA
1903	StL-NL	9	13	.409	26	201	231	7	59	83	2.60
1904	Chi-NL	15	10	.600	26	212.1	155	1	50	81	1.86
1905	Chi-NL	18	12	.600	30	249	219	3	44	89	2.17
1906	Chi-NL	26	6	.813	36	277.1	198	1	61	144	1.04
1907	Chi-NL	20	6	.769	34	233	180	2	40	107	1.39
1908	Chi-NL	29	9	.763	44	312.1	214	1	49	123	1.47
1909	Chi-NL	27	9	.750	50	342.2	246	1	53	172	1.31
1910	Chi-NL	25	13	.658	46	295.1	256	3	64	143	1.86
1911	Chi-NL	21	11	.656	53	270	267	5	55	129	2.80
1912	Chi-NL	5	6	.455	15	88.2	92	2	20	34	2.64
1913	Cin-NL	11	12	.478	39	173.1	174	7	44	41	2.91
1914	StL-F	12	6	.667	26	175	172	7	43	81	3.29
	Bro-F	2	5	.286	9	57.2	63	1	18	32	4.21
	Yr	14	11	.560	35	232.2	235	8	61	113	3.52
1915	Chi-F	17	8	.680	35	236.1	189	2	64	95	2.09
1916	Chi-NL	2	3	.400	12	48.1	52	0	9	21	3.91
Total	14	239	129	.649	481	3,172.1	2,708	43	673	1,375	2.06

Morgan G. Bulkeley

Executive (Morgan Gardner Bulkeley)
Born: December 26, 1837
Died: November 26, 1922

Morgan G. Bulkeley was the first president of the National League. The league was actually created by Chicago White Stockings owner William Hulbert in 1876 and Bulkeley (who owned the Hartford franchise) served as president for one year. Hulbert then took over the presidency in 1887.

At the end of the 1877 season Bulkeley dropped out of baseball to pursue a successful career in the insurance business. Later he become the governor of Connecticut and then served in the U.S. Senate.

In 1905 he was named to the infamous Mills Commission. It was this commission which, in 1908, erroneously named Abner Doubleday as the inventor of baseball.

Jesse Burkett

Outfielder (Jesse Cail Burkett)
Born: December 4, 1868, Wheeling, West Virginia
Died: May 27, 1953, Worcester, Massachusetts

Jesse Burkett batted over .400 two seasons in a row (in 1895 and '96). The only other players ever to perform such a feat were Ed Delahanty, Ty Cobb and Rogers Hornsby.

In his 16-year career he had more than 200 hits six times and led the National League in runs twice.

The left-handed outfielder was a clever bunter and his ability to foul off pitches brought about the introduction of the rule which makes foul balls strikes.

His testy disposition earned him the nickname of "Crab." He was as equally hostile to teammates and home fans as he was to rivals. For some reason he was sensitive about his physical resemblance to former Cleveland teammate Jack Glasscock, and would fly into a rage if it was suggested that they were father and son. When he coached for New York Giants in 1921, he was so disliked by the players that, when they won the World Series that year, they refused to vote him a share of the money. Manager John McGraw had to pay him out of his own pocket.

Jesse Burkett was inducted into the National Baseball Hall of Fame in 1946.

Burkett, Jesse Cail "Crab"
BL/TL, 5'8", 155 lbs. Deb: 4/22/1890

YEAR	TM/L	G	AB	R	H	2B	3B	HR	RBI	BB	SO	AVG
1890	NY-NL	101	401	67	124	23	13	4	60	33	52	.309
1891	Cle-NL	40	167	29	45	7	4	0	13	23	19	.269
1892	Cle-NL	145	608	119	167	15	14	6	66	67	59	.275
1893	Cle-NL	125	511	145	178	25	15	6	82	98	23	.348
1894	Cle-NL	125	523	138	187	27	14	8	94	84	27	.358
1895	Cle-NL	131	550	153	225	22	13	5	83	74	31	.409
1896	Cle-NL	133	586	160	240	27	16	6	72	49	19	.410
1897	Cle-NL	127	517	129	198	28	7	2	60	76	—	.383
1898	Cle-NL	150	624	114	213	18	9	0	42	69	—	.341
1899	StL-NL	141	558	116	221	21	8	7	71	67	—	.396
1900	StL-NL	141	559	88	203	11	15	7	68	62	—	.363
1901	StL-NL	142	601	142	226	20	15	10	75	59	—	.376
1902	StL-AL	138	553	97	169	29	9	5	52	71	—	.306
1903	StL-AL	132	515	73	151	20	7	3	40	52	—	.293
1904	StL-AL	147	575	72	156	15	10	2	27	78	—	.271
1905	Bos-AL	148	573	78	147	12	13	4	47	67	—	.257
Total	16	2,066	8,421	1,720	2,850	320	182	75	952	1,029	—	.338

YEAR	TM/L	W	L	PCT	G	IP	H	HR	BB	SO	ERA
1890	NY-NL	3	10	.231	21	118	134	3	92	82	5.57
1894	Cle-NL	0	0	—	1	4	6	0	1	0	4.50
1902	StL-AL	0	1	.000	1	1	4	0	1	2	9.00
Total	3	3	11	.214	23	123	144	3	94	84	5.56

Alexander Cartwright Jr.

Pioneer (Alexander Joy Cartwright Jr.)
Born: April 17, 1820
Died: July 12, 1892

Alexander Cartwright Jr. is truly the Father of Baseball. In 1845 he, along with members of his New York Knickerbocker Base Ball Club, devised the first rules and regulations for the modern game of baseball.

Baseball had first taken root on this continent in the mid 1700's when English lads brought an offshoot of the game of cricket to our shores. This game, where the fielders put out a runner by belting him with the ball as he ran from base to base, was called "rounders."

There were many variations of rounders, as the game had no "official" rules. It was usually played according to local custom, meaning the number of players on a side, the number of bases (usually anywhere from two to five), the way they were laid out, the distance between them and other rules would vary from place to place. It was basically a pickup game that was played by children.

In 1845 Cartwright took various elements that were used in these different forms of early baseball and, adding a few wrinkles of his own, fused them into regulations that stand today.

Cartwright gave us the baseball diamond and specified the distance between the bases (a measurement that we still use now). He did away with the practice of hitting the runner with the ball to achieve an out and replaced this with either tagging the runner with the ball or getting it to the base ahead of him. He specified the number of players on the field and invented the position of shortstop. He decided there would be three outs per side and the ball would be considered foul if knocked out of the 90-degree quadrant of the field. And these were just some of the things that Cartwright included when he wrote out baseball's first standardized set of rules.

Most important, Alexander Cartwright's rules and regulations added elements of precision, perfection, drama and excitement to the game, as he almost single-handedly transformed a simple children's game into a game that adults could play.

So, forget anything you ever heard about Abner Doubleday: it was, in fact, Alexander Cartwright Jr. who gave us the great game of baseball.

THE ORIGINAL RULES OF BASEBALL

As set down on paper by Alexander Cartwright, and adopted by the Knickerbocker Base Ball Club of New York on September 23, 1945. (Note: Explanations have been added in brackets where necessary.)

1. The bases shall be from "home" to second base, 42 paces; from first to third base, 42 paces, equidistant.

2. The game to consist of 21 counts, or aces *[runs]*; but at the conclusion an equal number of hands *[outs]* must be played.

3. The ball must be pitched *[underhand]*, and not thrown *[freehand]*, for the bat.

4. A ball knocked out of the field, or outside of the range of first or third base, is foul. *[Note — if it hit inside but rolled out it was considered to be fair.]*

5. If a ball be struck, or tipped, and caught, either flying or on the first bound, it is a hand out.

6. A player running the bases shall be out, if the ball is in the hands of an adversary on the base, or the runner is touched with it before he makes his base; it being understood, however, that in no instance is a ball to be thrown at him.

7. A player running who shall prevent an adversary from catching or getting the ball before making his base, is a hand out.

8. If two hands are already out, a player running home at the time a ball is struck cannot make an ace if the striker is thrown out.

9. Three hands out, all out.

10. Players must take their strike in regular turn.

11. All disputes and differences relative to the game, to be decided by the umpire, from which there is no appeal.

12. No ace or base can be made on a foul strike.

13. A runner cannot be put out in making one base, when a balk is made by the pitcher.

14. But one base allowed when a ball bounds out of the field when struck.

Bob Caruthers

Pitcher (Robert Lee Caruthers)
Born: January 5, 1864, Memphis, Tennessee
Died: August 5, 1911, Peoria, Illinois

Caruthers, P. Brooklyn's

In his major league debut with the A.A.'s St. Louis Browns on September 7, 1884, "Parisian Bob" Caruthers pitched a four hitter. The following year he led the league with a 40-13 record and a .207 ERA as the Browns took their first A.A. pennant. The next two seasons he had 30 and 29 wins and the Browns won the pennant two more times.

He was also an excellent hitter and St. Louis manager Charles Commiskey would stick him either in the outfield or at first base between starts. In 1886 he hit .334 in 106 appearances at the plate and in 1887 his .357 batting average was fifth highest in the league.

In the 1887 World Series he was responsible for four of the Browns' five victories (it was a travelling 15-game affair which Detroit eventually won ten games to five).

After the '87 season the Browns eccentric owner Chris Von der Ahe sold Caruthers to the Brooklyn Bridegrooms for $8,250. When Caruthers signed with Brooklyn for a $5,000 salary it made him the highest-paid player in the A.A. In 1888 his 29 wins helped Brooklyn finish in second place. The following year his 40 wins helped to give them their first pennant.

He ended up with the N.L.'s St. Louis Browns in 1892, and in addition to playing, he also managed the club for part of the year. In 1883, when the pitching distance was changed to the present 60' 6" from the previous 50', he complained of a sore arm and played only in the outfield. It was his last season in the majors though he went on to play in the minors for five more seasons.

Caruthers, Robert Lee "Parisian Bob"
BL/TR, 5'7", 138 lbs. Deb: 9/7/1884

YEAR	TM/L	W	L	PCT	G	IP	H	HR	BB	SO	ERA
1884	StL-AA	7	2	.778	13	82.2	61	1	15	58	2.61
1885	StL-AA	40	13	.755	53	482.1	430	3	57	190	2.07
1886	StL-AA	30	14	.682	44	387.1	323	3	86	166	2.32
1887	StL-AA	29	9	.763	39	341	337	6	61	74	3.30
1888	Bro-AA	29	15	.659	44	391.2	337	4	53	140	2.39
1889	Bro-AA	40	11	.784	56	445	444	16	104	118	3.13
1890	Bro-NL	23	11	.676	37	300	292	9	87	64	3.09
1891	Bro-NL	18	14	.563	38	297	323	7	107	69	3.12
1892	StL-NL	2	8	.200	16	101.2	131	10	27	21	5.84
Total	9	218	97	.692	340	2,828.2	2,678	59	597	900	2.83

YEAR	TM/L	G	AB	R	H	2B	3B	HR	RBI	BB	SO	AVG
1884	StL-AA	23	82	15	21	2	0	2	—	4	—	.256
1885	StL-AA	60	222	37	50	10	2	1	20	—	—	.225
1886	StL-AA	87	317	91	106	21	14	4	64	—	—	.334
1887	StL-AA	98	364	102	130	23	11	8	66	—	—	.357
1888	Bro-AA	94	335	58	77	10	5	5	53	45	—	.230
1889	Bro-AA	59	172	45	43	8	3	2	31	44	17	.250
1890	Bro-NL	71	238	46	63	7	4	1	29	47	18	.265
1891	Bro-NL	56	171	24	48	5	3	2	23	25	13	.281
1892	StL-NL	143	513	76	142	16	8	3	69	86	29	.277
1893	Chi-NL	1	3	0	0	0	0	0	0	0	1	.000
	Cin-NL	13	48	14	14	2	0	1	8	16	1	.292
	Yr	14	51	14	14	2	0	1	8	16	2	.275
Total	10	705	2,465	508	694	104	50	29	INC	417	INC	.282

Henry Chadwick

Writer
Born: October 6, 1824
Died: April 20, 1908

Henry Chadwick was the first full-time baseball writer, and is the inventor of the box score.

The British-born Chadwick, who as a teenager immigrated to the U.S. along with his family, saw his first baseball game in 1848 at Elysian Fields and immediately fell in love with the game. He then devoted his life to writing about, and promoting baseball.

Throughout the years, Chadwick wrote about baseball in such publications as the *New York Clipper*, the *New York Herald* and the *Brooklyn Eagle*, and he explained the game and its techniques in his own *Base Ball Manual*, *Beadle's Dime Base-Ball Player* and *De Witt's Base-Ball Guide*. He also edited *Spalding's Official Base-Ball Guide* from 1879 to 1908.

Chadwick, who sometimes is referred to as the "Father of Baseball," was inducted into the National Baseball Hall of Fame in 1938.

Aaron B. Champion

Executive

In 1869 local businessman Aaron Champion was the president of the Cincinnati Red Stockings when the club became baseball's first openly professional team. He hired English-born Harry Wright, a former professional cricket player and jeweler by trade, to manage the club. Wright imported players from all over the country and turned the Red Stockings into a top-caliber team.

That year the Red Stockings embarked on a nationwide tour, playing the best local teams they could find, and ran up a 79-game winning streak which finally ended in June of the following year. Several other defeats later on in the season caused interest in the team to drop off at home, and this, combined with the club's heavy travel expenses and mounting players salaries, forced Champion to disband the club.

But the Red Stockings had inspired the other great teams of the era to cast off their amateur disguises and this led directly to the formation of the the first professional baseball league, the National Association of Professional Base Ball Players, in 1871.

Frank Chance

Infielder - Manager (Frank Leroy Chance)
Born: September 9, 1877, Fresno, California
Died: September 15, 1924, Los Angeles, California

In the early 1900's Frank Chance played first base in the Chicago Cubs' legendary Tinker-to-Evers-to-Chance double-play combination.

He began his major league career with the Cubs as a catcher in 1898 and first teamed up with short-stop Joe Tinker and second baseman Johnny Evers in 1902 when manager Frank Selee stationed him at first base. He led the National League with 67 stolen bases in 1903, and 57 in 1906, when he also led the league in runs scored with 103.

In 1905 Chance became player-manager of the Cubs. He served in that capacity until 1912 and in that period of time the Cubs won four N.L. pennants and two World Championships. They also had four seasons in which they won 100 games or more.

In 1913 he left the Cubs to manage the Yankees, but was forced to retire in 1914 due to ill health. In 1923 he returned to the majors and managed the Red Sox for one season.

In 1946 Frank Chance, Joe Tinker and Johnny Evers were inducted into the National Baseball Hall of Fame.

Chance, Frank Leroy "Husk" or "The Peerless Leader"
BR/TR, 6', 190 lbs. Deb: 4/29/1898

YEAR	TM/L	G	AB	R	H	2B	3B	HR	RBI	BB	SO	AVG
1898	Chi-NL	53	147	32	41	4	3	1	14	7	—	.279
1899	Chi-NL	64	192	37	55	6	2	1	22	15	—	.286
1900	Chi-NL	56	149	26	44	9	3	0	13	15	—	.295
1901	Chi-NL	69	241	38	67	12	4	0	36	29	—	.278
1902	Chi-NL	75	240	39	69	9	4	1	31	35	—	.287
1903	Chi-NL	125	441	83	144	24	10	2	81	78	—	.327
1904	Chi-NL	124	451	89	140	16	10	6	49	36	—	.310
1905	Chi-NL	118	392	92	124	16	12	2	70	78	—	.316
1906	Chi-NL	136	474	103	151	24	10	3	71	70	—	.319
1907	Chi-NL	111	382	58	112	19	2	1	49	51	—	.293
1908	Chi-NL	129	452	65	123	27	4	2	55	37	—	.272
1909	Chi-NL	93	324	53	88	16	4	0	46	30	—	.272
1910	Chi-NL	88	295	54	88	12	8	0	36	37	15	.298
1911	Chi-NL	31	88	23	21	6	3	1	17	25	13	.239
1912	Chi-NL	2	5	2	1	0	0	0	0	3	0	.200
1913	NY-AL	12	24	3	5	0	0	0	6	8	1	.208
1914	NY-AL	1	0	0	0	0	0	0	0	0	0	—
Total	17	1,287	4,297	797	1,273	200	79	20	596	554	INC	.296

Jack Chapman

Outfielder - Manager (John Curtis Chapman)
Born: May 8, 1843, Brooklyn, New York
Died: June 10, 1916, Brooklyn, New York

In the 1860's Jack Chapman was an all-star outfielder for the Brooklyn Atlantics. He was known mainly for his fielding ability, and his many long running catches inspired his nickname "Death to Flying Things."

He played left field for the Atlantics on that fateful day, June 14, 1870, when the Atlantics defeated the Cincinnati Red Stockings in extra innings to bring the Red Stockings' monumental two-year, 79-game winning streak to an end.

He later played in the National Association for two years and in the National League for one. Chapman then spent 11 years managing in both the N.L and A.A. He managed the Louisville Cyclones to the A.A. pennant in 1890.

Chapman, John Curtis "Death To Flying Things"
TR, 5'11", 170 lbs. Deb: 5/5/1874

YEAR	TM/L	G	AB	R	H	2B	3B	HR	RBI	BB	SO	AVG
1874	Atl-NA	53	238	32	64	7	3	0	—	5	—	.269
1875	StL-NA	43	195	28	44	6	3	0	—	1	—	.226
Total	2 n	96	433	60	108	13	6	0	INC	—	—	.249
1876	Lou-NL	17	67	4	16	1	0	0	5	1	3	.239

Hal Chase

Infielder (Harold Homer Chase)
Born: February 13, 1883, Los Gatos, California
Died: May 18, 1947, Colusa, California

Considered by many to be the finest fielding first baseman in the history of the game, in 1916 "Prince Hal" Chase led the N.L. with 184 hits and a .339 batting average while playing for Cincinnati.

He was also one of the biggest crooks in the history of the game. Accusations from managers and teammates that the charming, charismatic Chase threw games for money were always swirling around him and in 1919, his behind-the-scenes involvement in the Black Sox scandal got him banned from baseball for life.

Chase, Harold Homer "Prince Hal"
BR/TL, 6', 175 lbs.   Deb: 4/14/05

YEAR	TM/L	G	AB	R	H	2B	3B	HR	RBI	BB	SO	AVG
1905	NY-AL	128	465	60	116	16	6	3	49	15	—	.249
1906	NY-AL	151	597	84	193	23	10	0	76	13	—	.323
1907	NY-AL	125	498	72	143	23	3	2	68	19	—	.287
1908	NY-AL	106	405	50	104	11	3	1	36	15	—	.257
1909	NY-AL	118	474	60	134	17	3	4	63	20	—	.283
1910	NY-AL	130	524	67	152	20	5	3	73	16	—	.290
1911	NY-AL	133	527	82	166	32	7	3	62	21	—	.315
1912	NY-AL	131	522	61	143	21	9	4	58	17	—	.274
1913	NY-AL	39	146	15	31	2	4	0	9	11	13	.212
	Chi-AL	102	384	49	110	11	10	2	39	16	41	.286
	Yr	141	530	64	141	13	14	2	48	27	54	.266
1914	Chi-AL	58	206	27	55	10	5	0	20	23	19	.267
	Buf-F	75	291	43	101	19	9	3	48	6	31	.347
1915	Buf-F	145	567	85	165	31	10	17	89	20	50	.291
1916	Cin-NL	142	542	66	184	29	12	4	82	19	48	.339
1917	Cin-NL	152	602	71	167	28	15	4	86	15	49	.277
1918	Cin-NL	74	259	30	78	12	6	2	38	13	15	.301
1919	NY-NL	110	408	58	116	17	7	5	45	17	40	.284
Total	15	1,919	7,417	980	2,158	322	124	57	941	276	INC	.291

YEAR	TM/L	W	L	PCT	G	IP	H	HR	BB	SO	ERA
1908	NY-AL	0	0	—	1	0.1	0	0	0	0	0.00

Jack Chesbro

Pitcher (John Dwight Chesbro)
Born: June 5, 1874, North Adams, Massachusetts
Died: November 6, 1931, Conway, Massachusetts

Spitballer "Happy Jack" Chesbro won 20 or more games five times in his 11-year career in the majors. His big year was in 1904 when he was with the New York Highlanders (later known as the Yankees). That season he had a 41-12 record (his 41 wins are the most in a single season in the twentieth century), and led the A.L. in games pitched (55), games completed (48) and innings pitched (454).

Unfortunately he will always be remembered for a wild pitch he unleashed on the last day of that season. The Highlanders needed to sweep a doubleheader with the Red Sox to win the pennant. When Chesbro's pitch sailed over the catcher's head in the top of the ninth inning of the first game it allowed a runner to score from third, breaking a 2-2 tie and giving the Red Sox the game ... and the pennant.

It was mainly because of his big 1904 season that Jack Chesbro was inducted into the National Baseball Hall of Fame in 1946.

Chesbro, John Dwight "Happy Jack"
BR/TR, 5'9", 180 lbs. Deb: 7/12/1899

YEAR	TM/L	W	L	PCT	G	IP	H	HR	BB	SO	ERA
1899	Pit-NL	6	9	.400	19	149	165	3	59	8	4.11
1900	Pit-NL	15	13	.536	32	215.2	220	4	79	6	3.67
1901	Pit-NL	21	10	.677	36	287.2	261	4	52	29	2.38
1902	Pit-NL	28	6	.824	35	286.1	242	1	62	36	2.17
1903	NY-AL	21	15	.583	40	324.2	300	7	74	47	2.77
1904	NY-AL	41	12	.774	55	454.2	338	4	88	39	1.82
1905	NY-AL	19	15	.559	41	303.1	262	5	71	56	2.20
1906	NY-AL	24	16	.600	49	325	314	2	75	52	2.96
1907	NY-AL	10	10	.500	30	206	192	0	46	8	2.53
1908	NY-AL	14	20	.412	45	288.2	271	6	67	24	2.93
1909	NY-AL	0	4	.000	9	49.2	70	2	13	7	6.34
	Bos-AL	0	1	.000	1	6	7	1	4	3	4.50
Yr		0	5	.000	10	55.2	77	3	17	20	6.14
Total	11	199	131	.603	392	2,896.2	2,642	39	690	265	2.68

Eddie Cicotte

Pitcher (Edward Victor Cicotte)
Born: June 19, 1884, Springwells, Michigan
Died: May 5, 1969, Detroit, Michigan

Eddie Cicotte spent 14 years pitching in the American League. The high point of his heartbreaking career was the year of 1917 when, while pitching for the White Sox, he led the A.L. with 28 wins and a 1.53 ERA. On April 14 of that season he hurled his only no-hitter, a 11-0 win over the St. Louis Browns. After an off year in 1918 he bounced back in 1919 to lead the A.L. in wins with 29, complete games (30) and innings pitched (306).

There is no doubt that this crafty control artist would have eventually ended up in the Hall of Fame if he hadn't accepted a $10,000 bribe to throw the first game of the 1919 World Series against Cincinnati. In 1921 Cicotte and seven Chicago teammates were banned from baseball for life for their involvement in the infamous 1919 Black Sox Scandal.

Cicotte, Edward Victor "Knuckles"
BB/TR, 5'9", 175 lbs. Deb: 9/3/05

YEAR	TM/L	W	L	PCT	G	IP	H	HR	BB	SO	ERA
1905	Det-AL	1	1	.500	3	18	25	0	5	6	3.50
1908	Bos-AL	11	12	.478	39	207.1	198	0	59	95	2.43
1909	Bos-AL	13	5	.722	27	159.2	117	3	56	82	1.97
1910	Bos-AL	15	11	.577	36	250	213	4	86	104	2.74
1911	Bos-AL	11	15	.423	35	220	236	2	73	106	2.82
1912	Bos-AL	1	3	.250	9	46	58	0	15	20	5.67
	Chi-AL	9	7	.563	20	152	159	3	37	70	2.84
Yr		10	10	.500	29	198	217	3	52	90	3.50
1913	Chi-AL	18	12	.600	41	268	224	2	73	121	1.58
1914	Chi-AL	11	16	.407	45	269.1	220	0	72	122	2.04
1915	Chi-AL	13	12	.520	39	223.1	216	2	48	106	3.02
1916	Chi-AL	15	7	.682	44	187	138	1	70	91	1.78
1917	Chi-AL	28	12	.700	49	346.2	246	2	70	150	1.53
1918	Chi-AL	12	19	.387	38	266	275	2	40	104	2.77
1919	Chi-AL	29	7	.806	40	306.2	256	5	49	110	1.82
1920	Chi-AL	21	10	.677	37	303.1	316	6	74	87	3.26
Total	14	208	149	.583	502	3,223.1	2,897	32	827	1,374	2.37

Fred Clarke

Outfielder - Manager (Fred Clifford Clarke)
Born: October 3, 1872, Winterset, Iowa
Died: August 14, 1960, Winfield, Kansas

Around the turn of the century Fred Clarke was one of baseball's fiercest competitors. This left-handed hitting outfielder was a first-rate hitter and an intrepid baserunner. In his major league debut with the N.L.'s Louisville Colonels on June 6, 1894, Clarke went 5 for 5, a major league record which still stands.

Clarke spent the next 21 years in the National League hitting better than .300 eleven times and finishing up with 506 stolen bases. His hard-nosed playing style was often compared to that of Ty Cobb.

In 1897, at the age of 24, he was appointed player-manager of the Colonels and spent three years managing that team and then 16 guiding Pittsburgh. In the early 1900's he managed the Pirates to four N.L. pennants and one World Championship.

Fred Clarke was inducted into the National Baseball Hall of Fame in 1945.

Clarke, Fred Clifford "Cap"
BL/TR, 5'10.5", 165 lbs. Deb: 6/30/1894

YEAR	TM/L	G	AB	R	H	2B	3B	HR	RBI	BB	SO	AVG
1894	Lou-NL	75	310	54	83	11	7	7	48	25	27	.268
1895	Lou-NL	132	550	96	191	21	5	4	82	34	24	.347
1896	Lou-NL	131	517	96	168	15	18	9	79	43	34	.325
1897	Lou-NL	128	518	120	202	30	13	6	67	45	—	.390
1898	Lou-NL	149	599	116	184	23	12	3	47	48	—	.307
1899	Lou-NL	148	602	122	206	23	9	5	70	49	—	.342
1900	Pit-NL	106	399	84	110	15	12	3	32	51	—	.276
1901	Pit-NL	129	527	118	171	24	15	6	60	51	—	.324
1902	Pit-NL	113	459	103	145	27	14	2	53	51	—	.316
1903	Pit-NL	104	427	88	150	32	15	5	70	41	—	.351
1904	Pit-NL	72	278	51	85	7	11	0	25	22	—	.306
1905	Pit-NL	141	525	95	157	18	15	2	51	55	—	.299
1906	Pit-NL	118	417	69	129	14	13	1	39	40	—	.309
1907	Pit-NL	148	501	97	145	18	13	2	59	68	—	.289
1908	Pit-NL	151	551	83	146	18	15	2	53	65	—	.265
1909	Pit-NL	152	550	97	158	16	11	3	68	80	—	.287
1910	Pit-NL	123	429	57	113	23	9	2	63	53	23	.263
1911	Pit-NL	110	392	73	127	25	13	5	49	53	27	.324
1913	Pit-NL	9	13	0	1	1	0	0	0	0	0	.077
1914	Pit-NL	2	2	0	0	0	0	0	0	0	0	.000
1915	Pit-NL	1	2	0	1	0	0	0	0	0	0	.500
Total	21	2,242	8,568	1,619	2,672	361	220	67	1,015	874	INC	.312

John Clarkson

Pitcher (John Gibson Clarkson)
Born: July 1, 1861, Cambridge, Massachusetts
Died: February 2, 1904, Belmont, Massachusetts

In the 1880's John Clarkson was one of baseball's premier pitchers. This brooding, sensitive righthander from Cambridge, Massachusetts, still ranks among the all-time leaders in wins, winning percentage, complete games and innings pitched, as well as various fielding categories.

Clarkson was a very crafty, scientific type of pitcher, who knew every batter's weakness and exploited it. In 1885 and '86 he helped the Chicago White Stockings win two N.L. pennants in a row. In 1885 he led the N.L. with 53 wins, 70 appearances, 68 complete games, 623 innings pitched and 308 strikeouts. And he also led the league in these five categories in 1887 and 1889.

On July 27, 1885, Clarkson pitched the only no-hitter of his career, a 4-0 win over the Providence Grays. At the end of the 1887 season he was sold to the Boston Beaneaters for the then-astronomical sum of $10,000 and spent several productive years with that club, racking up a 49-19 record in '89 and helping them win pennants in '91 and '92.

John Clarkson was inducted into the National Baseball Hall of Fame in 1963.

Clarkson, John Gibson
BR/TR, 5'10", 155 lbs. Deb: 5/2/1882

YEAR	TM/L	W	L	PCT	G	IP	H	HR	BB	SO	ERA
1882	Wor-NL	1	2	.333	3	24	49	0	2	3	4.50
1884	Chi-NL	10	3	.769	14	118	94	10	25	102	2.14
1885	Chi-NL	53	16	.768	70	623	497	21	97	308	1.85
1886	Chi-NL	36	17	.679	55	466.2	419	20	86	313	2.41
1887	Chi-NL	38	21	.644	60	523	513	20	92	237	3.08
1888	Bos-NL	33	20	.623	54	483.1	448	17	119	223	2.76
1889	Bos-NL	49	19	.721	73	620	589	16	203	284	2.73
1890	Bos-NL	26	18	.591	44	383	370	14	140	138	3.27
1891	Bos-NL	33	19	.635	55	460.2	435	18	154	141	2.79
1892	Bos-NL	8	6	.571	16	145.2	115	4	60	48	2.35
	Cle-NL	17	10	.630	29	243.1	235	4	72	91	2.55
Yr		25	16	.610	45	389	350	8	132	139	2.48
1893	Cle-NL	16	17	.485	36	295	358	11	95	62	4.45
1894	Cle-NL	8	10	.444	22	150.2	173	6	46	28	4.42
Total	12	328	178	.648	531	4,536.1	4,295	161	1,191	1,978	2.81

Ty Cobb

Outfielder-Manager (Tyrus Raymond Cobb)
Born: December 18, 1886, Narrows, Georgia
Died: July 17, 1961, Atlanta, Georgia

"The Georgia Peach" was famous for his spikes-first slides, his nasty disposition and for playing the game with an aggressiveness that was almost homicidal. He is also considered by many experts to have been the greatest player in the history of the game.

Starting in 1905, he spent 24 seasons in the American League (22 of them with Detroit). He won 12 batting titles, and from 1906 onwards hit better than .320 in 23 consecutive seasons. He topped the .400 mark three times.

His career batting average of .366 is the highest in major league history. When he retired in 1928 he held some 90 major league records and still ranks in the all-time top five in games played (3,035), at bats (11,434), runs scored (2,246), hits (4,189), doubles (724), triples (295), stolen bases (891), total bases (5,854) and runs batted in (1,937).

In 1907 he led the Tigers to the first of three consecutive A.L. pennants. In 1911 he hit over .400 for the first time and won his only Most Valuable Player Award. In 1912 he was involved in a bitter salary dispute with Tigers owner Frank Navin and did not sign until May 1 (for $11,332.55), but he nevertheless hit .409 that year.

In 1915 he stole 96 bases, a record that would stand until 1962 when Maury Wills of the Dodgers broke it with 104. In 1921 Cobb took over as manager of the Tigers and guided them to six straight winning seasons. After he retired in 1928 he became a very rich man due to wise investments he made during his playing days in real estate, automobiles, cotton and Coca-Cola stock.

Ty Cobb was a harsh, driving, lonely perfectionist, who throughout his career, fought with opposing players, umpires, his teammates and his family.

In 1936 Ty Cobb was one of the first players inducted into the National Baseball Hall of Fame.

Cobb, Tyrus Raymond "The Georgia Peach"
BL/TR, 6'1", 175 lbs. Deb: 8/30/05

YEAR	TM/L	G	AB	R	H	2B	3B	HR	RBI	BB	SO	AVG
1905	Det-AL	41	150	19	36	6	0	1	15	10	—	.240
1906	Det-AL	98	358	45	113	15	5	1	34	19	—	.316
1907	Det-AL	150	605	97	212	28	14	5	119	24	—	.350
1908	Det-AL	150	581	88	188	36	20	4	108	34	—	.324
1909	Det-AL	156	573	116	216	33	10	9	107	48	—	.377
1910	Det-AL	140	506	106	194	35	13	8	91	64	—	.383
1911	Det-AL	146	591	147	248	47	24	8	127	44	—	.420
1912	Det-AL	140	553	120	226	30	23	7	83	43	—	.409
1913	Det-AL	122	428	70	167	18	16	4	67	58	31	.390
1914	Det-AL	98	345	69	127	22	11	2	57	57	22	.368
1915	Det-AL	156	563	144	208	31	13	3	99	118	43	.369
1916	Det-AL	145	542	113	201	31	10	5	68	78	39	.371
1917	Det-AL	152	588	107	225	44	24	6	102	61	34	.383
1918	Det-AL	111	421	83	161	19	14	3	64	41	21	.382
1919	Det-AL	124	497	92	191	36	13	1	70	38	22	.384
1920	Det-AL	112	428	86	143	28	8	2	63	58	28	.334
1921	Det-AL	128	507	124	197	37	16	12	101	56	19	.389
1922	Det-AL	137	526	99	211	42	16	4	99	55	24	.401
1923	Det-AL	145	556	103	189	40	7	6	88	66	14	.340
1924	Det-AL	155	625	115	211	38	10	4	78	85	18	.338
1925	Det-AL	121	415	97	157	31	12	12	102	65	12	.378
1926	Det-AL	79	233	48	79	18	5	4	62	26	2	.339
1927	Phi-AL	134	490	104	175	32	7	5	93	67	12	.357
1928	Phi-AL	95	353	54	114	27	4	1	40	34	16	.323
Total	24	3,035	11,434	2,246	4,189	724	295	117	1,937	1,249	INC	.366

YEAR	TM/L	W	L	PCT	G	IP	H	HR	BB	SO	ERA
1918	Det-AL	0	0	—	2	4	6	0	2	0	4.50
1925	Det-AL	0	0	—	1	1	0	0	0	0	0.00
Total	2	0	0	—	3	5	6	0	2	0	3.60

John Coleman

Pitcher-Outfielder (John Francis Coleman)
Born: March 6, 1863, Saratoga Springs, New York
Died: May 31, 1922, Detroit, Michigan

As a pitcher John Coleman holds the major league record for most losses in a season — 48 in 1883 (he also managed to get 12 wins that year). It was his rookie season with the N.L.'s Philadelphia Quakers. He spent the rest of his eight-year career playing mostly in the outfield.

Coleman, John Francis
BL/TR, 5'9.5", 170 lbs. Deb: 5/1/1883

YEAR	TM/L	W	L	PCT	G	IP	H	HR	BB	SO	ERA
1883	Phi-NL	12	48	.200	65	538.1	772	17	48	159	4.87
1884	Phi-NL	5	15	.250	21	154.1	216	9	22	37	4.90
	Phi-AA	0	2	.000	3	21	28	0	2	5	3.43
1885	Phi-AA	2	2	.500	8	60.1	82	0	5	12	3.43
1886	Phi-AA	1	1	.500	3	20.2	18	1	5	2	2.61
1889	Phi-AA	3	2	.600	5	34	38	2	14	6	2.91
1890	Pit-NL	0	2	.000	2	14	28	1	6	3	9.64
Total	6	23	72	.242	107	842.2	1,182	30	102	224	4.68

YEAR	TM/L	G	AB	R	H	2B	3B	HR	RBI	BB	SO	AVG
1883	Phi-NL	90	354	33	83	12	8	0	32	15	39	.234
1884	Phi-NL	43	171	16	42	7	2	0	22	8	20	.246
	Phi-AA	28	107	16	22	2	3	2	—	5	—	.206
1885	Phi-AA	96	398	71	119	15	11	3	—	25	—	.299
1886	Phi-AA	121	492	67	121	18	16	0	—	33	—	.246
	Pit-AA	11	43	3	15	2	1	0	—	2	—	.349
	Yr	132	535	70	136	20	17	0	—	35	—	.254
1887	Pit-NL	115	475	75	139	21	11	2	54	31	40	.293
1888	Pit-NL	116	438	49	101	11	4	0	26	29	52	.231
1889	Phi-AA	6	19	1	1	0	0	0	1	1	3	.053
1890	Pit-NL	3	11	1	2	0	0	0	0	3	0	.182
Total	8	629	2,508	332	645	88	56	7	INC	152	INC	.257

Eddie Collins

Infielder-Manager (Edward Trowbridge Collins Sr.)
Born: May 2, 1887, Millerton, New York
Died: March 25, 1951, Boston, Massachusetts

Eddie Collins played for the Athletics and then for the White Sox from 1906 to 1930 and his 25-year career is the longest in American League history. Though he won no batting titles (mainly because he played at the same time as Ty Cobb) he nevertheless batted .333 lifetime, led the league in stolen bases four times and in runs scored three consecutive seasons (1912-14). He finished his career with 743 stolen bases and 3,312 hits (eighth all-time).

This fleet-footed, left-handed hitting second baseman was part of Connie Mack's famed $100,000 infield. Collins, along with shortstop Jack Barry, first baseman Stuffy McInnis and third baseman Frank "Home Run" Baker. They steered the A's to four pennants and three World Championships from 1910 to 1914.

He was sold to the White Sox in 1915 and led that club to a World Championship in 1917. In 1919 he was one on the "honest players" on the infamous Chicago "Black Sox" club.

In 1924 Collins was appointed manager of the White Sox and piloted the club for three years, winning more games than he lost. After he retired as a player he served as general manager of the Boston Red Sox from 1932 until his death in 1951 and was responsible for bringing such players as Jimmie Foxx and Ted Williams to Boston.

Eddie Collins was inducted into the National Baseball Hall of Fame in 1939.

Collins, Edward Trowbridge Sr. "Cocky" (a.k.a. Edward T. Sullivan in 1906)
BL/TR, 5'9", 175 lbs.   Deb: 9/17/06

YEAR	TM/L	G	AB	R	H	2B	3B	HR	RBI	BB	SO	AVG
1906	Phi-AL	6	15	2	3	0	0	0	0	0	—	.200
1907	Phi-AL	14	20	0	5	0	0	0	2	0	—	.250
1908	Phi-AL	102	330	39	90	18	7	1	40	16	—	.273
1909	Phi-AL	153	572	104	198	30	10	3	56	62	—	.346
1910	Phi-AL	153	583	81	188	16	15	3	81	49	—	.322
1911	Phi-AL	132	493	92	180	22	13	3	73	62	—	.365
1912	Phi-AL	153	543	137	189	25	11	0	64	101	—	.348
1913	Phi-AL	148	534	125	184	23	13	3	73	85	37	.345
1914	Phi-AL	152	526	122	181	23	14	2	85	97	31	.344
1915	Chi-AL	155	521	118	173	22	10	4	77	119	27	.332
1916	Chi-AL	155	545	87	168	14	17	0	52	86	36	.308
1917	Chi-AL	156	564	91	163	18	12	0	67	89	16	.289
1918	Chi-AL	97	330	51	91	8	2	2	30	73	13	.276
1919	Chi-AL	140	518	87	165	19	7	4	80	68	27	.319
1920	Chi-AL	153	602	117	224	38	13	3	76	69	19	.372
1921	Chi-AL	139	526	79	177	20	10	2	58	66	11	.337
1922	Chi-AL	154	598	92	194	20	12	1	69	73	16	.324
1923	Chi-AL	145	505	89	182	22	5	5	67	84	8	.360
1924	Chi-AL	152	556	108	194	27	7	6	86	89	16	.349
1925	Chi-AL	118	425	80	147	26	3	3	80	87	8	.346
1926	Chi-AL	106	375	66	129	32	4	1	62	62	8	.344
1927	Phi-AL	95	226	50	76	12	1	1	15	56	9	.336
1928	Phi-AL	36	33	3	10	3	0	0	7	4	4	.303
1929	Phi-AL	9	7	0	0	0	0	0	0	2	0	.000
1930	Phi-AL	3	2	1	1	0	0	0	0	0	0	.500
Total	25	2,826	9,949	1,821	3,312	438	186	47	1,300	1,499	INC	.333

Jimmy Collins

Infielder-Manager (James Joseph Collins)
Born: Jan 16, 1870, Buffalo, New York
Died: March 6 1943, Buffalo, New York

JAMES J. COLLINS, Third Baseman.
BOSTON CLUB, 1891.

Jimmy Collins was one of the greatest third basemen to ever play the game. At the turn of the century he revolutionized the way the position was played. At a time when bunting was a big part of baseball, he was the first man to charge bunts and play them barehanded, flipping the ball to first base in one motion. He would also range far from his base to field the ball, instead of playing close to the bag, as was the custom in those days. His 601 chances accepted at third base in 1899, and his 252 putouts in 1900 remain among the longest-standing fielding records.

He was no slouch at the plate either. In his 14-year career, he hit better than .300 five times, had over 100 RBI twice and scored over 100 runs four times.

After starring with the N.L.'s Boston Beaneaters in the late 1890's, Collins jumped to the American League, when it was formed in 1901, to become player-manager for the Boston Red Sox. He held that position for the first six years of the team's existence and lead the club to its first pennant in 1903. That October the Red Sox then went on to defeat Pittsburgh in the first modern-day World Series. The following year he led the Red Sox to a second pennant, but there was no World Series that year due to a feud between the A.L. and N.L. In 1907 he was relieved of his managerial duties and traded to Philadelphia. He retired from the majors in 1908.

Jimmy Collins was inducted into the National Baseball Hall of Fame in 1945.

Collins, James Joseph
BR/TR, 5'9", 178 lbs. Deb: 4/19/1895

YEAR	TM/L	G	AB	R	H	2B	3B	HR	RBI	BB	SO	AVG
1895	Bos-NL	11	38	10	8	3	0	1	8	4	4	.211
	Lou-NL	96	373	65	104	17	5	6	49	33	16	.279
	Yr	107	411	75	112	20	5	7	57	37	20	.273
1896	Bos-NL	84	304	48	90	10	9	1	46	30	12	.296
1897	Bos-NL	134	529	103	183	28	13	6	132	41	—	.346
1898	Bos-NL	152	597	107	196	35	5	15	111	40	—	.328
1899	Bos-NL	151	599	98	166	28	11	5	92	40	—	.277
1900	Bos-NL	142	586	104	178	25	5	6	95	34	—	.304
1901	Bos-AL	138	564	108	187	42	16	6	94	34	—	.332
1902	Bos-AL	108	429	71	138	21	10	6	61	24	—	.322
1903	Bos-AL	130	540	88	160	33	17	5	72	24	—	.296
1904	Bos-AL	156	631	85	171	33	13	3	67	27	—	.271
1905	Bos-AL	131	508	66	140	26	5	4	65	37	—	.276
1906	Bos-AL	37	142	17	39	8	4	1	16	4	—	.275
1907	Bos-AL	41	158	13	46	8	0	0	10	10	—	.291
	Phi-AL	100	365	38	100	22	0	0	35	24	—	.274
	Yr	141	523	51	146	30	0	0	45	34	—	.279
1908	Phi-AL	115	433	34	94	14	3	0	30	20	—	.217
Total	14	1,726	6,796	1,055	2,000	353	116	65	983	426	INC	.294

Charles Commiskey

Infielder - Manager - Owner (Charles Albert Commiskey)
Born: August 15, 1959, Chicago, Illinois
Died: October 26, 1931, Eagle River, Wisconsin

COR. NINTH & FRANKLIN AVE.,
ST. LOUIS, MO.

In the 1880's Charlie Commiskey managed and played first base for the American Association's St. Louis Browns. Although he had to put up with constant interference from club owner Chris Von der Ahe, who was basically ignorant about baseball, Commiskey nevertheless guided the club to four consecutive A.A. pennants from 1885-88.

Charles Commiskey's exploits as Browns first baseman and manager are legendary. He is generally credited for revolutionizing the way the position of first base was played. Until he came along, it was customary for all the basemen to stay very near their bases, so when Commiskey ventured out to short right field to catch a fly ball, or when he would gobble up a hot grounder while playing away from the bag and then have the pitcher go over to first to cover the play, it changed baseball forever. He was also the first manager to shift his infield in or out, depending on the situation and stage of the game.

Commiskey is the only player in the history of the game to become sole owner of a major league franchise. In 1901, when the American League was born, he established the Chicago White Sox and was president of the club until 1931.

Under Commiskey's ownership the club won four American League pennants and two World Championships. In 1919 the club was rocked by the infamous "Black Sox" scandal in which eight White Sox players were caught taking bribes to throw the World Series to Cincinnati.

As it turned out, Chicago's poorly paid players (Commiskey was one of the stingiest men in baseball) were easy pickings for the gamblers who had offered the eight teammates $100,000 (but who actually only paid $10,000) to lose the series.

Charles Commiskey was inducted into the National Baseball Hall of Fame in 1939.

Commiskey, Charles Albert "Commy" or "The Old Roman"
BR/TR, 6', 180 lbs. Deb: 5/2/1882

YEAR	TM/L	G	AB	R	H	2B	3B	HR	RBI	BB	SO	AVG
1882	StL-AA	78	329	58	80	9	5	1	—	4	—	.243
1883	StL-AA	96	401	87	118	17	9	2	—	11	—	.294
1884	StL-AA	108	460	76	110	17	6	2	—	5	—	.239
1885	StL-AA	83	340	68	87	15	7	2	—	14	—	.256
1886	StL-AA	131	578	95	147	15	9	3	—	10	—	.254
1887	StL-AA	125	538	139	180	22	5	4	—	27	—	.335
1888	StL-AA	137	576	102	157	22	5	6	83	12	—	.273
1889	StL-AA	137	587	105	168	28	10	3	102	19	19	.286
1890	Chi-PL	88	377	53	92	11	3	0	59	14	17	.244
1891	StL-AA	141	580	86	152	16	2	3	93	33	25	.262
1892	Cin-NL	141	551	61	125	14	6	3	71	32	16	.227
1893	Cin-NL	64	259	38	57	12	1	0	26	11	2	.220
1894	Cin-NL	61	220	26	58	8	0	0	33	5	5	.264
Total	13	1,390	5,796	994	1,531	206	68	29	INC	197	INC	.264

YEAR	TM/L	W	L	PCT	G	IP	H	HR	BB	SO	ERA
1882	StL-AA	0	1	.000	2	8	12	0	3	2	0.00
1884	StL-AA	0	0	—	1	4	1	0	0	4	2.25
1889	StL-AA	0	0	—	1	0.1	0	0	0	0	0.00
Total	3	0	1	.000	4	12.1	13	0	3	6	0.73

Roger Connor

Infielder
Born: July 1, 1857, Waterbury, Connecticut
Died: January 4, 1931, Waterbury, Connecticut

Roger Connor was the pre-eminent home-run hitter of the 1800's. His lifetime record of 138 homers was a major league record until Babe Ruth broke it in 1921. This towering 6'3", 220 lb. first baseman started his career in 1880 with the N.L.'s Troy Haymakers and, in 1881, hit the first grand slam in major league history while with that club. The franchise was shifted to New York in 1883 and Connor played for the Giants for the rest of the decade. In 1885 he won the batting title with a .371 average and in 1889 his 130 RBI led the league.

He is probably best remembered for a towering home-run he hit in 1889 which cleared the right-field wall of the Polo Grounds and sailed out onto 112th St. A group of Wall Street brokers, watching from the stands, were so impressed that they collected $500 and bought him an inscribed gold watch from Tiffany's.

After defecting to the Players League in 1890 (and leading that league in home runs) he returned to the Giants in 1891. He spent the following seven seasons alternating among New York, Philadelphia and St. Louis and retired from the majors in 1897.

Roger Connor was inducted into the National Baseball Hall of Fame in 1976.

Connor, Roger
BL/TL, 6'3", 220 lbs. Deb: 5/1/1880

YEAR	TM/L	G	AB	R	H	2B	3B	HR	RBI	BB	SO	AVG
1880	Tro-NL	83	340	53	113	18	8	3	47	13	21	.332
1881	Tro-NL	85	367	55	107	17	6	2	31	15	20	.292
1882	Tro-NL	81	349	65	115	22	18	4	42	13	20	.330
1883	NY-NL	98	409	80	146	28	15	1	50	25	16	.357
1884	NY-NL	116	477	98	151	28	4	4	82	38	32	.317
1885	NY-NL	110	455	102	169	23	15	1	65	51	8	.371
1886	NY-NL	118	485	105	172	29	20	7	71	41	15	.355
1887	NY-NL	127	471	113	134	26	22	17	104	75	50	.285
1888	NY-NL	134	481	98	140	15	17	14	71	73	44	.291
1889	NY-NL	131	496	117	157	32	17	13	130	93	46	.317
1890	NY-PL	123	484	133	169	24	15	14	103	88	32	.349
1891	NY-NL	129	479	112	139	29	13	7	94	83	39	.290
1892	Phi-NL	155	564	123	166	37	11	12	73	116	39	.294
1893	NY-NL	135	511	111	156	25	8	11	105	91	26	.305
1894	NY-NL	22	82	10	24	7	0	1	14	8	0	.293
	StL-NL	99	380	83	122	28	25	7	79	51	17	.321
	Yr	121	462	93	146	35	25	8	93	59	17	.316
1895	StL-NL	103	398	78	131	29	9	8	77	63	10	.329
1896	StL-NL	126	483	71	137	21	9	11	72	52	14	.284
1897	StL-NL	22	83	13	19	3	1	1	12	13	—	.229
Total	18	1,997	7,794	1,620	2,467	441	233	138	1,322	1,002	INC	.317

Jack Coombs

Pitcher (John Wesley Coombs)
Born: November 18, 1882, LeGrand, Iowa
Died: April 15, 1957, Palestine, Texas

"Colby Jack" Coombs pitched the Philadelphia Athletics to the 1910 World championship with a league-leading 31 regular-season victories, and three post-season wins. He also pitched a major league record 13 shutouts that year.

Coombs helped the A's win another World championship the following season, leading the league in victories once again with 28. He had one World Series win that year. Another post-season win in 1916 while he was with the Dodgers gave him the all-time major league record of five World Series wins without a loss.

Coombs, John Wesley "Colby Jack"
BB/TR, 6', 185 lbs. Deb: 7/5/06

YEAR	TM/L	W	L	PCT	G	IP	H	HR	BB	SO	ERA
1906	Phi-AL	10	10	.500	23	173	144	0	68	90	2.50
1907	Phi-AL	6	9	.400	23	132.2	109	2	64	73	3.12
1908	Phi-AL	7	5	.583	26	153	130	1	64	80	2.00
1909	Phi-AL	12	11	.522	30	205.2	156	1	73	97	2.32
1910	Phi-AL	31	9	.775	45	353	248	0	115	224	1.30
1911	Phi-AL	28	12	.700	47	336.2	360	8	119	185	3.53
1912	Phi-AL	21	10	.677	40	262.1	227	5	94	120	3.29
1913	Phi-AL	1	0	.000	2	5.1	5	0	6	0	10.13
1914	Phi-AL	0	1	.000	2	8	8	0	3	1	4.50
1915	Bro-NL	15	10	.600	29	195.2	166	1	91	56	2.58
1916	Bro-NL	13	8	.619	27	159	136	3	44	47	2.66
1917	Bro-NL	7	11	.389	31	141	147	7	49	34	3.96
1918	Bro-NL	8	14	.364	27	189	191	10	49	44	3.81
1920	Det-AL	0	0	—	2	5.2	7	0	2	1	3.18
Total	14	159	110	.591	354	2,320	2,034	38	841	1,052	2.78

YEAR	TM/L	G	AB	R	H	2B	3B	HR	RBI	BB	SO	AVG
1906	Phi-AL	24	67	9	16	2	0	0	3	1	—	.239
1907	Phi-AL	24	48	4	8	0	0	1	4	0	—	.167
1908	Phi-AL	78	220	24	56	9	5	1	23	9	—	.255
1909	Phi-AL	37	83	4	14	4	0	0	10	4	—	.169
1910	Phi-AL	46	132	20	29	3	0	0	9	7	—	.220
1911	Phi-AL	52	141	31	45	6	1	2	23	8	—	.319
1912	Phi-AL	56	110	10	28	2	0	0	13	14	—	.255
1913	Phi-AL	2	3	1	1	1	0	0	0	0	2	.333
1914	Phi-AL	5	11	0	3	1	0	0	2	1	1	.273
1915	Bro-NL	29	75	8	21	1	1	0	5	2	17	.280
1916	Bro-NL	27	61	2	11	2	0	0	3	2	10	.180
1917	Bro-NL	32	44	4	10	0	1	0	2	4	9	.227
1918	Bro-NL	46	113	6	19	3	2	0	3	7	5	.168
1920	Det-AL	2	2	0	0	0	0	0	0	0	0	.000
Total	14	460	1,110	123	261	34	10	4	100	59	—	.235

Larry Corcoran

Pitcher (Lawrence J. Corcoran)
Born: August 10, 1859, Brooklyn, New York
Died: October 14, 1891, Newark, New York

LARRY CORCORAN, PITCHER.

Larry Corcoran was one of the premier pitchers of the early 1880's when he starred for the N.L.'s Chicago White Stockings. In the five seasons from 1880 to 1884 he had a 170-83 record and became the first pitcher to hurl three no-hitters. He led the White Stockings to three consecutive N.L. pennants during this period.

He was the first pitcher to work out a set of signals with his catcher. By shifting the wad of chewing tobacco in his mouth he was able to tell his receiver what he was going to throw. In 1891 he died of Bright's disease at the age of 32.

Corcoran, Lawrence J.
BL/TB, 120 lbs. Deb: 5/1/1880

YEAR	TM/L	W	L	PCT	G	IP	H	HR	BB	SO	ERA
1880	Chi-NL	43	14	.754	63	536.1	404	6	99	268	1.95
1881	Chi-NL	31	14	.689	45	396.2	380	10	78	150	2.31
1882	Chi-NL	27	13	.675	39	355.2	281	5	63	170	1.95
1883	Chi-NL	34	20	.630	56	473.2	483	7	82	216	2.49
1884	Chi-NL	35	23	.603	60	516.2	473	35	116	272	2.40
1885	Chi-NL	5	2	.714	7	59.1	63	2	24	10	3.64
	NY-NL	2	1	.667	3	25	24	1	11	10	2.88
Yr		7	3	.700	10	84.1	87	3	35	20	3.42
1886	Was-NL	0	1	.000	2	14	16	0	4	3	5.79
1887	Ind-NL	0	2	.000	2	15	23	3	19	4	12.60
Total	8	177	90	.663	277	2,392.1	2,147	69	496	1,103	2.36

YEAR	TM/L	G	AB	R	H	2B	3B	HR	RBI	BB	SO	AVG
1880	Chi-NL	72	286	41	66	11	1	0	25	10	33	.231
1881	Chi-NL	47	189	25	42	8	0	0	9	5	22	.222
1882	Chi-NL	40	169	23	35	10	2	1	24	6	18	.207
1883	Chi-NL	68	263	40	55	12	7	0	25	6	62	.209
1884	Chi-NL	64	251	43	61	3	4	1	19	10	33	.243
1885	Chi-NL	7	22	6	6	1	0	0	4	6	1	.273
	NY-NL	3	14	3	5	0	0	0	2	0	1	.357
	Yr	10	36	9	11	1	0	0	6	6	2	.306
1886	NY-NL	1	4	0	0	0	0	0	0	0	2	.000
	Was-NL	21	81	9	15	2	1	0	3	7	14	.185
	Yr	22	85	9	15	2	1	0	3	7	16	.176
1887	Ind-NL	3	10	2	2	0	0	0	0	2	1	.200
Total	8	326	1,289	192	287	47	15	2	111	52	187	.223

Sam Crawford

Outfielder (Samuel Earl Crawford)
Born: Apr 18, 1880, Wahoo, Nebraska
Died: June 15, 1968, Hollywood, California

"Wahoo Sam" Crawford is the only player to lead both major leagues in home runs and triples. He started out with the Cincinnati Reds in 1899 and led the N.L. in homers in 1901 with 16. He jumped to the A.L. in 1903 and spent 15 seasons with the Detroit Tigers. Crawford led that league in triples five times and RBI three times.

While with the Tigers he played in the shadow of teammate Ty Cobb. Although he despised "The Georgia Peach," the two of them were nevertheless part of one of the greatest outfields in A.L. history, and when they were on base together they had a double steal routine worked out which was usually quite successful.

Sam Crawford was inducted into the National Baseball Hall Of Fame in 1957.

Crawford, Samuel Earl "Wahoo Sam"
BL/TL, 6', 190 lbs. Deb: 9/10/1899H

YEAR	TM/L	G	AB	R	H	2B	3B	HR	RBI	BB	SO	AVG
1899	Cin-NL	31	127	25	39	3	7	1	20	2	—	.307
1900	Cin-NL	101	389	68	101	15	15	7	59	28	—	.260
1901	Cin-NL	131	515	91	170	20	16	16	104	37	—	.330
1902	Cin-NL	140	555	92	185	18	22	3	78	47	—	.333
1903	Det-AL	137	550	88	184	23	25	4	89	25	—	.335
1904	Det-AL	150	562	49	143	22	16	2	73	44	—	.254
1905	Det-AL	154	575	73	171	38	10	6	75	50	—	.297
1906	Det-AL	145	563	65	166	25	16	2	72	38	—	.295
1907	Det-AL	144	582	102	188	34	17	4	81	37	—	.323
1908	Det-AL	152	591	102	184	33	16	7	80	37	—	.311
1909	Det-AL	156	589	83	185	35	14	6	97	47	—	.314
1910	Det-AL	154	588	83	170	26	19	5	120	37	—	.289
1911	Det-AL	146	574	109	217	36	14	7	115	61	—	.378
1912	Det-AL	149	581	81	189	30	21	4	109	42	—	.325
1913	Det-AL	153	609	78	193	32	23	9	83	52	28	.317
1914	Det-AL	157	582	74	183	22	26	8	104	69	31	.314
1915	Det-AL	156	612	81	183	31	19	4	112	66	29	.299
1916	Det-AL	100	322	41	92	11	13	0	42	37	10	.286
1917	Det-AL	61	104	6	18	4	0	2	12	4	6	.173
Total	19	2,517	9,570	1,391	2,961	458	309	97	1,525	760	INC	.309

James Creighton

Pitcher
Born: April 15, 1841
Died: October 18, 1862

Jim Creighton was baseball's first great pitcher. He played from 1857 to 1862, an era before there were any organized leagues, when all players were considered to be amateurs. At this time pitches were delivered underhanded, in a stiff-armed, stiff-wristed fashion. Creighton employed an illegal but yet imperceptible wrist snap which added speed to the ball. He then learned to change speeds to fool the batters.

He also became baseball's first professional player when he surreptitiously accepted money to play for the Excelsior club of Brooklyn in 1860. On November 8th of that year he threw baseball's first recorded shutout.

Creighton was also an excellent hitter, scoring 47 runs in 20 games in 1860, while being retired only 56 times. In the 1862 season he was retired a mere four times.

James Creighton died on October 18, 1862, at the age of 21, four days after rupturing his bladder while hitting a home run for the Excelsiors in a game against Union club of Morrisania, N.Y.

Candy Cummings

Pitcher (William Arthur Cummings)
Born: October 18, 1848, Ware, Massachusetts
Died: May 16, 1924, Toledo, Ohio

Candy Cummings is generally credited with inventing the curveball, though there is some dispute about this. He claimed he came up with the idea as a 14-year-old in 1863 while throwing clam shells on a New England beach. He observed the irregular flight of the shells and attempted to duplicate the movement with a baseball by flicking his wrist and releasing the ball late from his fingers.

In the 1860's the diminutive (5'9", 120 lbs.) Cummings pitched for the Excelsior and Star clubs of Brooklyn. Opposing players were stunned by the odd behavior of his pitches. In 1872, after the National Association was formed, he joined the Mutual club of New York and spent four years in the N.A., never winning fewer than 28 games a season.

In the National League's inaugural season in 1876, he won 16 games for the Hartford Blues. On September 9 of that year he pitched both games of the first major league doubleheader (and won them both).

In spite of a claim by Fred Goldsmith, another early pitcher, to have been the inventor of the curveball, it was Cumming's 1908 article "How I Pitched the First Curve" and the endorsement of baseball writer Henry Chadwick that eventually led to his induction into the Hall of Fame in 1939 as the curve's inventor.

Cummings, William Arthur
BR/TR, 5'9", 120 lbs. Deb: 4/22/1872

YEAR	TM/L	W	L	PCT	G	IP	H	HR	BB	SO	ERA
1872	Mut-NA	33	20	.623	55	497	600	2	30	43	2.52
1873	Bal-NA	28	14	.667	42	382	475	4	33	31	2.66
1874	Phi-NA	28	26	.519	54	482	602	4	21		2.88
1875	Har-NA	35	12	.745	48	417	396	0	6		1.60
Total	4n	124	72	.633	199	1,778	2,073	10	90	74	2.43
1876	har-NL	16	8	.667	24	216	215	0	14	26	1.67
1877	Cin-NL	5	14	.263	19	155.2	219	2	13	11	4.34
Total	2	21	22	.488	43	371.2	434	2	27	37	2.78

Ed Delahanty

Outfielder (Edward James Delahanty)
Born: October 30, 1867, Cleveland, Ohio
Died: July 2, 1903, Niagara Falls, Ontario, Canada

"Big Ed" Delahanty was one of the finest hitters of the 1800's. His lifetime batting average of .346 is fourth best of all-time. In his 16-year career he hit better than .400 three times and is the only player to win batting championships in both the American and National Leagues.

He was one of five brothers who played in the majors. The 6'1", 170 lb. slugger starred for the Philadelphia Phillies in the 1890's, driving in better than 100 runs seven times and leading the league in doubles four times. On July 13, 1896, he became the second player in baseball history to hit four homers in one game (all of them off of Chicago's Adonis Terry).

In 1902 he jumped to the American League to play for the Washington Nationals and led the league with 43 doubles and a .376 batting average that year.

Though Delahanty was well known for his playing achievements, he was almost as famous for his off-the-field ability to consume beer, and in June of 1903 Washington manager Tom Loftus suspended him for excessive drinking. This led to his untimely and rather mysterious death.

On July 2, Delahanty, who also had marital and financial troubles, left the club in Detroit and took a train to New York City to visit his wife. At the International Bridge near Niagara Falls the conductor put him off the train for being drunk and disorderly. It is not quite clear what happened next but apparently Delahanty staggered along the tracks in the dark in a desperate attempt to catch up with the train, fell through an open drawbridge, and was then swept over the falls to his death.

Ed Delahanty was inducted into the National Baseball Hall of Fame in 1945.

Delahanty, Edward James "Big Ed"
BR/TR, 6'1", 170 lbs. Deb: 5/22/1888

YEAR	TM/L	G	AB	R	H	2B	3B	HR	RBI	BB	SO	AVG
1888	Phi-NL	74	290	40	66	12	2	1	31	12	26	.228
1889	Phi-NL	56	246	37	72	13	3	0	27	14	17	.293
1890	Cle-PL	115	517	107	154	26	13	3	64	24	30	.298
1891	Phi-NL	128	543	92	132	19	9	5	86	33	50	.243
1892	Phi-NL	123	477	79	146	30	21	6	91	31	32	.306
1893	Phi-NL	132	595	145	219	35	18	19	146	47	20	.368
1894	Phi-NL	114	489	147	199	39	18	4	131	60	16	.407
1895	Phi-NL	116	480	149	194	49	10	11	106	86	31	.404
1896	Phi-NL	123	499	131	198	44	17	13	126	62	22	.397
1897	Phi-NL	129	530	109	200	40	15	5	96	60	—	.377
1898	Phi-NL	144	548	115	183	36	9	4	92	77	—	.334
1899	Phi-NL	146	581	135	238	55	9	9	137	55	—	.410
1900	Phi-NL	131	539	82	174	32	10	2	109	41	—	.323
1901	Phi-NL	139	542	106	192	38	16	8	108	65	—	.354
1902	Was-AL	123	473	103	178	43	14	10	93	62	—	.376
1903	Was-AL	42	156	22	52	11	1	1	21	12	—	.333
Total	16	1,835	7,505	1,599	2,597	522	185	101	1,464	741	INC	.346

Hugh Duffy

Outfielder - Manager
Born: November 26, 1866, Cranston, Rhode Island
Died: October 19, 1954, Boston, Massachusetts

When Duffy joined the N.L.'s Boston Beaneaters in 1892 he became center fielder and captain of the club and joined with right fielder Tommy McCarthy to form Boston's "Heavenly Twins," a deadly hit-and-run combination. The Beaneaters won the pennant that year and went on to defeat the Cleveland Spiders in the World Series.

Duffy hit over .300 in seven of the nine seasons he spent with Boston, and his 1894 batting average of .440 is the highest of all-time. That year he won baseball's first Triple Crown with 18 home runs and 145 RBI.

In 1897 he helped the Beaneaters win another N.L. pennant. He left the club in 1901 to play in the newly formed American League and became player-manager of the first edition of the Milwaukee Brewers, but the club folded at the end of the season. Duffy then went on to manage in Philadelphia, Chicago and Boston. Later in life he became a batting instructor with the Red Sox and tutored a young Ted Williams in the art of hitting.

Hugh Duffy was inducted into the National Baseball Hall of Fame in 1945.

Duffy, Hugh
BR/TR, 5'7", 168 lbs. Deb: 6/23/1888

YEAR	TM/L	G	AB	R	H	2B	3B	HR	RBI	BB	SO	AVG
1888	Chi-NL	71	298	60	84	10	4	7	41	9	32	.282
1889	Chi-NL	136	584	144	172	21	7	12	89	46	30	.295
1890	Chi-PL	138	596	161	191	36	16	7	82	59	20	.320
1891	Bos-AA	127	536	134	180	20	8	9	110	61	29	.336
1892	Bos-NL	147	612	125	184	28	12	5	81	60	37	.301
1893	Bos-NL	131	560	147	203	23	7	6	118	50	13	.363
1894	Bos-NL	125	539	160	237	51	16	18	145	66	15	.440
1895	Bos-NL	130	531	110	187	30	6	9	100	63	16	.352
1896	Bos-NL	131	527	97	158	16	8	5	113	52	19	.300
1897	Bos-NL	134	550	130	187	25	10	11	129	52	—	.340
1898	Bos-NL	152	568	97	169	13	3	8	108	59	—	.298
1899	Bos-NL	147	588	103	164	29	7	5	102	39	—	.279
1900	Bos-NL	55	181	27	55	5	4	2	31	16	—	.304
1901	Mil-AL	79	285	40	86	15	9	2	45	16	—	.302
1904	Phi-NL	18	46	10	13	1	1	0	5	13	—	.283
1905	Phi-NL	15	40	7	12	2	1	0	3	1	—	.300
1906	Phi-NL	1	1	0	0	0	0	0	0	0	—	.000
Total	17	1,737	7,042	1,552	2,282	325	119	106	1,302	662	INC	.324

Johnny Evers

Infielder - Manager (John Joseph Evers)
Born: July 21, 1881, Troy, New York
Died: March 28, 1947, Albany, New York

Johnny Evers played second base in the Chicago Cubs' famed Tinker-to-Evers-to-Chance double-play combination of the early 1900's. This slick-fielding infield helped the Cubs win three straight N.L. pennants starting in 1906. Chicago won the World Series in 1907 and 1908 with Evers hitting .350 in both series. In the 1908 series he knocked in the winning run in the fifth and final game.

The slightly built (5'9", 125 lb.) Evers was nicknamed "The Crab" both for the way he sidled up to grounders and for his testy disposition. Not only was he constantly at war with the umpires, but in their final years together, due to some minor dispute, Evers and Joe Tinker didn't speak to each other off the field, and the two often traded punches.

Joe Tinker, Johnny Evers and Frank Chance were certainly not the greatest double-play combination in the history of baseball but they were nevertheless immortalized in the annals of the game when New York columnist Franklin P. Adams wrote a famous poem about the trio in 1910.

Evers took over as manager of the Cubs in 1913 and was traded to Boston the following year were he formed another slick-fielding double-play combination with shortstop Rabbit Maranville. The Braves won the pennant that year and then went on to sweep the Athletics in the World Series in four straight games with Evers hitting .438.

Johnny Evers was inducted into the National Baseball Hall of Fame in 1946.

Evers, John Joseph "Crab" or "Trojan"
BL/TR, 5'9", 125 lbs. Deb: 9/1/02

YEAR	TM/L	G	AB	R	H	2B	3B	HR	RBI	BB	SO	AVG
1902	Chi-NL	26	90	7	20	0	0	0	2	3	—	.222
1903	Chi-NL	124	464	70	136	27	7	0	52	19	—	.293
1904	Chi-NL	152	532	49	141	14	7	0	47	28	—	.265
1905	Chi-NL	99	340	44	94	11	2	1	37	27	—	.276
1906	Chi-NL	154	533	65	136	17	6	1	51	36	—	.255
1907	Chi-NL	151	508	66	127	18	4	2	51	38	—	.250
1908	Chi-NL	126	416	83	125	19	6	0	37	66	—	.300
1909	Chi-NL	127	463	88	122	19	6	1	24	73	—	.263
1910	Chi-NL	125	433	87	114	11	7	0	28	108	18	.263
1911	Chi-NL	46	155	29	35	4	3	0	7	34	10	.226
1912	Chi-NL	143	478	73	163	23	11	1	63	74	18	.341
1913	Chi-NL	136	446	81	127	20	5	3	49	50	14	.285
1914	Bos-NL	139	491	81	137	20	3	1	40	87	26	.279
1915	Bos-NL	83	278	38	73	4	1	1	22	50	16	.263
1916	Bos-NL	71	241	33	52	4	1	0	15	40	19	.216
1917	Bos-NL	24	83	5	16	0	0	0	0	13	8	.193
	Phi-NL	56	183	20	41	5	1	1	12	30	13	.224
	Yr	80	266	25	57	5	1	1	12	43	21	.214
1922	Chi-AL	1	3	0	0	0	0	0	1	2	0	.000
1929	Bos-NL	1	0	0	0	0	0	0	0	0	0	—
Total	18	1,784	6,137	919	1,659	216	70	12	538	778	INC	.270

Buck Ewing

Catcher - Manager (William Ewing)
Born: October 17, 1859, Hoagland, Ohio
Died: October 20, 1906, Cincinnati, Ohio

For most of the 1880's and '90's Buck Ewing was considered to be the best catcher in baseball. He revolutionized the way the position was played. Ewing was one of the first catchers to switch from an unpadded glove to the modern "pillow style" mitt and he was the first catcher to throw to second base from the crouch position, thereby saving precious time when attempting to throw out base stealers.

Ewing spent 18 years in the majors, most of with the New York Giants, and hit .303 lifetime. In 1895 he took over as manager of the Cincinnati Reds and spent five years with that club. He retired in 1900 after returning to the Giants and managing that team for one season.

Buck Ewing was inducted into the National Baseball Hall of Fame in 1939.

Ewing, William
BR/TR, 5'10", 188 lbs. Deb: 9/9/1880

YEAR	TM/L	G	AB	R	H	2B	3B	HR	RBI	BB	SO	AVG
1880	Tro-NL	13	45	1	8	1	0	0	5	1	3	.178
1881	Tro-NL	67	272	40	68	14	7	0	25	7	8	.250
1882	Tro-NL	74	328	67	89	16	11	2	29	10	15	.271
1883	NY-NL	88	376	90	114	11	13	10	41	20	14	.303
1884	NY-NL	94	382	90	106	15	20	3	41	28	22	.277
1885	NY-NL	81	342	81	104	15	12	6	63	13	17	.304
1886	NY-NL	73	275	59	85	11	7	4	31	16	17	.309
1887	NY-NL	77	318	83	97	17	13	6	44	30	33	.305
1888	NY-NL	103	415	83	127	18	15	6	58	24	28	.306
1889	NY-NL	99	407	91	133	23	13	4	87	37	32	.327
1890	NY-PL	83	352	98	119	19	15	8	72	39	12	.338
1891	NY-NL	14	49	8	17	2	1	0	18	5	5	.347
1892	NY-NL	105	393	58	122	10	15	8	76	38	26	.310
1893	Cle-NL	116	500	117	172	28	15	6	122	41	18	.344
1894	Cle-NL	53	211	32	53	12	4	2	39	24	9	.251
1895	Cin-NL	105	434	90	138	24	13	5	94	30	22	.318
1896	Cin-NL	69	263	41	73	14	4	1	38	29	13	.278
1897	Cin-NL	1	1	0	0	0	0	0	0	0	—	.000
Total	18	1,315	5,363	1,129	1,625	250	178	71	883	392	INC	.303

YEAR	TM/L	W	L	PCT	G	IP	H	HR	BB	SO	ERA
1882	Tro-NL	0	0	—	1	1	2	0	1	0	9.00
1884	NY-NL	0	1	.000	1	8	7	0	4	3	1.13
1885	NY-NL	0	1	.000	1	2	4	0	3	0	4.50
1888	NY-NL	0	0	—	2	7	8	1	4	6	2.57
1889	NY-NL	2	0	1.000	3	20	23	0	8	12	4.05
1890	NY-PL	0	1	.000	1	9	11	1	3	2	4.00
Total	6	2	3	.400	9	47	55	2	23	23	3.45

Elmer Flick

Outfielder (Elmer Harrison Flick)
Born: January 11, 1876, Bedford, Ohio
Died: January 9, 1971, Bedford, Ohio

At the turn of the century Elmer Flick was one of baseball's top all-round players. He began his major league career with the Philadelphia Phillies in 1898 and hit .302 in his rookie season. In his second year, this left-hand-hitting outfielder was among the top ten hitters in the the N.L. with a .342 average. And in the following season of 1900 he led the league with 110 RBI and his .367 batting average was second only to Honus Wagner's .381.

ELMER H. FLICK,
RIGHTFIELDER, BOSTON, 1899.

In 1902 Flick, like many of the N.L.'s top players of the day, jumped to the upstart American League. In 1905, while with Cleveland he led the A.L. in hitting with a .308 average. He also led the league in triples three straight years from 1905 to 1907, and in stolen bases in 1904 and 1906 (the fleet-footed Flick finished his 13-year career with 330 stolen bases).

In 1907 the Detroit Tigers offered to trade 21-year-old Ty Cobb to Cleveland for the then 31-year-old Flick in a one for one deal. Cleveland owner Charlie Sommers figured that Cobb would be too much trouble and declined the offer.

The following year Flick came down with a mysterious stomach ailment which plagued him for the rest of his career. He retired from the major leagues in 1910.

Elmer Flick was inducted into the National Baseball Hall of Fame in 1963.

Flick, Elmer Harrison
BL/TR, 5'9", 168 lbs. Deb: 5/2/1898

YEAR	TM/L	G	AB	R	H	2B	3B	HR	RBI	BB	SO	AVG
1898	Phi-NL	134	453	84	137	16	13	8	81	86	—	.302
1899	Phi-NL	127	485	98	166	22	11	2	98	42	—	.342
1900	Phi-NL	138	545	106	200	32	16	11	110	56	—	.367
1901	Phi-NL	138	540	112	180	32	17	8	88	52	—	.333
1902	Phi-AL	11	37	15	11	2	1	0	3	6	—	.297
	Cle-AL	110	424	70	126	19	11	2	61	47	—	.297
	Yr	121	461	85	137	21	12	2	64	53	—	.297
1903	Cle-AL	140	523	81	155	23	16	2	51	51	—	.296
1904	Cle-AL	150	579	97	177	31	17	6	56	51	—	.306
1905	Cle-AL	132	500	72	154	29	18	4	64	53	—	.308
1906	Cle-AL	157	624	98	194	34	22	1	62	54	—	.311
1907	Cle-AL	147	549	78	166	15	18	3	58	64	—	.302
1908	Cle-AL	9	35	4	8	1	1	0	2	3	—	.229
1909	Cle-AL	66	235	28	60	10	2	0	15	22	—	.255
1910	Cle-AL	24	68	5	18	2	1	1	7	10	—	.265
Total	13	1,483	5,597	948	1,752	268	164	48	756	597	—	.313

Pud Galvin

Pitcher (James Francis Galvin)
Born: December 25, 1856, St. Louis, Missouri
Died: March 7, 1902, Pittsburgh, Pennsylvania

Jim "Pud" Galvin was baseball's first 300-game winner. In the 1880's Galvin, a hefty right-hander with a blazing fastball, was a pitching mainstay for both the Buffalo Bisons and Pittsburgh Alleghenys.

In 1979, his first season in the N.L., he went 37-27 for Buffalo. It was the first of six straight seasons in which he would win more than 20 games for the Bisons. On August 20 of the following year he pitched the first of his two no-hitters, a 1-0 win over the Worchester Ruby Legs.

Galvin's best seasons were 1883 and 1884. In '83 he went 46-29, leading the league in games pitched (76), complete games (72) shutouts (5) and innings pitched (656). In 1884 he went 46-22, had an ERA of 1.99, and threw his second no-hitter, a 18-0 win over Detroit.

In 1885 Buffalo sold him to the Pittsburgh Alleghenys of the American Association, a club that would join the N.L. in 1887 and later become known as the Pittsburgh Pirates. From 1886 to 1889, while with Pittsburgh, Galvin had four more straight 20-win seasons. After a fling in the Players League in 1890, he returned to the Pirates in 1891 and went 14-14 that year. A finger injury ended his baseball career in 1892.

Pud Galvin was inducted into the National Baseball Hall of Fame in 1965.

Galvin, James Francis "Pud", "Gentle Jeems" or "The Little Steam Engine"
BR/TR, 5'8", 190 lbs. Deb: 5/22/1875

YEAR	TM/L	W	L	PCT	G	IP	H	HR	BB	SO	ERA
1879	Buf-NL	37	27	.578	66	593	585	3	31	136	2.28
1880	Buf-NL	20	35	.364	58	458.2	528	5	32	128	2.71
1881	Buf-NL	29	24	.547	56	474	546	4	46	136	2.37
1882	Buf-NL	28	23	.549	52	445.1	476	8	40	162	3.17
1883	Buf-NL	46	29	.613	76	656.1	676	9	50	279	2.72
1884	Buf-NL	46	22	.676	72	636.1	566	23	63	369	1.99
1885	Buf-NL	13	19	.406	33	284	356	8	37	93	4.09
	Pit-AA	3	7	.300	11	88.1	97	2	7	27	3.67
1886	Pit-AA	29	21	.580	50	434.2	457	3	75	72	2.67
1887	Pit-NL	28	21	.571	49	440.2	490	12	67	76	3.29
1888	Pit-NL	23	25	.479	50	437.1	446	9	53	107	2.63
1889	Pit-NL	23	16	.590	41	341	392	19	78	77	4.17
1890	Pit-PL	12	13	.480	26	217	275	3	49	35	4.35
1891	Pit-NL	14	14	.500	33	246.2	256	10	62	46	2.88
1892	Pit-NL	5	6	.455	12	96	104	0	28	29	2.63
	StL-NL	5	6	.455	12	92	102	4	26	27	3.23
	Yr	10	12	.455	24	188	206	4	54	56	2.92
Total	14	361	308	.540	697	5,941.1	6,352	122	744	1,799	2.87

Jack Glasscock

Infielder (John Wesley Glasscock)
Born: July 22, 1859, Wheeling, West Virginia
Died: February 24, 1947, Wheeling, West Virginia

In the late 1800's Jack Glasscock was one of baseball's premier shortstops. He played the position barehanded and was one of the first short-stops to back up throws to the second baseman.

Glasscock, who was nicknamed "Pebbly Jack" for his habit of picking up and tossing away peb-bles while playing his position, spent 17 years in the majors. He hit better than .300 five times and, in 1889 while with the Indianapolis Hoosiers, he led the N.L. with 205 hits. The following season, playing for the New York Giants, he led the N.L. in hits (172) and batting average (.336).

Jack Glasscock finished his career in 1895 with a lifetime .290 batting average.

Glasscock, John Wesley "Pebbly Jack"
BR/TR, 5'8", 160 lbs. Deb: 5/1/1879

YEAR	TM/L	G	AB	R	H	2B	3B	HR	RBI	BB	SO	AVG
1879	Cle-NL	80	325	31	68	9	3	0	29	6	24	.209
1880	Cle-NL	77	296	37	72	13	3	0	27	2	21	.243
1881	Cle-NL	85	335	49	86	9	5	0	33	15	8	.257
1882	Cle-NL	84	358	66	104	27	9	4	46	13	9	.291
1883	Cle-NL	96	383	67	110	19	6	0	46	13	23	.287
1884	Cle-NL	72	281	45	70	4	4	1	22	25	16	.249
	Cin-UA	38	172	48	72	9	5	2	—	8	—	.419
1885	StL-NL	111	446	66	125	18	3	1	40	29	10	.280
1886	StL-NL	121	486	96	158	29	7	3	40	38	13	.325
1887	Ind-NL	122	483	91	142	18	7	0	40	41	8	.294
1888	Ind-NL	113	442	63	119	17	3	1	45	14	17	.269
1889	Ind-NL	134	582	128	205	40	3	7	85	31	10	.352
1890	NY-NL	124	512	91	172	32	9	1	66	41	8	.336
1891	NY-NL	97	369	46	89	12	6	0	55	36	11	.241
1892	StL-NL	139	566	83	151	27	5	3	72	44	19	.267
1893	StL-NL	48	195	32	56	8	1	1	26	25	3	.287
	Pit-NL	66	293	49	100	7	11	1	74	17	4	.341
	Yr	114	488	81	156	15	12	2	100	42	7	.320
1894	Pit-NL	86	332	46	93	10	7	1	63	31	4	.280
1895	Lou-NL	18	74	9	25	3	1	1	6	3	1	.338
	Was-NL	25	100	20	23	2	0	0	10	7	3	.230
	Yr	43	174	29	48	5	1	1	16	10	4	.276
Total	17	1,736	7,030	1,163	2,040	313	98	27	INC	439	INC	.290

YEAR	TM/L	W	L	PCT	G	IP	H	HR	BB	SO	ERA
1884	Cle-NL	0	0	—	2	5	8	0	2	1	5.40
1887	Ind-NL	0	0	—	1	1	0	0	0	1	0.00
1888	Ind-NL	0	0	—	1	0.1	1	0	2	1	54.00
1889	Ind-NL	0	0	—	1	0.2	3	0	3	0	0.00
Total	4	0	0	—	5	7	12	0	7	3	6.43

Kid Gleason

Pitcher - Infielder - Manager (William J. Gleason)
Born: October 26, 1866, Camden, New Jersey
Died: January 2, 1933, Philadelphia, Pennsylvania

Beginning in 1888, Kid Gleason spent 22 years playing major league ball. He then spent five more seasons as a manager. The feisty Gleason began his career as a pitcher, and in 1890 went 38-17 for the Philadelphia Phillies. It was the first of four consecutive seasons of 20 or more wins.

In 1895 he came down with a sore arm and switched to second base just in time to help the Baltimore Orioles win a second straight N.L. pennant. Known mostly for his defensive and base-stealing skills, he had his best offensive year in 1897, hitting .319 with 172 hits and 106 RBI while with the Giants.

In 1919 he took over as manager of the Chicago White Sox. The club won the A.L. pennant that year but Gleason was betrayed by the team that autumn when they threw the World Series to Cincinnati in the infamous Black Sox scandal. He spent four more years as manager of the White Sox and then left in 1923 to coach for Connie Mack in Philadelphia.

Gleason, William J.
BB/TR, 5'7", 158 lbs. Deb: 4/20/1888

YEAR	TM/L	G	AB	R	H	2B	3B	HR	RBI	BB	SO	AVG
1888	Phi-NL	24	83	4	17	2	0	0	5	3	16	.205
1889	Phi-NL	30	99	11	25	5	0	0	8	8	12	.253
1890	Phi-NL	63	224	22	47	3	0	0	17	12	21	.210
1891	Phi-NL	65	214	31	53	5	2	0	17	20	17	.248
1892	StL-NL	66	233	35	50	4	2	3	25	34	23	.215
1893	StL-NL	59	199	25	51	6	4	0	20	19	8	.256
1894	StL-NL	9	28	3	7	0	1	0	1	2	1	.250
	Bal-NL	26	86	22	30	5	1	0	17	7	2	.349
	Yr	35	114	25	37	5	2	0	18	9	3	.325
1895	Bal-NL	112	421	90	130	14	12	0	74	33	18	.309
1896	NY-NL	133	541	79	162	17	5	4	89	42	13	.299
1897	NY-NL	131	540	85	172	16	4	1	106	26	—	.319
1898	NY-NL	150	570	78	126	8	5	0	62	39	—	.221
1899	NY-NL	146	576	72	152	14	4	0	59	24	—	.264
1900	NY-NL	111	420	60	104	11	3	1	29	17	—	.248
1901	Det-AL	135	547	82	150	16	12	3	75	41	—	.274
1902	Det-AL	118	441	42	109	11	4	1	38	25	—	.247
1903	Phi-NL	106	412	65	117	19	6	1	49	23	—	.284
1904	Phi-NL	153	587	61	161	23	6	0	42	37	—	.274
1905	Phi-NL	155	608	95	150	17	7	1	50	45	—	.247
1906	Phi-NL	135	494	47	112	17	2	0	34	36	—	.227
1907	Phi-NL	36	126	11	18	3	0	0	6	7	—	.143
1908	Phi-NL	2	1	0	0	0	0	0	0	0	—	.000
1912	Chi-AL	1	2	0	1	0	0	0	0	0	—	.500
Total	22	1,966	7,452	1,020	1,944	216	80	15	823	500	INC	.261

YEAR	TM/L	W	L	PCT	G	IP	H	HR	BB	SO	ERA
1888	Phi-NL	7	16	.304	24	199.2	199	11	53	89	2.84
1889	Phi-NL	9	15	.375	29	205	242	8	97	64	5.58
1890	Phi-NL	38	17	.691	60	506	479	8	167	222	2.63
1891	Phi-NL	24	22	.522	53	418	431	10	165	100	3.51
1892	StL-NL	16	24	.400	47	400	389	11	151	133	3.33
1893	StL-NL	21	25	.457	48	380.1	436	18	187	86	4.61
1894	StL-NL	2	6	.250	8	58	75	2	21	9	6.05
	Bal-NL	15	5	.750	21	172	224	3	44	35	4.45
	Yr	17	11	.607	29	230	299	5	65	44	4.85
1895	Bal-NL	2	4	.333	9	50.1	77	4	21	6	6.97
Total	8	134	134	.500	299	2,389.1	2,552	75	906	744	3.79

Clark Griffith

Pitcher - Manager - Owner (Clark Calvin Griffith)
Born: November 20, 1869, Clear Creek, Missouri (Mo?)
Died: October 27, 1955, Washington, D.C.

Clark Griffith spent 64 years in major league baseball as a player, manager and owner. He earned his nickname "The Old Fox" while pitching for Cap Anson's Chicago Colts in the 1890's. In his first full season with the club in 1894 he went 21-14. He followed this with five straight 20-win seasons and in 1898 he led the N.L. with a 1.88 ERA.

Griffith, who claimed to have invented the screwball, was known to have scuffed, scratched, cut and spit upon almost every ball he pitched. Ironically, in 1920 he was one of the leaders of the movement to ban the spitball.

Griffith had been a star in the N.L. for seven seasons when he jumped to the new American League in 1901. He was offered the job of managing the Chicago club and that year he went 24-7 on the mound and managed the team to a first-place finish.

In the interests of the American League he left the White Sox in 1903 to become the manager of the newly established New York Highlanders (later to become known as the Yankees). It was imperative that the A.L. establish a strong franchise in New York City to compete with John McGraw's Giants.

In 1904 he went 14-11 and managed the club to a second-place finish. His pitching powers soon started to diminish and in 1906 Griffith won his final game, yet he managed to make appearances on the mound up until 1914.

Griffith remained with the Highlanders until 1909, then he went back to the N.L. to manage Cincinnati. After three years with the Reds he returned to the A.L. in 1912 and found a home for life with the Washington Nationals (later known as the Senators). From 1912 to 1920 he managed, and gradually purchased control of the franchise. He then ran the club until his death at the age of 88 in 1955.

Clark Griffith was inducted into the National Baseball Hall of Fame in 1946.

Griffith, Clark Calvin "The Old Fox"
BR/TR, 5'6.5", 156 lbs. Deb: 4/11/1891

YEAR	TM/L	W	L	PCT	G	IP	H	HR	BB	SO	ERA
1891	StL-AA	14	6	.700	27	186.1	195	8	58	68	3.33
	Bos-AA	3	1	.750	7	40	47	3	15	20	5.62
	Yr	17	7	.708	34	226.1	242	11	73	88	3.74
1893	Chi-NL	1	2	.333	4	19.2	24	1	5	9	5.03
1894	Chi-NL	21	14	.600	36	261.1	328	12	85	71	4.92
1895	Chi-NL	26	14	.650	42	353	434	11	91	79	3.93
1896	Chi-NL	23	11	.676	36	317.2	370	3	70	81	3.54
1897	Chi-NL	21	18	.538	41	343.2	410	3	86	102	3.72
1898	Chi-NL	24	10	.706	38	325.2	305	1	64	97	1.88
1899	Chi-NL	22	14	.611	38	319.2	329	5	65	73	2.79
1900	Chi-NL	14	13	.519	30	248	245	6	51	61	3.05
1901	Chi-AL	24	7	.774	35	266.2	275	4	50	67	2.67
1902	Chi-AL	15	9	.625	28	213	247	11	47	51	4.18
1903	NY-AL	14	11	.560	25	213	201	3	33	69	2.70
1904	NY-AL	7	5	.583	16	100.1	91	3	16	36	2.87
1905	NY-AL	9	6	.600	25	101.2	82	1	15	46	1.68
1906	NY-AL	2	2	.500	17	59.2	58	0	15	16	3.02
1907	NY-AL	0	0	—	4	8.1	15	0	6	5	8.64
1909	Cin-NL	0	1	.000	1	6	11	0	2	3	6.00
1912	Was-AL	0	0	—	1	0	1	1	0	0	\
1913	Was-AL	0	0	—	1	1	1	0	0	0	0.00
1914	Was-AL	0	0	—	1	1	1	0	0	1	0.00
Total	20	240	144	.625	453	3,385.2	3,670	76	774	955	3.31

Billy Hamilton

Outfielder (William Robert Hamilton)
Born: February 16, 1866, Newark, New Jersey
Died: December 16, 1940, Worcester, Massachusetts

When Billy Hamilton retired from big league baseball in 1901 his lifetime record of 912 stolen bases was a major league record that stood until 1974 when it was broken by Lou Brock. In his 14-year career, this five-time stolen-base champion scored 1,690 runs in 1,591 games ... better than a run a game!

Unfortunately, stolen bases in Hamilton's era can't be compared with those of today: from 1886 to 1897 a runner was credited with a stolen base if he advanced an extra base on a hit. For example, if a batter singled a base runner from first to third, the runner was credited with a stolen base. Also, the art of holding runners on base had not yet been perfected by pitchers; and the catchers of that era usually stood much farther back from the plate than those of today, often catching the ball on the first bounce. As a result, a throw to second base took longer to get there. Nevertheless, when compared to the base stealers of his time, Hamilton was the best there was.

In 1889, his first full season in the majors, he hit .301 and stole a league-leading 111 bases for the A.A.'s Kansas City Cowboys. The next year he signed with Philadelphia in the National League and led that circuit with 102 stolen bases. During the next 11 seasons, while with the Phillies and the Boston Braves, the left-handed hitting Hamilton combined patience at the plate, excellent hitting ability and daring baserunning to become baseball's first great leadoff hitter.

Hamilton led the N.L. in stolen bases four times, walks five times, batting average twice and runs scored four times (he holds the all-time record with 192 in 1894). He finished his career with a .344 lifetime batting average (sixth best of all-time).

Billy Hamilton was inducted into the National Baseball Hall of Fame in 1961.

Hamilton, William Robert "Sliding Billy"
BL/TR, 5'6", 165 lbs. Deb: 7/31/1888

YEAR	TM/L	G	AB	R	H	2B	3B	HR	RBI	BB	SO	AVG
1888	KC-AA	35	129	21	34	4	4	0	11	4	—	.264
1889	KC-AA	137	534	144	161	17	12	3	77	87	41	.301
1890	Phi-NL	123	496	133	161	13	9	2	49	83	37	.325
1891	Phi-NL	133	527	141	179	23	7	2	60	102	28	.340
1892	Phi-NL	139	554	132	183	21	7	3	53	81	29	.330
1893	Phi-NL	82	355	110	135	22	7	5	44	63	7	.380
1894	Phi-NL	129	544	192	220	25	15	4	87	126	17	.404
1895	Phi-NL	123	517	166	201	22	6	7	74	96	30	.389
1896	Bos-NL	131	523	152	191	24	9	3	52	110	29	.365
1897	Bos-NL	127	507	152	174	17	5	3	61	105	—	.343
1898	Bos-NL	110	417	110	154	16	5	3	50	87	—	.369
1899	Bos-NL	84	297	63	92	7	1	1	33	72	—	.310
1900	Bos-NL	136	520	103	173	20	5	1	47	107	—	.333
1901	Bos-NL	102	348	71	100	11	2	3	38	64	—	.287
Total	14	1,591	6,268	1,690	2,158	242	94	40	736	1,187	INC	.344

Harry Hooper

Outfielder (Harry Bartholomew Hooper)
Born: August 24, 1887, Bell Station, California
Died: December 18, 1974, Santa Cruz, California

Harry Hooper was the leadoff hitter for the Boston Red Sox from 1909 to 1920. He was a graceful fielder who is credited with inventing the sliding catch. Hooper played right field in Boston's fabled "Million Dollar Outfield" along with Tris Speaker and Duffy Lewis.

The left-handed hitting Hooper's .281 lifetime batting average and exceptional fielding ability helped the Red Sox win four world championships during the period from 1912 to 1918. In 1915 he became the first player to hit two home runs in a single World Series game.

In 1918 Hooper became captain of the Red Sox and is credited with convincing manager Ed Barrow to move pitching ace Babe Ruth into left field between starts ... a move that changed both Ruth's career and baseball forever.

Hooper was traded to the White Sox in 1921 and hit a career high of .321 that year. He hit better than .300 in two of the next four years that he spent with Chicago and retired from major league baseball in 1925 when cheapskate owner Charles Commiskey tried to cut his $13,250 per year salary down to $7,000.

Harry Hooper was inducted into the National Baseball Hall of Fame in 1971.

Hooper, Harry Bartholomew
BL/TR, 5'10", 168 lbs. Deb: 4/16/09

YEAR	TM/L	G	AB	R	H	2B	3B	HR	RBI	BB	SO	AVG
1909	Bos-AL	81	255	29	72	3	4	0	12	16	—	.282
1910	Bos-AL	155	584	81	156	9	10	2	27	62	—	.267
1911	Bos-AL	130	524	93	163	20	6	4	45	73	—	.311
1912	Bos-AL	147	590	98	143	20	12	2	53	66	—	.242
1913	Bos-AL	148	586	100	169	29	12	4	40	60	51	.288
1914	Bos-AL	142	530	85	137	23	15	1	41	58	47	.258
1915	Bos-AL	149	566	90	133	20	13	2	51	89	36	.235
1916	Bos-AL	151	575	75	156	20	11	1	37	80	35	.271
1917	Bos-AL	151	559	89	143	21	11	3	45	80	40	.256
1918	Bos-AL	126	474	81	137	26	13	1	44	75	25	.289
1919	Bos-AL	128	491	76	131	25	6	3	49	79	28	.267
1920	Bos-AL	139	536	91	167	30	17	7	53	88	27	.312
1921	Chi-AL	108	419	74	137	26	5	8	58	55	21	.327
1922	Chi-AL	152	602	111	183	35	8	11	80	68	33	.304
1923	Chi-AL	145	576	87	166	32	4	10	65	68	22	.288
1924	Chi-AL	130	476	107	156	27	8	10	62	65	26	.328
1925	Chi-AL	127	442	62	117	23	5	6	55	54	21	.265
Total	17	2,309	8,785	1,429	2,466	389	160	75	817	1,136	INC	.281

YEAR	TM/L	W	L	PCT	G	IP	H	HR	BB	SO	ERA
1913	Bos-AL	0	0	—	1	2	2	0	1	0	0.00

Dummy Hoy

Outfielder (William Ellsworth Hoy)
Born: May 23, 1862, Houcktown, Ohio
Died: January 15, 1961, Cincinnati, Ohio

Dummy Hoy, a better than average outfielder who played in the late 1800's, left quite a legacy.

William Ellsworth "Dummy" Hoy couldn't talk or hear, and in these politically correct times he'd probably be called "verbally challenged" and "aurally deprived," but in 1888 when he entered the major leagues he was just plain deaf and dumb.

Dummy, who played for seven different clubs in four different leagues, was no dummy when it came to getting on base; he led the American Association with 119 walks in 1891 and the American League with 86 walks in 1901. And when he got on base he knew what to do, as the diminutive (5'4"-148 lb) outfielder led the National League in stolen bases in 1888 with 82, and had a total of 594 in his 14-year career.

It is Dummy Hoy who is responsible for umpires raising their hands when calling balls and strikes. When Dummy was at the plate, he couldn't hear the call, so he would turn and look at the umpire. The umpires would oblige him by raising the right hand to signal a strike and the left hand to signify a ball. The practice caught on ... and the umps have have been waving their arms and signaling their calls ever since!

Hoy, William Ellsworth
BL/TR, 5'4", 148 lbs. Deb: 4/20/1888

YEAR	TM/L	G	AB	R	H	2B	3B	HR	RBI	BB	SO	AVG
1888	Was-NL	136	503	77	138	10	8	2	29	69	48	.274
1889	Was-NL	127	507	98	139	11	6	0	39	75	30	.274
1890	Buf-PL	122	493	107	147	17	8	1	53	94	36	.298
1891	StL-AA	141	567	136	165	14	5	5	66	119	25	.291
1892	Was-NL	152	593	108	166	19	8	3	75	86	23	.280
1893	Was-NL	130	564	106	138	12	6	0	45	66	9	.245
1894	Cin-NL	126	495	114	148	22	13	5	70	87	18	.299
1895	Cin-NL	107	429	93	119	21	12	3	55	52	8	.277
1896	Cin-NL	121	443	120	132	23	7	4	57	65	13	.298
1897	Cin-NL	128	497	87	145	24	6	2	42	54	—	.292
1898	Lou-NL	148	582	104	177	15	16	6	66	49	—	.304
1899	Lou-NL	154	633	116	194	17	13	5	49	61	—	.306
1901	Chi-AL	132	527	112	155	28	11	2	60	86	—	.294
1902	Cin-NL	72	279	48	81	15	2	2	20	41	—	.290
Total	14	1,796	7,112	1,426	2,044	248	121	40	726	1,004		.287

Arthur Irwin

Infielder (Arthur Albert Irwin)
Born: February 14, 1858, Toronto, Ontario, Canada
Died: August 16, 1921, Atlantic Ocean

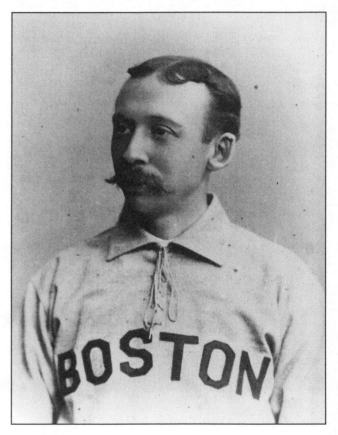

Arthur Irwin was a journeyman shortstop who played in the big leagues from 1880 to 1894. He is generally credited with inventing the modern baseball glove in 1883.

Gloves without padding, which were intended for the protection of the hands only, had been worn by players as early as 1878. In order to protect two broken fingers, while playing for the N.L.'s Providence Grays in 1885, the Canadian-born Irwin added padding to a buckskin glove. He then discovered that he could field his position much better with his new invention. This style of glove soon caught on with his teammates and then throughout all of baseball.

Irwin, Arthur Albert "Doc" or "Sandy"
BL/TR, 5'8.5", 158 lbs. Deb: 5/1/1880

YEAR	TM/L	G	AB	R	H	2B	3B	HR	RBI	BB	SO	AVG
1880	Wor-NL	85	352	53	91	19	4	1	35	11	27	.259
1881	Wor-NL	50	206	27	55	8	2	0	24	7	4	.267
1882	Wor-NL	84	333	30	73	12	4	0	30	14	34	.219
1883	Pro-NL	98	406	67	116	22	7	0	44	12	38	.286
1884	Pro-NL	102	404	73	97	14	3	2	44	28	52	.240
1885	Pro-NL	59	218	16	39	2	1	0	14	14	29	.179
1886	Phi-NL	101	373	51	87	6	6	0	34	35	39	.233
1887	Phi-NL	100	374	65	95	14	8	2	56	48	26	.254
1888	Phi-NL	125	448	51	98	12	4	0	28	33	56	.219
1889	Phi-NL	18	73	9	16	5	0	0	10	6	6	.219
	Was-NL	85	313	49	73	10	5	0	32	42	37	.233
	Yr	103	386	58	89	15	5	0	42	48	43	.231
1890	Bos-PL	96	354	60	92	17	1	0	45	57	29	.260
1891	Bos-AA	6	17	1	2	0	0	0	0	2	1	.118
1894	Phi-NL	1	0	0	0	0	0	0	0	0	0	—
Total	13	1,010	3,871	552	934	141	45	5	396	309	378	.241

YEAR	TM/L	W	L	PCT	G	IP	H	HR	BB	SO	ERA
1884	Pro-NL	0	0	—	1	3	5	0	1	0	3.00
1889	Was-NL	0	0	—	1	1	1	0	0	0	0.00
Total	2	0	0	—	2	4	6	0	1	0	2.25

Joe Jackson

Outfielder (Joseph Jefferson Jackson)
Born: July 16, 1889, Pickens Country, South Carolina
Died: December 5, 1951, Greenville, South Carolina

"Shoeless Joe" Jackson was an illiterate farm boy from South Carolina whose lifetime batting average of .356 and outstanding running and fielding abilities would have eventually put him in the Hall of Fame if he hadn't been been involved in the infamous Black Sox scandal of 1919.

Jackson spent 13 years in the American League. In 1911, his first full season with Cleveland, he hit .408 and then followed this up with seasons of .395 and .373. In 1915 he was traded to the White Sox and, while with that club, put together five more .300 seasons between 1916 and 1920.

In 1919 the Chicago White Sox were the hottest thing in baseball. They won the American League pennant that year with a 88-52 record and were 5-1 favorites to beat the Cincinnati Reds in the World Series.

But even before the Series began there were rumors swirling that a "fix" was in. And when Cincinnati took the best of nine series 5 games to 3, it didn't sit well with a lot of baseball fans. One year later a Chicago Grand Jury blew the whole thing wide open, naming eight Chicago players as having conspired with gamblers to throw the series.

One of those players was "Shoeless Joe," who admitted accepting $5,000 from gamblers but claimed that it didn't affect his play, and his .375 batting average and club-leading 6 RBI during the series tends to bear him out.

Nevertheless, in 1921 baseball's newly appointed commissioner Kenesaw Mountain Landis banned Jackson and the other seven co-conspirators from baseball for life.

Jackson, Joseph Jefferson "Shoeless Joe"
BL/TR, 6'1", 200 lbs. Deb: 8/25/08

YEAR	TM/L	G	AB	R	H	2B	3B	HR	RBI	BB	SO	AVG
1908	Phi-AL	5	23	0	3	0	0	0	3	0	—	.130
1909	Phi-AL	5	17	3	3	0	0	0	3	1	—	.176
1910	Cle-AL	20	75	15	29	2	5	1	11	8	—	.387
1911	Cle-AL	147	571	126	233	45	19	7	83	56	—	.408
1912	Cle-AL	154	572	121	226	44	26	3	90	54	—	.395
1913	Cle-AL	148	528	109	197	39	17	7	71	80	26	.373
1914	Cle-AL	122	453	61	153	22	13	3	53	41	34	.338
1915	Cle-AL	83	303	42	99	16	9	3	45	28	11	.327
	Chi-AL	45	158	21	43	4	5	2	36	24	12	.272
	Yr	128	461	63	142	20	14	5	81	52	23	.308
1916	Chi-AL	155	592	91	202	40	21	3	78	46	25	.341
1917	Chi-AL	146	538	91	162	20	17	5	75	57	25	.301
1918	Chi-AL	17	65	9	23	2	2	1	20	8	1	.354
1919	Chi-AL	139	516	79	181	31	14	7	96	60	10	.351
1920	Chi-AL	146	570	105	218	42	20	12	121	56	14	.382
Total	13	1,332	4,981	873	1,772	307	168	54	785	519	—	.356

Hughie Jennings

Infielder (Hugh Ambrose Jennings)
Born: April 2, 1869, Pittston, Pennsylvania
Died: February 1, 1928, Scranton, Pennsylvania

During Hughie Jennings' 35-year career in baseball he was a star infielder with the legendary Baltimore Orioles of the National League in the 1890's, and later on spent 14 years as manager of the Detroit Tigers.

In 1884, his first full season with the Orioles, the feisty shortstop hit .335 and was appointed captain of the club. That year the Orioles won the first of three straight N.L. pennants. During his five years with Baltimore he never hit under .328. His all-time best year was 1896 when he batted .401. In 1899 and 1900, while with the Brooklyn Superbas, he played on two more pennant-winning clubs.

Jennings took over as skipper of the Tigers in 1907, and although he didn't get along well with temperamental superstar Ty Cobb, he managed the club to three straight A.L. pennants in his first three years. He would direct the team from the third-base coaching box and was famous for cheering them on with his piercing cry of "Ee-yah!"

During the off-season Jennings studied law, earned a law degree and built up a successful practice.

After he left the Tigers in 1920 he became a coach with John McGraw's New York Giants and helped that club win four straight pennants from 1921 to 1924. In 1925 he suffered a nervous breakdown and left baseball for good.

Hughie Jennings was inducted into the National Baseball Hall of Fame in 1945.

Jennings, Hugh Ambrose "Ee-Yah"
BR/TR, 5'8.5", 165 lbs. Deb: 6/1/1891

YEAR	TM/L	G	AB	R	H	2B	3B	HR	RBI	BB	SO	AVG
1891	Lou-AA	90	360	53	105	10	8	1	58	17	36	.292
1892	Lou-NL	152	594	65	132	16	4	2	61	30	30	.222
1893	Lou-NL	23	88	6	12	3	0	0	9	3	3	.136
	Bal-NL	16	55	6	14	0	0	1	6	4	3	.255
	Yr	39	143	12	26	3	0	1	15	7	6	.182
1894	Bal-NL	128	501	134	168	28	16	4	109	37	17	.335
1895	Bal-NL	131	529	159	204	41	7	4	125	24	17	.386
1896	Bal-NL	130	521	125	209	27	9	0	121	19	11	.401
1897	Bal-NL	117	439	133	156	26	9	2	79	42	—	.355
1898	Bal-NL	143	534	135	175	25	11	1	87	78	—	.328
1899	Bro-NL	16	41	7	7	0	2	0	6	9	—	.171
	Bal-NL	2	8	2	3	0	2	0	2	0	—	.375
	Bro-NL	51	175	35	57	3	8	0	34	13	—	.326
	Yr	69	224	44	67	3	12	0	42	22	—	.299
1900	Bro-NL	115	441	61	120	18	6	1	69	31	—	.272
1901	Phi-NL	82	302	38	79	21	2	1	39	25	—	.262
1902	Phi-NL	78	290	32	79	13	4	1	32	14	—	.272
1903	Bro-NL	6	17	2	4	0	0	0	1	1	—	.235
1907	Det-AL	1	4	0	1	1	0	0	0	0	—	.250
1909	Det-AL	2	4	1	2	0	0	0	2	0	—	.500
1912	Det-AL	1	1	0	0	0	0	0	0	0	—	.000
1918	Det-AL	1	0	0	0	0	0	0	0	0	0	—
Total	17	1,285	4,904	994	1,527	232	88	18	840	347	INC	.311

Walter Johnson

Pitcher - Manager (Walter Perry Johnson)
Born: November 6, 1887, Humboldt, Kansas
Died: December 10, 1946, Washington, D.C.

Walter Johnson was the hardest-throwing pitcher of his era. In his 21 seasons with Washington from 1907 to 1927 he won 417 games, an American League record. "The Big Train" won more than 30 games twice, had 10 consecutive years of 20 or more wins, led the league in strikeouts 12 times, in ERA five times, and wins six times. All while playing for a perennially lousy team.

Johnson's best season was 1913 when he went 36-7, had a league leading 1.14 ERA, and struck out 243 batters while walking only 38. He also led the league with 11 shutouts (he holds the all-time major league record with 110).

Johnson, a shy, humble man who didn't smoke, drink or swear, never got a chance to play in a World Series until he was 37 years old. In 1924 Washington managed to win its first pennant. They then faced the Giants in the series and Johnson, after pitching a complete game two days earlier, made a relief appearance in the seventh and deciding game, pitching four scoreless innings to get his only win and give Washington a world championship. The following season he won 20 games as the club won another pennant.

After his pitching career ended in 1927, he came back to Washington in 1929 as the manager. He ran the club for four years and then spent another three years managing Cleveland.

In 1936 Walter Johnson was one of the first players to be inducted into the National Baseball Hall of Fame.

Johnson, Walter Perry "Barney" or "The Big Train"
BR/TR, 6'1", 200 lbs. Deb: 8/2/07

YEAR	TM/L	W	L	PCT	G	IP	H	HR	BB	SO	ERA
1907	Was-AL	5	9	.357	14	110.1	100	1	20	71	1.88
1908	Was-AL	14	14	.500	36	256.1	194	0	53	160	1.65
1909	Was-AL	13	25	.342	40	296.1	247	1	84	164	2.22
1910	Was-AL	25	17	.595	45	370	262	1	76	313	1.36
1911	Was-AL	25	13	.658	40	322.1	292	8	70	207	1.90
1912	Was-AL	33	12	.733	50	369	259	2	76	303	1.39
1913	Was-AL	36	7	.837	48	346	232	9	38	243	1.14
1914	Was-AL	28	18	.609	51	371.2	287	3	74	225	1.72
1915	Was-AL	27	13	.675	47	336.2	258	1	56	203	1.55
1916	Was-AL	25	20	.556	48	369.2	290	0	82	228	1.90
1917	Was-AL	23	16	.590	47	326	248	3	68	188	2.21
1918	Was-AL	23	13	.639	39	326	241	2	70	162	1.27
1919	Was-AL	20	14	.588	39	290.1	235	0	51	147	1.49
1920	Was-AL	8	10	.444	21	143.2	135	5	27	78	3.13
1921	Was-AL	17	14	.548	35	264	265	7	92	143	3.51
1922	Was-AL	15	16	.484	41	280	283	8	99	105	2.99
1923	Was-AL	17	12	.586	42	261.1	263	9	73	130	3.48
1924	Was-AL	23	7	.767	38	277.2	233	10	77	158	2.72
1925	Was-AL	20	7	.741	30	229	217	7	78	108	3.07
1926	Was-AL	15	16	.484	33	260.2	259	13	73	125	3.63
1927	Was-AL	5	6	.455	18	107.2	113	7	26	48	5.10
Total	21	417	279	.599	802	5,914.2	4,913	97	1,363	3,509	2.17

YEAR	TM/L	G	AB	R	H	2B	3B	HR	RBI	BB	SO	AVG
1907	Was-AL	14	36	3	4	0	1	0	1	1	—	.111
1908	Was-AL	36	79	7	13	3	2	0	5	6	—	.165
1909	Was-AL	40	101	6	13	3	0	1	6	1	—	.129
1910	Was-AL	45	137	14	24	6	1	2	12	4	—	.175
1911	Was-AL	42	128	18	30	5	3	1	15	0	—	.234
1912	Was-AL	55	144	16	38	6	4	2	20	7	—	.264
1913	Was-AL	54	134	12	35	5	6	2	14	5	14	.261
1914	Was-AL	55	136	23	30	4	1	3	16	10	27	.221
1915	Was-AL	64	147	14	34	7	4	2	17	8	34	.231
1916	Was-AL	58	142	13	32	2	4	1	7	11	28	.225
1917	Was-AL	57	130	15	33	12	1	0	15	9	30	.254
1918	Was-AL	65	150	10	40	4	4	1	18	9	18	.267
1919	Was-AL	56	125	13	24	1	3	1	8	12	17	.192
1920	Was-AL	33	64	6	17	1	3	1	7	3	10	.266
1921	Was-AL	38	111	10	30	7	0	0	10	6	14	.270
1922	Was-AL	43	108	8	22	3	0	1	15	2	12	.204
1923	Was-AL	42	93	11	18	3	3	0	13	4	15	.194
1924	Was-AL	39	113	18	32	9	0	1	14	3	11	.283
1925	Was-AL	36	97	12	42	6	1	2	20	3	6	.433
1926	Was-AL	35	103	6	20	5	0	1	12	3	11	.194
1927	Was-AL	26	46	6	16	2	0	2	10	3	4	.348
Total	21	933	2,324	241	547	94	41	24	255	110	INC	.235

Addie Joss

Pitcher (Adrian Joss)
Born: April 12, 1880, Woodland, Wisconsin
Died: April 14, 1911, Toledo, Ohio

Addie Joss spent his nine-year major league career with the Cleveland Indians. When he joined the club in 1902 he threw a one hitter in his first start and then went on to lead the A.L. with five shutouts that year.

Joss was a 6'3" righthander who had a stinging fastball and an outstanding curve. In his career he won 20 games four times, had at least 100 strikeouts six times, finished with ERA's of 1.83 or less five times, and completed a remarkable 236 of 260 starts. His lifetime ERA of 1.89 is second all-time to Big Ed Walsh.

What has to be Joss's greatest game took place on October 2, 1908, when he engaged in a pitching duel with Walsh (who won 40 games for Chicago that year). Both clubs were locked in a pennant race. Even though Walsh threw a four-hitter in which he struck out 15 batters and gave up only one run, he was no match for Joss who retired 27 batters in a row for a perfect game. In 1910 Joss threw his second career no-hitter, once again defeating Chicago 1-0.

In April of 1911 Joss died of tubercular meningitis at the age of 31. Though he played for only nine years, he was such an outstanding performer that in 1978, the Veterans Committee waived the 10-year minimum rule and inducted Addie Joss into the National Baseball Hall of Fame.

Addie Joss
BR/TR, 6'3", 185 lbs. Deb: 4/26/02

YEAR	TM/L	W	L	PCT	G	IP	H	HR	BB	SO	ERA
1902	Cle-AL	17	13	.567	32	269.1	225	2	75	106	2.77
1903	Cle-AL	18	13	.581	32	283.2	232	3	37	120	2.15
1904	Cle-AL	14	10	.583	25	192.1	160	0	30	83	1.59
1905	Cle-AL	20	12	.625	33	286	246	4	46	132	2.01
1906	Cle-AL	21	9	.700	34	282	220	3	43	106	1.72
1907	Cle-AL	27	11	.711	42	338.2	279	3	54	127	1.83
1908	Cle-AL	24	11	.686	42	325	232	2	30	130	1.16
1909	Cle-AL	14	13	.519	33	242.2	198	0	31	67	1.71
1910	Cle-AL	5	5	.500	13	107.1	96	2	18	49	2.26
Total	9	160	97	.623	286	2,327	1,888	19	364	920	1.88

Tim Keefe

Pitcher (Timothy John Keefe)
Born: January 1, 1857, Cambridge, Massachusetts
Died: April 23, 1933, Cambridge, Massachusetts

Tim Keefe was one of baseball's best and most durable pitchers of the late 1800's. In his 14-year career he completed 554 of the 593 games he started, winning 342.

In his first major league season with the N.L.'s Troy (NY) Trojans in 1880, Keefe started and completed 12 games, finishing the year with an amazing 0.86 ERA. That year the pitching distance was 45 feet. The following season it was increased to 50 feet and remained that way through most of Keefe's 14-year career. It wasn't until 1893, which was Keefe's final season, that it was increased to the the present 60' 6".

In 1883, while with the A.A.'s New York Metropolitans, Keefe won 41 games, completing 68 games in 68 starts. On July 4th of that year he won both games of a doubleheader against the Columbus Buckeyes, giving up a grand total of three hits in the two games.

In 1884 he had a record of 37-17 and, that October, had the distinction of pitching in the first World Series game ever played. (He lost 6-0 to Providence's Old Hoss Radbourn.)

In 1885 he was transferred from the Mets to the N.L.'s Giants (John B. Day owned both teams). He had four 30-or-more win seasons in his next five years with the Giants, taking them to the World Series twice.

In 1890 he helped establish the Players League and pitched for the New York franchise. When the league folded after one season he went back to the N.L. and retired from playing in 1893. He then umpired in the National League for two years.

Tim Keefe was inducted into the National Baseball Hall of Fame in 1964.

Keefe, Timothy John "Smiling Tim" or "Sir Timothy"
BR/TR, 5'10.5", 185 lbs. Deb: 8/6/1880

YEAR	TM/L	W	L	PCT	G	IP	H	HR	BB	SO	ERA
1880	Tro-NL	6	6	.500	12	105	71	0	17	43	0.86
1881	Tro-NL	18	27	.400	45	402	442	4	81	103	3.25
1882	Tro-NL	17	26	.395	43	375	368	4	81	116	2.50
1883	NY-AA	41	27	.603	68	619	486	6	98	361	2.41
1884	NY-AA	37	17	.685	57	482.2	378	5	75	317	2.26
1885	NY-NL	32	13	.711	46	400	300	6	102	227	1.58
1886	NY-NL	42	20	.677	64	535	479	9	102	297	2.56
1887	NY-NL	35	19	.648	56	476.2	428	11	108	189	3.12
1888	NY-NL	35	12	.745	51	434.1	317	5	90	335	1.74
1889	NY-NL	28	13	.683	47	364	319	9	151	225	3.31
1890	NY-PL	17	11	.607	30	229	228	6	85	88	3.38
1891	NY-NL	2	5	.286	8	55	71	1	27	29	5.24
	Phi-NL	3	6	.333	11	78.1	84	2	28	35	3.91
	Yr	5	11	.313	19	133.1	155	3	55	64	4.45
1892	Phi-NL	19	16	.543	39	313.1	264	4	100	127	2.36
1893	Phi-NL	10	7	.588	22	178	202	3	79	53	4.40
Total	14	342	225	.603	599	5,047.1	4,437	75	1,224	2,545	2.62

Wee Willie Keeler

Outfielder (William Henry Keeler)
Born: March 3, 1872, Brooklyn, New York
Died: January 1, 1923, Brooklyn, New York

Wee Willie "Hit 'em where they ain't" Keeler was the leadoff hitter for the legendary Baltimore Orioles of the National League in the 1890's. The 5'4", 140 lb. Keeler is probably the greatest slap hitter of all time. He was the master of the "Baltimore Chop," pounding high bouncers over infielder's heads as they charged potential bunts. He also had an uncanny ability to aim the ball at vacated spots in the infield. And once on base he was a base-stealing threat: he stole 495 lifetime with a high of 67 in 1896.

Starting in 1894 Keeler began eight consecutive seasons of 200 or more hits, something that no other player has ever done. Keeler's biggest year was 1897 when he led the league in batting (with a .424 average) and hits (with 239). He also had a 44-game hitting streak, a major league record which stood until Joe Dimaggio broke it in 1941.

At Baltimore, Keeler teamed up with fellow future Hall of Famers Hughie Jennings, John McGraw, Joe Kelley, Wilbert Robinson and Dan Brouthers to form one of the greatest teams in baseball history. The feisty Orioles made baseball into a real team sport, specializing in relays and cut-offs — and pioneering the hit and run. The Orioles participated in the Temple Cup "World Series" four straight years from 1894 to '97.

When the Oriole franchise was broken up after the 1898 season Keeler went to Brooklyn where he helped the Superbas win two pennants in 1899 and 1900. He later spent eight seasons in the American League with New York Highlanders. Keeler ended his 19-year career in 1910 with a lifetime batting average of .341. A sportswriter once asked Willie his hitting secret and he replied, "Keep your eye clear and hit 'em where they ain't."

Wee Willie Keeler was inducted into the National Baseball Hall of Fame in 1939.

Keeler, William Henry "Wee Willie" (b: William Henry O'Kelleher)
BL/TL, 5'4.5", 140 lbs. Deb: 9/30/1892

YEAR	TM/L	G	AB	R	H	2B	3B	HR	RBI	BB	SO	AVG
1892	NY-NL	14	53	7	17	3	0	0	6	3	3	.321
1893	NY-NL	7	24	5	8	2	1	1	7	5	1	.333
	Bro-NL	20	80	14	25	1	1	1	9	4	4	.313
	Yr	27	104	19	33	3	2	2	16	9	5	.317
1894	Bal-NL	129	590	165	219	27	22	5	94	40	6	.371
1895	Bal-NL	131	565	162	213	24	15	4	78	37	12	.377
1896	Bal-NL	126	544	153	210	22	13	4	82	37	9	.386
1897	Bal-NL	129	564	145	239	27	19	0	74	35	—	.424
1898	Bal-NL	129	561	126	216	7	2	1	44	31	—	.385
1899	Bro-NL	141	570	140	216	12	13	1	61	37	—	.379
1900	Bro-NL	136	563	106	204	13	12	4	68	30	—	.362
1901	Bro-NL	136	595	123	202	18	12	2	43	21	—	.339
1902	Bro-NL	133	559	86	186	20	5	0	38	21	—	.333
1903	NY-AL	132	512	95	160	14	7	0	32	32	—	.313
1904	NY-AL	143	543	78	186	14	8	2	40	35	—	.343
1905	NY-AL	149	560	81	169	14	4	4	38	43	—	.302
1906	NY-AL	152	592	96	180	8	3	2	33	40	—	.304
1907	NY-AL	107	423	50	99	5	2	0	17	15	—	.234
1908	NY-AL	91	323	38	85	3	1	1	14	31	—	.263
1909	NY-AL	99	360	44	95	7	5	1	32	24	—	.264
1910	NY-NL	19	10	5	3	0	0	0	0	3	1	.300
Total	19	2,123	8,591	1,719	2,932	241	145	33	810	524	INC	.341

Joe Kelley

Outfielder - Manager (Joseph James Kelley)
Born: December 9, 1871, Cambridge, Massachusetts
Died: August 14, 1943, Baltimore, Maryland

Joe Kelley was a turn-of-the-century all-star outfielder who played for the legendary Baltimore Orioles of the 1890's and later became player-manager of the Cincinnati Reds in the early 1900's.

Beginning in 1893, his second year with the Orioles, Kelley had 12 straight seasons where he hit better than .300. In 1894 he batted .393 with 199 hits and 46 stolen bases. On September 3rd he went a record setting 9 for 9 in a double header, hitting four doubles in one game. The Orioles won the pennant that year, but lost in the Temple Cup postseason series. It was the first of four straight years that the Orioles would play for the Temple Cup.

In 1896 Kelley hit .364 and led the league with 87 stolen bases. When the Oriole franchise was broken up after the 1898 season Kelley, along with teammates Wee Willie Keeler and Hughie Jennings, went to Brooklyn where they helped the Superbas win two pennants in 1899 and 1900.

In 1902 Kelley came back to Baltimore to play for the new American League version of the Orioles. He left in mid-season to become player-manager of the Reds, a position he held for the next four years. He spent his last major league season with the Boston Braves in 1908 and retired with a .317 lifetime batting average.

Joe Kelley was inducted into the National Baseball Hall of Fame in 1971.

Kelley, Joseph James
BR/TR, 5'11", 190 lbs. Deb: 7/27/1891

YEAR	TM/L	G	AB	R	H	2B	3B	HR	RBI	BB	SO	AVG
1891	Bos-NL	12	45	7	11	1	1	0	3	2	7	.244
1892	Pit-NL	56	205	26	49	7	7	0	28	17	21	.239
	Bal-NL	10	33	3	7	0	0	0	4	4	7	.212
	Yr	66	238	29	56	7	7	0	32	21	28	.235
1893	Bal-NL	125	502	120	153	27	16	9	76	77	44	.305
1894	Bal-NL	129	507	165	199	48	20	6	111	107	36	.393
1895	Bal-NL	131	518	148	189	26	19	10	134	77	29	.365
1896	Bal-NL	131	519	148	189	31	19	8	100	91	19	.364
1897	Bal-NL	131	505	113	183	31	9	5	118	70	—	.362
1898	Bal-NL	124	464	71	149	18	15	2	110	56	—	.321
1899	Bro-NL	143	538	108	175	21	14	6	93	70	—	.325
1900	Bro-NL	121	454	90	145	23	17	6	91	53	—	.319
1901	Bro-NL	120	492	77	151	22	12	4	65	40	—	.307
1902	Bal-AL	60	222	50	69	17	7	1	34	34	—	.311
	Cin-NL	40	156	24	50	9	2	1	12	15	—	.321
1903	Cin-NL	105	383	85	121	22	4	3	45	51	—	.316
1904	Cin-NL	123	449	75	126	21	13	0	63	49	—	.281
1905	Cin-NL	90	321	43	89	7	6	1	37	27	—	.277
1906	Cin-NL	129	465	43	106	19	11	1	53	44	—	.228
1908	Bos-NL	73	228	25	59	8	2	2	17	27	—	.259
Total	17	1,853	7,006	1,421	2,220	358	194	65	1,194	911	INC	.317

King Kelly

Outfielder - Catcher (Michael Joseph Kelly)
Born: December 31, 1857, Troy, New York
Died: November 8, 1894, Boston, Massachusetts

In the 1880's a hard-playing, hard-drinking catcher-outfielder by the name of Mike Kelly became baseball's first genuine superstar. This handsome, mustachioed son of Irish immigrants helped lead the Chicago White Stockings to five N.L. pennants from 1880 to 1886, and his fans nicknamed him the "King."

The flamboyant Kelly had perfected the hook slide and whenever he got on base he would be greeted by chants of "Slide Kelly Slide" from the stands.

King Kelly played big league baseball for 16 years, had a lifetime batting average of .307, led the N.L. in hitting twice and three times in runs scored, and was a master base stealer in an age when, unfortunately, complete statistics were not kept on the tactic. But we do know that he stole 84 bases in the 1887 season and in 1890 he swiped six bases in one game.

Kelly, who had a fondness for

strong drink, fine food and having a good time, was just as famous for his off-field antics as for his playing ability. He liked to bet on the horses and spent many a night carousing in Chicago's saloons. Kelly even took a crack at vaudeville. He would appear on stage and tell baseball stories and perform in skits, usually to thunderous applause.

Although Kelly hit .388 in 1886, after the season was over Chicago owner Al Spalding shook up the baseball world by selling Kelly to the Boston club for the then unheard-of sum of $10,000. This caused the press to dub Kelly "the Ten Thousand Dollar Beauty."

Kelly spent three creditable years playing for Boston (batting over .300 each season). After spending the 1890 season in the ill-fated Players League he then went back to the N.L. where he played and managed in Cincinnati for awhile, and finally ended up with New York in 1893.

But his many years of high living and hard drinking finally did him in. In 1894 Mike Kelly came down with pneumonia and died at the age of 36.

Mike "King" Kelly was the most colorful and best-known player of his day, and was baseball's first true superstar.

King Kelly was inducted into the National Baseball Hall of Fame in 1945.

Slide, Kelly, slide!
Your running's a disgrace!
Slide, Kelly, slide!
Stay there, hold your base!
If someone doesn't steal ya,
And your batting doesn't fail ya,
They'll take you to Australia!
Slide, Kelly, slide!
> *—Anonymous*

Kelly, Michael Joseph
BR/TR, 5'10", 170 lbs. Deb: 5/1/1878

YEAR	TM/L	G	AB	R	H	2B	3B	HR	RBI	BB	SO	AVG
1878	Cin-NL	60	237	29	67	7	1	0	27	7	7	.283
1879	Cin-NL	77	345	78	120	20	12	2	47	8	14	.348
1880	Chi-NL	84	344	72	100	17	9	1	60	12	22	.291
1881	Chi-NL	82	353	84	114	27	3	2	55	16	14	.323
1882	Chi-NL	84	377	81	115	37	4	1	55	10	27	.305
1883	Chi-NL	98	428	92	109	28	10	3	61	16	35	.255
1884	Chi-NL	108	452	120	160	28	5	13	95	46	24	.354
1885	Chi-NL	107	438	124	126	24	7	9	75	46	24	.288
1886	Chi-NL	118	451	155	175	32	11	4	79	83	33	.388
1887	Bos-NL	116	484	120	156	34	11	8	63	55	40	.322
1888	Bos-NL	107	440	85	140	22	11	9	71	31	39	.318
1889	Bos-NL	125	507	120	149	41	5	9	78	65	40	.294
1890	Bos-PL	89	340	83	111	18	6	4	66	52	22	.326
1891	Cin-AA	82	283	56	84	15	7	1	53	51	28	.297
	Bos-AA	4	15	2	4	0	0	1	4	0	2	.267
	Yr	86	298	58	88	15	7	2	57	51	30	.295
	Bos-NL	16	52	7	12	1	0	0	5	6	10	.231
1892	Bos-NL	78	281	40	53	7	0	2	41	39	31	.189
1893	NY-NL	20	67	9	18	1	0	0	15	6	5	.269
Total	16	1,455	5,894	1,357	1,813	359	102	69	950	549	417	.308

YEAR	TM/L	W	L	PCT	G	IP	H	HR	BB	SO	ERA
1880	Chi-NL	0	0	—	1	3	3	0	1	1	0.00
1883	Chi-NL	0	0	—	1	1	1	0	0	0	0.00
1884	Chi-NL	0	1	.000	2	5.1	12	2	2	1	8.44
1887	Bos-NL	1	0	1.000	3	13	17	1	14	0	3.46
1890	Bos-PL	1	0	1.000	1	2	1	0	2	2	4.50
1891	Cin-AA	0	1	.000	3	15.1	21	2	7	0	5.28
1892	Bos-NL	0	0	—	1	6	8	0	4	0	1.50
Total	7	2	2	.500	12	45.2	63	5	30	4	4.14

Nap Lajoie

Infielder - Manager (Napoleon Lajoie)
Born: September 5, 1874 , Woonsocket, Rhode Island
Died: February 7, 1959, Daytona Beach, Florida

At the turn of the century Nap Lajoie was a superstar in both major leagues. He was known for the stinging line-drives that he hit, and is considered by many to be the greatest second baseman of all-time. Lajoie (pronounced either Lajwa or Lajaway depending on who you talk to) began his 21-year big league career with the Phillies in 1896. He never hit less than .324 in the five years he was with the club. In 1898 he led the National League with 43 doubles and 127 RBI.

When the American League was formed in 1901 Lajoie jumped across town to play for Connie Mack's Athletics and that year, became the A.L.'s first Triple Crown winner, leading the league in homers (14), RBI (125) and batting average (.426 — the highest in A.L. history). The following season the Phillies obtained a court injunction prohibiting Lajoie from playing for any other team but the Phillies in the state of Pennsylvania. So the A.L. transferred him to Cleveland where he spent the next 13 years, and he became so popular both as a player and a manager that they named the team after him!

Lajoie led the league in batting average in 1903 and '04 and was appointed manager of the Cleveland club in 1905, at which time the team changed its nickname to the Cleveland Naps in his honor.

But the burdens of managing seemed to affect his performance on the field. His batting average plummeted below .300 for the first time in his career in 1907 and remained that way in 1908. In 1909 he gave up his managerial duties to become a full-time player once again and finished the season with a .324 average.

In a legendary incident at the end of the 1910 season the well-loved Lajoie challenged the much-loathed Ty Cobb for the A.L. batting championship. Cobb had sat out the last two games of the season to protect his .385 average and in a season-ending doubleheader Lajoie managed to get eight hits (six of which were bunts that he obtained in a rather dubious manner because St. Louis third baseman Red Corriden intentionally played deep). But it wasn't enough. Lajoie finished one point behind Cobb. In 1981 a *Sporting News* researcher discovered that Cobb's average had been inflated because one of his games had inadvertently been counted twice and the title should have gone to Lajoie after all, but Commissioner Bowie Kuhn ruled that the mistake would not be corrected.

Lajoie left Cleveland after the 1914 season to spend his last two years in the big leagues with the A's. He retired from major league baseball in 1916 with a .338 lifetime batting average.

Nap Lajoie was inducted into the National Baseball Hall of Fame in 1937.

Lajoie, Napoleon "Larry"
BR/TR, 6'1", 195 lbs. Deb: 8/12/1896

YEAR	TM/L	G	AB	R	H	2B	3B	HR	RBI	BB	SO	AVG
1896	Phi-NL	39	175	36	57	12	7	4	42	1	11	.326
1897	Phi-NL	127	545	107	197	40	23	9	127	15	—	.361
1898	Phi-NL	147	608	113	197	43	11	6	127	21	—	.324
1899	Phi-NL	77	312	70	118	19	9	6	70	12	—	.378
1900	Phi-NL	102	451	95	152	33	12	7	92	10	—	.337
1901	Phi-AL	131	544	145	232	48	14	14	125	24	—	.426
1902	Phi-AL	1	4	0	1	0	0	0	1	0	—	.250
	Cle-AL	86	348	81	132	35	5	7	64	19	—	.379
	Yr	87	352	81	133	35	5	7	65	19	—	.378
1903	Cle-AL	125	485	90	167	41	11	7	93	24	—	.344
1904	Cle-AL	140	553	92	208	49	15	6	102	27	—	.376
1905	Cle-AL	65	249	29	82	12	2	2	41	17	—	.329
1906	Cle-AL	152	602	88	214	48	9	0	91	30	—	.355
1907	Cle-AL	137	509	53	152	30	6	2	63	30	—	.299
1908	Cle-AL	157	581	77	168	32	6	2	74	47	—	.289
1909	Cle-AL	128	469	56	152	33	7	1	47	35	—	.324
1910	Cle-AL	159	591	94	227	51	7	4	76	60	—	.384
1911	Cle-AL	90	315	36	115	20	1	2	60	26	—	.365
1912	Cle-AL	117	448	66	165	34	4	0	90	28	—	.368
1913	Cle-AL	137	465	66	156	25	2	1	68	33	17	.335
1914	Cle-AL	121	419	37	108	14	3	0	50	32	15	.258
1915	Phi-AL	129	490	40	137	24	5	1	61	11	16	.280
1916	Phi-AL	113	426	33	105	14	4	2	35	14	26	.246
Total	21	2480	9589	1504	3242	657	163	83	1599	516	INC	.338

Connie Mack

Catcher - Manager - Owner (Cornelius McGillicuddy)
Born: December 22, 1862, East Brookfield, Massachusetts
Died: February 8, 1956, Philadelphia, Pennsylvania

From 1901 to 1950 Connie Mack spent 50 years as manager of the Philadelphia Athletics, winning nine American League pennants and five world championships along the way. When he retired at the age of 88, he held the major league record for most victories by a manager (3,731) and most losses (3,948).

Mack did not wear a uniform while piloting his club; instead he wore a suit and tie. During the game he would stand on the top step of the dugout and position his players by waiving a folded scorecard at them.

Mack was born Cornelius McGillicuddy in East Brookfield, Massachusetts, on December 22, 1862. In 1883, while playing minor league ball for Meriden in the Connecticut State League, he shortened his name to Connie Mack so it would fit into the newspaper box scores.

Young Connie Mack was an excellent defensive catcher, and beginning in 1886 spent 11 years playing in the major leagues. Mack got his first chance to manage while with Pittsburgh in 1894. When the club fired him after a sixth-place finish in 1896, he went on to manage Milwaukee in the minor Western League for the next four years. When the Western League upgraded itself to major league status and became the American League in 1901, Mack was appointed manager of the new Philadelphia franchise and given a 25 percent interest in the club. He eventually became sole owner of the team.

Mack soon built the A's into a dynasty that won four pennants and three world championships from 1910 to 1914. The team featured the famous "$100,000 Infield" of Stuffy McInnis, Eddie Collins and Frank "Home Run" Baker. After the 1914 season Mack dismantled this great team of his to go with younger, lower-paid players, and the A's spent the next seven years in last place.

But Mack eventually put together another dynasty that won three straight pennants from 1929-31. Once again he tore his club apart, and gradually sold off such future Hall of Famers as Al Simmons, Mickey Cochrane, Lefty Grove and Jimmie Foxx to pay off a $500,000 debt. Mack never won another pennant and the club spent most of the next two decades in the second division. Although he never made much money with his club, Connie Mack spent 50 years doing what he liked best. He was inducted into the National Baseball Hall of Fame in 1937.

Mack, Cornelius Alexander "The Tall Tactician"
BR/TR, 6'1", 150 lbs. Deb: 9/11/1886

YEAR	TM/L	G	AB	R	H	2B	3B	HR	RBI	BB	SO	AVG
1886	Was-NL	10	36	4	13	2	1	0	5	0	2	.361
1887	Was-NL	82	314	35	63	6	1	0	20	8	17	.201
1888	Was-NL	85	300	49	56	5	6	3	29	17	18	.187
1889	Was-NL	98	386	51	113	16	1	0	42	15	12	.293
1890	Buf-PL	123	503	95	134	15	12	0	53	47	13	.266
1891	Pit-NL	75	280	43	60	10	0	0	29	19	11	.214
1892	Pit-NL	97	346	39	84	9	4	1	31	21	22	.243
1893	Pit-NL	37	133	22	38	3	1	0	15	10	9	.286
1894	Pit-NL	69	228	32	57	7	1	1	21	20	14	.250
1895	Pit-NL	14	49	12	15	2	0	0	4	7	1	.306
1896	Pit-NL	33	120	9	26	4	1	0	16	5	8	.217
Total	11	723	2,695	391	659	79	28	5	265	169	127	.245

Rube Marquard

Pitcher (Richard William Marquard)
Born: October 9, 1889, Cleveland, Ohio
Died: June 1, 1980, Baltimore, Maryland

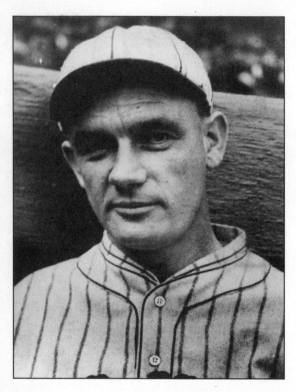

Rube Marquard and teammate Christy Mathewson were the core of the N.Y. Giants pitching staff when the Giants won three consecutive N.L. pennants from 1911 to 1913.

Marquard began his major league career in 1908 when the Giants brought him up as a 18-year-old rookie. After three rather unspectacular seasons he finally began to blossom in 1911 when he went 24-7. In the World Series that year he lost his only decision when Frank "Home Run" Baker beat him with a long ball.

In 1912 Marquard led the league with 26 wins, winning his first 19 games in a row (under present-day rules it would have been 20: in a game in which the Giants overcame a deficit to win while he was on the mound in relief, the win was awarded to the starter). Then in the World Series he pitched two complete game victories over Boston. The following year he finished the season with a 23-10 record. During the off-season he would team up with his wife, actress Blossom Seeley, to perform a vaudeville act.

On April 15, 1915, Marquard threw the only no-hitter of his career, beating Brooklyn 2-0 in a game that lasted only one hour and 16 minutes. That same year, with the Giants' approval, he arranged for his own sale to Brooklyn for $7,500 and went on to play in two more World Series with the Robins (Dodgers), but never got to wear a Series ring. Marquard spent the 1921 season at Cincinnati where he posted a 17-14 record and then finished off his 18-year major league career with Boston. He retired in 1925 with a lifetime record of 201-177 and a 3.08 ERA.

Rube Marquard was inducted into the National Baseball Hall of Fame in 1971.

Marquard, Richard William
BB/TL, 6'3", 180 lbs. Deb: 9/25/08

YEAR	TM/L	W	L	PCT	G	IP	H	HR	BB	SO	ERA
1908	NY-NL	0	1	.000	1	5	6	0	2	2	3.60
1909	NY-NL	5	13	.278	29	173	155	2	73	109	2.60
1910	NY-NL	4	4	.500	13	70.2	65	2	40	52	4.46
1911	NY-NL	24	7	.774	45	277.2	221	9	106	237	2.50
1912	NY-NL	26	11	.703	43	294.2	286	9	80	175	2.57
1913	NY-NL	23	10	.697	42	288	248	10	49	151	2.50
1914	NY-NL	12	22	.353	39	268	261	9	47	92	3.06
1915	NY-NL	9	8	.529	27	169	178	8	33	79	3.73
	Bro-NL	2	2	.500	6	24.2	29	0	5	13	6.20
	Yr	11	10	.524	33	193.2	207	8	38	92	4.04
1916	Bro-NL	13	6	.684	36	205	169	2	38	107	1.58
1917	Bro-NL	19	12	.613	37	232.2	200	5	60	117	2.55
1918	Bro-NL	9	18	.333	34	239	231	7	59	89	2.64
1919	Bro-NL	3	3	.500	8	59	54	1	10	29	2.29
1920	Bro-NL	10	7	.588	28	189.2	181	5	35	89	3.23
1921	Cin-NL	17	14	.548	39	265.2	291	8	50	88	3.39
1922	Bos-NL	11	15	.423	39	198	255	12	66	57	5.09
1923	Bos-NL	11	14	.440	38	239	265	10	65	78	3.73
1924	Bos-NL	1	2	.333	6	36	33	3	13	10	3.00
1925	Bos-NL	2	8	.200	26	72	105	5	27	19	5.75
Total	18	201	177	.532	536	3,306.2	3,233	107	858	1,593	3.08

Christy Mathewson

Pitcher (Christopher Mathewson)
Born: August 12, 1880, Factoryville, Pennsylvania
Died: October 7, 1925, Saranac Lake, New York

Tall, blond, clean-living, college-educated Christy Mathewson pitched in the big leagues in a era when baseball players were considered to be crude, tobacco-chewing dolts. He was baseball's pre-eminent pitcher in the first part of the twentieth century.

Pitching for the Giants, Mathewson had 13 seasons of 20 or more wins from 1901 to 1914. He topped the 30 mark four times. His best season was 1908 when he led the league in wins (37), complete games (34), strikeouts (259), shutouts (11) and ERA (1.43). Christy, who threw a screwball (he called it his "fadeaway") which he mixed in with other outstanding pitches, racked up 373 wins in his 17-year career, tying him with Grover Cleveland Alexander for the N.L. record.

His last big year was 1914 when he went 24-13. The following season he won only eight games and in 1916, after only three wins, he was traded to Cincinnati, where he pitched in one game and then was appointed manager of the club. Mathewson managed the Reds until 1918 when he was called for military service. While overseas he was gassed in a training exercise and suffered permanent lung damage. After he returned home he coached for the Giants for three years, and then was appointed president of the Boston Braves in 1923, a post he held until his death from tuberculosis in 1925.

In 1936 — along with Ty Cobb, Babe Ruth, Honus Wagner and Walter Johnson — Christy Mathewson was part of the first group of men elected to the National Baseball Hall of Fame.

Mathewson, Christopher "Matty" or "Big Six"
BR/TR, 6'1.5", 195 lbs. Deb: 7/17/00

YEAR	TM/L	W	L	PCT	G	IP	H	HR	BB	SO	ERA
1900	NY-NL	0	3	.000	6	33.2	37	1	20	15	5.08
1901	NY-NL	20	17	.541	40	336	288	3	97	221	2.41
1902	NY-NL	14	17	.452	34	276.2	241	3	73	159	2.11
1903	NY-NL	30	13	.698	45	366.1	321	4	100	267	2.26
1904	NY-NL	33	12	.733	48	367.2	306	7	78	212	2.03
1905	NY-NL	31	9	.775	43	338.2	252	4	64	206	1.28
1906	NY-NL	22	12	.647	38	266.2	262	3	77	128	2.97
1907	NY-NL	24	12	.667	41	315	250	6	53	178	2.00
1908	NY-NL	37	11	.771	56	390.2	285	5	42	259	1.43
1909	NY-NL	25	6	.806	37	275.1	192	2	36	149	1.14
1910	NY-NL	27	9	.750	38	318.1	292	5	60	184	1.89
1911	NY-NL	26	13	.667	45	307	303	5	38	141	1.99
1912	NY-NL	23	12	.657	43	310	311	6	34	134	2.12
1913	NY-NL	25	11	.694	40	306	291	8	21	93	2.06
1914	NY-NL	24	13	.649	41	312	314	16	23	80	3.00
1915	NY-NL	8	14	.364	27	186	199	9	20	57	3.58
1916	NY-NL	3	4	.429	12	65.2	59	3	7	16	2.33
	Cin-NL	1	0	1.000	1	9	15	1	1	3	8.00
	Yr	4	4	.500	13	74.2	74	4	8	19	3.01
Total	17	373	188	.665	635	4,780.2	4,218	91	844	2,502	2.13

Joe McGinnity

Pitcher (Joseph Jerome McGinnity)
Born: March 19, 1871, Rock Island, Illinois
Died: November 14, 1929, Brooklyn, New York

Joe McGinnity was nicknamed "Iron Man" for good reason. In August, 1903, this tough-as-nails N.Y. Giant righthander pitched both ends of a doubleheader three times ... and won all six games! (And none of the games lasted longer than two hours.) Previously, in 1900, when he was with the N.L.'s Brooklyn Superbas he once pitched five games in six days and won them all. That year he also led the league in innings pitched (343) and wins (28).

McGinnity began his big league career in 1899 when he was 28 years old, and pitched for ten seasons, completing 314 of the 381 games he started. Six times, he led the league in games pitched — five times in wins and four times in innings pitched. In 1905 he led the National League with a 1.61 ERA in the regular season, and then when the Giants faced the Athletics in the World Series that year (and beat them four games to one), McGinnity pitched two complete games and did not allow an earned run!

In his ten seasons in the majors Joe McGinnity had seven seasons of 20 or more wins and finished with a lifetime record of 246-142 and a ERA of 2.66. Back in a day and age when doubleheaders were commonplace and relief pitchers were rare, durable Joe McGinnity established himself as baseball's original "Iron Man."

Joe McGinnity was inducted into the National Baseball Hall of Fame in 1946.

McGinnity, Joseph Jerome "Iron Man"
BR/TR, 5'11", 206 lbs. Deb: 4/18/1899

YEAR	TM/L	W	L	PCT	G	IP	H	HR	BB	SO	ERA
1899	Bal-NL	28	16	.636	48	366.1	358	3	93	74	2.68
1900	Bro-NL	28	8	.778	44	343	350	5	113	93	2.94
1901	Bal-AL	26	20	.565	48	382	412	7	96	75	3.56
1902	Bal-AL	13	10	.565	25	198.2	219	3	46	39	3.44
	NY-NL	8	8	.500	19	153	122	1	32	67	2.06
1903	NY-NL	31	20	.608	55	434	391	4	109	171	2.43
1904	NY-NL	35	8	.814	51	408	307	8	86	144	1.61
1905	NY-NL	21	15	.583	46	320.1	289	6	71	125	2.87
1906	NY-NL	27	12	.692	45	339.2	316	1	71	105	2.25
1907	NY-NL	18	18	.500	47	310.1	320	6	58	120	3.16
1908	NY-NL	11	7	.611	37	186	192	8	37	55	2.27
Total	10	246	142	.634	465	3,441.1	3,276	52	812	1,068	2.66

John McGraw

Infielder - Manager (John Joseph McGraw)
Born: April 7, 1873, Truxton, New York
Died: February 25, 1934, New Rochelle, New York

Although John McGraw played major league ball for 16 seasons he was best known as the fiery third baseman of the legendary Baltimore Oriole club of the mid-1890's. During this period, he and outfielder Wee Willie Keeler teamed up to perfect the hit-and-run. McGraw fielded his position brilliantly and when the Orioles won the N.L. pennant three straight years from 1894-96 he never hit under .325.

But it was as a manager that he achieved his greatest success. In 1902 he took over as skipper of the New York Giants and ran the club for 29 years, winning 10 pennants and finishing second 11 times. He drove his players hard and his abrasive and pugnacious personality earned him the nickname "Little Napoleon." He was famous for abusing opponents and umpires, both verbally and occasionally physically. But he had his compassionate moments, too; after the famous "Merkle's Boner" incident in 1908 when the Giants narrowly lost the pennant because infielder Fred Merkle failed to touch second base in a crucial game, McGraw stoutly defended the young player and gave him a raise the following year.

McGraw, who was considered a managerial genius, called pitches from the bench, favored the hit-and-run, had no use for the sacrifice bunt and was one of the first managers to grasp the concept of relief pitching.

McGraw's Giants won three consecutive N.L. pennants from 1911 to 1913, but lost all three World Series. They won their next pennant in 1917 and lost that World Series to the White Sox.

From 1921 to 1924 the Giants won an unprecedented four pennants in a row and beat the rival New York Yankees in the 1921 and '22 World Series.

After spending 33 years as a big league manager, John McGraw retired in 1932 with a record of 2,784 wins and 1,959 losses. He was inducted into the National Baseball Hall of Fame in 1937.

McGraw, John Joseph "Mugsy" or "Little Napoleon"
BL/TR, 5'7", 155 lbs. Deb: 8/26/1891

YEAR	TM/L	G	AB	R	H	2B	3B	HR	RBI	BB	SO	AVG
1891	Bal-AA	33	115	17	31	3	5	0	14	12	17	.270
1892	Bal-NL	79	286	41	77	13	2	1	26	32	21	.269
1893	Bal-NL	127	480	123	154	9	10	5	64	101	11	.321
1894	Bal-NL	124	512	156	174	18	14	1	92	91	12	.340
1895	Bal-NL	96	388	110	143	13	6	2	48	60	9	.369
1896	Bal-NL	23	77	20	25	2	2	0	14	11	4	.325
1897	Bal-NL	106	391	90	127	15	3	0	48	99	—	.325
1898	Bal-NL	143	515	143	176	8	10	0	53	112	—	.342
1899	Bal-NL	117	399	140	156	13	3	1	33	124	—	.391
1900	StL-NL	99	334	84	115	10	4	2	33	85	—	.344
1901	Bal-AL	73	232	71	81	14	9	0	28	61	—	.349
1902	Bal-AL	20	63	14	18	3	2	1	3	17	—	.286
	NY-NL	35	107	13	24	0	0	0	5	26	—	.224
1903	NY-NL	12	11	2	3	0	0	0	1	1	—	.273
1904	NY-NL	5	12	0	4	0	0	0	0	3	—	.333
1905	NY-NL	3	0	0	0	0	0	0	0	0	—	—
1906	NY-NL	4	2	0	0	0	0	0	0	1	—	.000
Total	16	1,099	3,924	1,024	1,308	121	70	13	462	836	INC	.333

Kid Nichols

Pitcher (Charles Augustus Nichols)
Born: September 14, 1869, Madison, Wisconsin
Died: April 11, 1953, Kansas City, Missouri

In the 1890's Kid Nichols was one of baseball's premier pitchers. In his rookie season of 1890, the 20-year-old Nichols won 27 games for the N.L.'s Boston Beaneaters. During the next nine seasons, this durable righthander who threw no curve (he depended on control and speed) averaged 30 wins per season.

Nowadays it's a fairly rare occurrence when a starting pitcher actually pitches a complete game, but this wasn't always the case. Back in the 1890's, relief pitchers were almost as rare as hen's teeth. When a pitcher started a game, he was expected to finish it. In a pitching career that spanned 15 years, Kid Nichols started 561 games and completed 531 of them — that's right, only 30 times did he fail to finish the game!

In his 12 years with Boston he helped the club win five National League pennants and one world championship. After pitching for and managing the St. Louis Cardinals in 1904 and '05, Nichols retired from the big leagues in 1906 with 361 wins under his belt and a lifetime ERA of 2.95.

Kid Nichols was inducted into the National Baseball Hall of Fame in 1949.

Nichols, Charles Augustus
BB/TR, 5'10.5", 175 lbs. Deb: 4/23/1890

YEAR	TM/L	W	L	PCT	G	IP	H	HR	BB	SO	ERA
1890	Bos-NL	27	19	.587	48	424	374	8	112	222	2.21
1891	Bos-NL	30	17	.638	52	425.1	413	15	103	240	2.39
1892	Bos-NL	35	16	.686	53	453	404	15	121	187	2.83
1893	Bos-NL	34	14	.708	52	425	426	15	118	94	3.52
1894	Bos-NL	32	13	.711	50	407	488	23	121	113	4.75
1895	Bos-NL	26	16	.619	47	379.2	417	15	86	140	3.29
1896	Bos-NL	30	14	.682	49	372.1	387	14	101	102	2.81
1897	Bos-NL	31	11	.738	46	368	362	9	68	127	2.64
1898	Bos-NL	31	12	.721	50	388	316	7	85	138	2.13
1899	Bos-NL	21	19	.525	42	343.1	326	11	82	108	2.94
1900	Bos-NL	13	16	.448	29	231.1	215	11	72	53	3.07
1901	Bos-NL	19	16	.543	38	321	306	8	90	143	3.22
1904	StL-NL	21	13	.618	36	317	268	3	50	134	2.02
1905	StL-NL	1	5	.167	7	51.2	64	1	18	16	5.40
	Phi-NL	10	6	.625	17	138.2	129	1	28	50	2.26
	Yr	11	11	.500	24	190.1	193	2	46	66	3.11
1906	Phi-NL	0	1	.000	4	11	17	0	13	1	9.82
Total	15	361	208	.634	620	5,056.1	4912	156	1,268	1,868	2.94

Tip O'Neill

Outfielder (James Edward O'Neill)
Born: May 24, 1858, Woodstock, Ontario, Canada
Died: December 31, 1915, Montreal, Quebec, Canada

When the St. Louis Browns won four straight American Association pennants from 1885 to '88 their offence was bolstered by outfielder Tip O'Neill who led the league with a .435 batting average in 1887. (He was originally credited with hitting .492, as walks were counted as hits for that one season.)

O'Neill, who spent 10 years in the majors and finished his career with a lifetime batting average of .326, not only led the league in batting average in '87, but he also led the league in doubles (52), triples (19), home runs (14), hits (225) and runs scored (167). He is the only player to lead a major league in all six categories in a single season.

O'Neill, James Edward
BR/TR, 6'1.5", 167 lbs.Deb: 5/5/1883

YEAR	TM/L	G	AB	R	H	2B	3B	HR	RBI	BB	SO	AVG
1883	NY-NL	23	76	8	15	3	0	0	5	315	—	.197
1884	StL-AA	78	297	49	82	13	11	3	12	—	—	.276
1885	StL-AA	52	206	44	72	7	4	3	13	—	—	.350
1886	StL-AA	138	579	106	190	28	14	3	47	—	—	.328
1887	StL-AA	124	517	167	225	52	19	14	50	—	—	.435
1888	StL-AA	130	529	96	177	24	10	5	98	44	—	.335
1889	StL-AA	134	534	123	179	33	8	9	110	72	37	.335
1890	Chi-PL	137	577	112	174	20	16	3	75	65	36	.302
1891	StL-AA	129	521	112	167	28	4	10	95	62	33	.321
1892	Cin-NL	109	419	63	105	14	6	2	52	53	25	.251
Total	10	1,054	4,255	880	1,386	222	92	52	557	421	INC	.326

Jim O'Rourke

Outfielder - Infielder - Catcher - Manager (James Henry O'Rourke)
Born: September 1, 1850, Bridgeport, Connecticut
Died: January 8, 1919, Bridgeport, Connecticut

J. H. O'ROURKE, CATCHER AND CENTRE FIELD.

Jim O'Rourke began his professional career in 1872 with the Middletown Mansfields of the National Association and then spent the next three N.A. seasons with Harry Wright's Boston Red Stockings, helping the club to win an N.A. pennant each year. When the National League was formed in 1876, O'Rourke played for the Boston franchise, and in the first inning of the the first N.L. game ever played (Boston at Philadelphia — April 22, 1876), he walloped a line drive into left field to record the first hit in N.L. history.

O'Rourke, who was nicknamed "Orator" because of his astonishing vocabulary and verbosity, hit over .300 in 15 of the 19 seasons that he played. He also served as manager when he was with the N.L.'s Buffalo Bisons from 1881 to 1884. In 1888 and '89 he helped the New York Giants win their first two N.L. pennants (they also went on to win the World Series both years). In 1890 O'Rourke was one of the first players to join the ill-fated Players League.

Although O'Rourke retired from the big leagues in 1893, New York Giant manager John McGraw nevertheless brought him in to catch the first part of a doubleheader on September 22, 1904, making O'Rourke, at the age of 52, the oldest man to complete a major league game.

Jim O'Rourke was inducted into the National Baseball Hall of Fame in 1945.

O'Rourke, James Henry "Orator Jim"
BR/TR, 5'8", 185 lbs. Deb: 4/26/1872

YEAR	TM/L	G	AB	R	H	2B	3B	HR	RBI	BB	SO	AVG
1876	Bos-NL	70	312	61	102	17	3	2	43	15	17	.327
1877	Bos-NL	61	265	68	96	14	4	0	23	20	9	.362
1878	Bos-NL	60	255	44	71	17	7	1	29	5	21	.278
1879	Pro-NL	81	362	69	126	19	9	1	46	13	10	.348
1880	Bos-NL	86	363	71	100	20	11	6	45	21	8	.275
1881	Buf-NL	83	348	71	105	21	7	0	30	27	18	.302
1882	Buf-NL	84	370	62	104	15	6	2	37	13	13	.281
1883	Buf-NL	94	436	102	143	29	8	1	38	15	13	.328
1884	Buf-NL	108	467	119	162	33	7	5	63	35	17	.347
1885	NY-NL	112	477	119	143	21	16	5	42	40	21	.300
1886	NY-NL	105	440	106	136	26	6	1	34	39	21	.309
1887	NY-NL	103	397	73	113	15	13	3	88	36	11	.285
1888	NY-NL	107	409	50	112	16	6	4	50	24	30	.274
1889	NY-NL	128	502	89	161	36	7	3	81	40	34	.321
1890	NY-PL	111	478	112	172	37	5	9	115	33	20	.360
1891	NY-NL	136	555	92	164	28	7	5	95	26	29	.295
1892	NY-NL	115	448	62	136	28	5	0	56	30	30	.304
1893	Was-NL	129	547	75	157	22	5	2	95	49	26	.287
1904	NY-NL	1	4	1	1	0	0	0	—	0	0	.250
Total	19	1,774	7,435	1,446	2,304	414	132	50	1,010	481	348	.310

Dickey Pearce

Infielder (Richard J. Pearce)
Born: February 29, 1836, Brooklyn, New York
Died: October 12, 1908, Wareham, Massachusetts

RICHARD J. PEARCE,
The Veteran Base Ball Player, and Short Stop of the Mutual Nine.

Dickey Pearce was one of baseball's best known early players. He broke in with the Brooklyn Atlantics in 1856 and became one of the first players to be paid for his services. He played for 22 years and is credited with inventing the bunt (which he called the "tricky hit").

Pearce was one of baseball's first shortstops and helped to pioneer the way the position is played. He played in baseball's first professional league, the National Association, from the time it was formed in 1871 until it folded in 1875, and then spent two years in the National League. Following his playing days he umpired in the N.L. for several years.

Pearce, Richard J.
BR/TR, 5'3.5", 161 lbs.Deb: 5/18/1871

YEAR	TM/L	G	AB	R	H	2B	3B	HR	RBI	BB	SO	AVG
1876	StL-NL	25	102	12	21	1	0	0	10	3	5	.206
1877	StL-NL	8	29	1	5	0	0	0	4	1	4	.172
Total	2	33	131	13	26	1	0	0	14	4	9	.198

Deacon Phillippe

Pitcher (Charles Louis Phillippe)
Born: May 23, 1872, Rural Retreat, Virginia
Died: March 30, 1952, Avalon, Pennsylvania

On May 25, 1899, exactly one month and four days after he made his major league debut, Deacon Phillippe pitched a no-hitter for the N.L.'s Louisville Colonels, defeating the New York Giants 7-0 in a game played at Louisville's Eclipse Park. Phillippe went on to win 21 games that year for the Colonels. It was the first of six 20 or more win seasons that he would have in his 13-year major league career.

The Louisville franchise folded at the end of the 1899 season and Phillippe was transferred to Pittsburgh where he spent the rest of his career with the Pirates. He helped the Pirates win three straight N.L. pennants from 1901 to 1903 and when Pittsburgh met Boston in the first modern-day World Series in 1903, Phillippe beat Cy Young in the first game of the series and went on to win two more games in the best of nine affair, which Boston eventually won.

The big righthander was one of the great control artists of all time, averaging just over one walk per game throughout his career. Deacon Phillippe retired from big-league baseball in 1911 with a lifetime ERA of 2.59.

Phillippe, Charles Louis
BR/TR, 6'0.5", 180 lbs. Deb: 4/21/1899

YEAR	TM/L	W	L	PCT	G	IP	H	HR	BB	SO	ERA
1899	Lou-NL	21	17	.553	42	321	331	10	64	68	3.17
1900	Pit-NL	20	13	.606	38	279	274	7	42	75	2.84
1901	Pit-NL	22	12	.647	37	296	274	7	38	103	2.22
1902	Pit-NL	20	9	.690	31	272	265	1	26	122	2.05
1903	Pit-NL	24	7	.774	36	289.1	269	4	29	123	2.43
1904	Pit-NL	10	10	.500	21	166.2	183	1	26	82	3.24
1905	Pit-NL	22	13	.629	38	279	235	0	48	133	2.19
1906	Pit-NL	15	10	.600	33	218.2	216	3	26	90	2.47
1907	Pit-NL	13	11	.542	35	214	214	2	36	61	2.61
1908	Pit-NL	0	0	—	5	12	20	0	3	1	11.25
1909	Pit-NL	8	3	.727	22	131.2	121	2	14	38	2.32
1910	Pit-NL	14	2	.875	31	121.2	111	4	9	30	2.29
1911	Pit-NL	0	0	—	3	6	5	0	2	3	7.50
Total	13	189	107	.639	372	2,607	2,518	41	363	929	2.59

Eddie Plank

Pitcher (Edward Stewart Plank)
Born: Aug 31, 1875, Gettysburg, Pennsylvania
Died: February 24, 1926, Gettysburg, Pennsylvania

In 1901, at the age of 25, Eddie Plank was signed straight out of college by Connie Mack to pitch for the Philadelphia Athletics. It was the first year that Mack's A's and the American League were in existence. Plank won 17 games that season and had a 20-15 record the following year. He became the mainstay of the A's pitching staff, winning 20 or more games seven times in his 14 years with the club.

On the mound Plank had a slow, deliberate style that annoyed opponents, umpires and fans. He threw a fastball and a sidearm curve, and had superb control, averaging less than two walks per nine innings. Altogether he appeared in four World Series for the A's, and although he had a career World Series ERA of 1.32 he only managed to win two games while losing five. And he didn't pitch at all in the 1910 Series due to a sore arm.

In 1915 Plank jumped to the Federal League's St. Louis Terriers, much to the chagrin of Mack, who was trying to deal him to the Yankees at the time. He returned to the A.L. the following season and spent two years with the St. Louis Browns. In 1918 the Browns tried to send him to the Yankees as part of a package deal, but he refused to go and chose to retire from major league baseball instead.

With 326 wins under his belt, Plank was the winningest lefthander of all time until Warren Spahn surpassed his record in 1962.

Eddie Plank was inducted into the National Baseball Hall of Fame in 1946.

Plank, Edward Stewart "Gettysburg Eddie"
BL/TL, 5'11.5", 175 lbs. Deb: 5/13/01

YEAR	TM/L	W	L	PCT	G	IP	H	HR	BB	SO	ERA
1901	Phi-AL	17	13	.567	33	260.2	254	2	68	90	3.31
1902	Phi-AL	20	15	.571	36	300	319	5	61	107	3.30
1903	Phi-AL	23	16	.590	43	336	317	5	65	176	2.38
1904	Phi-AL	26	16	.619	44	357.1	311	2	86	201	2.14
1905	Phi-AL	25	12	.676	41	346.2	287	3	75	201	2.14
1906	Phi-AL	19	6	.760	26	211.2	173	1	51	210	2.26
1907	Phi-AL	24	16	.600	43	343.2	282	5	85	108	2.25
1908	Phi-AL	14	16	.467	34	244.2	202	1	46	183	2.20
1909	Phi-AL	19	10	.655	34	265.1	215	1	62	135	2.17
1910	Phi-AL	16	10	.615	38	250.1	218	3	55	132	1.70
1911	Phi-AL	23	8	742	40	256.2	237	2	77	123	2.01
1912	Phi-AL	26	6	.813	37	259.2	234	1	83	149	2.10
1913	Phi-AL	18	10	.643	41	242.2	211	3	57	110	2.22
1914	Phi-AL	15	7	.682	34	185.1	178	2	42	151	2.60
1915	StL-F	21	11	.656	42	268.1	212	1	54	110	2.87
1916	StL-AL	16	15	.516	37	235.2	203	2	67	147	2.08
1917	StL-AL	5	6	—	—	—	—	—	—	88	2.33
Total	17	327	193	.629	623	4,495.2	3,958	41	1,072	2,246	2.34

Old Hoss Radbourn

Pitcher (Charles Gardner Radbourn)
Born: December 11, 1854, Rochester, New York
Died: February 5, 1897, Bloomington, Illinois

Charles "Old Hoss" Radbourn was one of the premier pitchers of the 1880's. He began his 11-year major league career with the N.L.'s Providence Grays in 1881 and finished the season with a 25-11 record (and a league-leading won-lost percentage of .694). Dubbed "Old Hoss" for his durability and dependability, Radbourn started in 68 games in 1883 and won a league-leading 48 of them, including a 8-0 no-hitter over Cleveland on July 25.

The temperamental righthander had his biggest year in 1884; it was in fact the greatest single season of any nineteenth-century pitcher. Radbourn won 60 games for Providence that year, leading the league in strikeouts (441) and ERA (1.38), and then he went on to lead the Grays to victory over the A.A.'s New York Metropolitans in the very first World Series. Radbourn pitched, and won all three games of the Series.

Earlier, in July of that season, Radbourn had been suspended by the Grays after a run-in with manager Frank Bancroft, but when Frank Sweeney, the club's other pitcher (they only carried two in those days), jumped to the St. Louis Maroons of the Union Association a few days later, it left the Grays without a pitcher. Bancroft begged Radbourn to return and he agreed to do so for more money, offering to pitch all remaining games that season. And Old Hoss pitched every game on the schedule from July 23 to September 24. He won 18 consecutive games, lost one and then won eight more. At the end of the season he couldn't lift his arm above his head.

Radbourn used a cricket-style pitching motion that included a running start, and throughout his career he always threw underhanded, even though the rule was changed to allow overhand delivery in 1883.

After the Grays folded at the end of the 1885 season, Radbourn joined the Boston Beaneaters and spent four years with that club. He jumped to the Players League in 1890 to pitch for the Boston club and then came back to the N.L. in 1891 to spend his final major league season with Cincinnati.

Charles "Old Hoss" Radbourn was inducted into the National Baseball Hall of Fame in 1939.

Radbourn, Charles Gardner "Old Hoss"
BR/TR, 5'9", 168 lbs. Deb: 5/5/1880

YEAR	TM/L	W	L	PCT	G	IP	H	HR	BB	SO	ERA
1881	Pro-NL	25	11	.694	41	325.1	309	1	64	117	2.43
1882	Pro-NL	33	20	.623	55	474	429	6	51	201	2.09
1883	Pro-NL	48	25	.658	76	632.1	563	7	56	315	2.05
1884	Pro-NL	59	12	.831	75	678.2	528	18	98	441	1.38
1885	Pro-NL	28	21	.571	49	445.2	423	4	83	154	2.20
1886	Bos-NL	27	31	.466	58	509.1	521	18	111	218	3.00
1887	Bos-NL	24	23	.511	50	425	505	20	133	87	4.55
1888	Bos-NL	7	16	.304	24	207	187	8	45	64	2.87
1889	Bos-NL	20	11	.645	33	277	282	14	72	99	3.67
1890	Bos-PL	27	12	.692	41	343	352	8	100	80	3.31
1891	Cin-NL	11	13	.458	26	218	236	13	62	54	4.25
Total	11	309	195	.613	528	4,535.1	4,335	117	875	1,830	2.67

Wilbert Robinson

Catcher - Manager - Executive
Born: June 29, 1863, Bolton, Massachusetts
Died: August 8, 1934, Atlanta, Georgia

Wilbert Robinson began his 30-year career in baseball (17 years as a player, 23 years as a manager and executive) as a catcher for the American Association's Philadelphia Athletics in 1886. After five rather unspectacular years with the A's he was transferred to the Baltimore Orioles in 1890 and it was there, in Baltimore, that he finally blossomed as the catcher for the legendary Baltimore Oriole club that won four straight National League championships in the mid-1890's.

During the Orioles' glory years Robinson was the cornerstone of the club, teaming up with such future Hall of Famers as Wee Willie Keeler, Hughie Jennings, John McGraw and manager "Foxy" Ned Hanlon to help create baseball's first "greatest team of all time." During the '90's Robertson hit better than .300 four different seasons, and in a game against St. Louis on June 10, 1892 he went 7-for-7, driving in 11 runs, a record that's still on the books today.

On one occasion during the 1896 season the durable Robinson caught all three games of a triple header on one day and both games of a double header the following day. On another occasion that year Robinson had to have a finger amputated due to an injury. He nevertheless finished the season with a .347 batting average.

After his playing career ended in 1902, Robinson came back to the game in 1911 as a pitching coach for his buddy John McGraw's New York Giants. After a falling out with McGraw after the 1913 season he left the Giants to become the manager of the Brooklyn Dodgers in 1914, a position he held for the next 18 years. The fiery, profane and colorful Robinson immediately became a favorite with the Brooklyn fans, so much so that they took to calling him "Uncle Robbie" and the club

became known as the Brooklyn Robins, in his honor.

Robinson's club won N.L. pennants in 1916 and 1920, but lost both World Series. They almost won another pennant in 1924, losing to McGraw's Giants by a game and a half. In 1925 Robinson was appointed president of the club, and served in a dual capacity as both chief officer and manager of the franchise until 1929 when, due to a clash with club half-owner Steve McKeever, he was forced to give up the presidency. He still remained as manager of the team until he retired from major league baseball following the 1931 season. Robinson then moved to Georgia where he owned and managed a minor league club in Atlanta from 1932 until his death in 1934.

Wilbert Robinson was inducted into the National Baseball Hall of Fame in 1945.

Robinson, Wilbert "Uncle Robby"
BR/TR, 5'8.5", 215 lbs. Deb: 4/19/1886

YEAR	TM/L	G	AB	R	H	2B	3B	HR	RBI	BB	SO	AVG
1886	Phi-AA	87	342	57	69	11	3	1	21	—	—	.202
1887	Phi-AA	68	264	28	60	6	2	1	14	—	—	.227
1888	Phi-AA	66	254	32	62	7	2	1	31	9	—	.244
1889	Phi-AA	69	264	31	61	13	2	0	28	6	34	.231
1890	Phi-AA	82	329	32	78	13	4	4	16	—	—	.237
	Bal-AA	14	48	7	13	1	0	0	3	—	—	.271
	Yr	96	377	39	91	14	4	4	19	—	—	.241
1891	Bal-AA	93	334	25	72	8	5	2	46	16	37	.216
1892	Bal-NL	90	330	36	88	14	4	2	57	15	35	.267
1893	Bal-NL	95	359	49	120	21	3	3	57	26	22	.334
1894	Bal-NL	109	414	69	146	21	4	1	98	46	18	.353
1895	Bal-NL	77	282	38	74	19	1	0	48	12	19	.262
1896	Bal-NL	67	245	43	85	9	6	2	38	14	13	.347
1897	Bal-NL	48	181	25	57	9	0	0	23	8	—	.315
1898	Bal-NL	79	289	29	80	12	2	0	38	16	—	.277
1899	Bal-NL	108	356	40	101	15	2	0	47	31	—	.284
1900	StL-NL	60	210	26	52	5	1	0	28	11	—	.248
1901	Bal-AL	68	239	32	72	12	3	0	26	10	—	.301
1902	Bal-AL	91	335	38	98	16	7	1	57	12		.293
Total	17	1,371	5,075	637	1,388	212	51	18	695	INC	INC	.273

Amos Rusie

Pitcher (Amos Wilson Rusie)
Born: May 30, 1871, Mooresville, Indiana
Died: December 6, 1942, Seattle, Washington

Nicknamed "The Hoosier Thunderbolt" because of his blazing fastball, Amos Rusie was one of the hardest-throwing pitchers of the 1890's and is considered to be the principal reason that the mound was moved back from 50' to the present 60'6" in 1893.

The big righthander began his major league career at the age of 18 when he joined his home-town Indianapolis Hoosiers of the National League in 1889. That year Rusie posted a 12-10 record, and when the Hoosiers folded at the end of the season he was dispatched to the New York Giants. He went 29-34 in his first season with the Giants and began a string of eight 20 or more win seasons in a row.

Rusie was a workhorse, pitching an average of 377 innings per season during his 10-year career. He led the league in strikeouts five times, shutouts four times and in 1893 he completed a league-leading 50 of 56 starts.

In 1894 Amos led the N.L. with 36 wins, and even though the Giants finished second that year, they went on to defeat the Baltimore Orioles in the first Temple Cup post-season series, winning four straight games. Rusie won two of the contests, allowing only one earned run in 18 innings.

In 1896 Rusie sat out the entire season due to a dispute over a $200 fine that he felt Giants owner Andrew Freeman had wrongly levied against him. He sued the Giants for $5,000 in lost salary and damages in a legal action that challenged the reserve clause, and even though Freeman refused to give in on the matter, the other N.L. owners chipped in for a $3,000 settlement, rather than have the reserve clause issue brought up in a court of law.

The year off didn't seem to bother Rusie as he went 28-10 in 1897 and led the league with a 2.54 ERA. After a 20-11 season in 1898, he was sidelined for the 1899 season due to a torn shoulder muscle. In 1900 Rusie was involved in what is probably the most one-sided trade in baseball history. The Cincinnati Reds dealt a young pitching prospect by the name of Christy Mathewson to the Giants for the 29-year-old, still-injured Rusie. Mathewson went on to win 373 games for the Giants, but Rusie only managed a 0-1 record in three games for the Reds in 1901 and was forced to retire from the game.

Amos Rusie was inducted into the National Baseball Hall of Fame in 1977.

Rusie, Amos Wilson "The Hoosier Thunderbolt"
BR/TR, 6'1", 200 lbs. Deb: 5/9/1889

YEAR	TM/L	W	L	PCT	G	IP	H	HR	BB	SO	ERA
1889	Ind-NL	12	10	.545	33	225	246	12	116	109	5.32
1890	NY-NL	29	34	.460	67	548.2	436	3	289	341	2.56
1891	NY-NL	33	20	.623	61	500.1	391	7	262	337	2.55
1892	NY-NL	31	31	.500	64	532	405	7	267	288	2.88
1893	NY-NL	33	21	.611	56	482	451	15	218	208	3.23
1894	NY-NL	36	13	.735	54	444	426	10	200	195	2.78
1895	NY-NL	23	23	.500	49	393.1	384	9	159	201	3.73
1897	NY-NL	28	10	.737	38	322.1	314	6	87	135	2.54
1898	NY-NL	20	11	.645	37	300	288	6	103	114	3.03
1901	Cin-NL	0	1	.000	3	22	43	1	3	6	8.59
Total	10	245	174	.585	462	3,769.2	3,384	76	1,704	1,934	3.07

Babe Ruth

Outfielder - Pitcher (George Herman Ruth Jr.)
Born: February 6, 1895, Baltimore, Maryland
Died: August 16, 1948, New York, New York

Babe Ruth survived a stormy childhood, growing up mostly in a Baltimore orphanage and reform school where his parents had abandoned him at the age of seven, to become the biggest celebrity in American sports history.

In 1914, the 19-year-old Ruth started his major league career as a pitcher with the Boston Red Sox and soon became the club's best hurler. In 1916 he lead the A.L. with a 1.75 ERA and nine shutouts while posting a 23-12 record.

But his ability to handle the bat caught the Red Sox management's eye and they gradually moved him into the outfield. In 1918 his 66 RBI was third best in the league, and when he walloped a league-leading 29 homers the following season his career as a pitcher was over.

That winter Boston sold him to the New York Yankees and in 1920 (the year that a livelier ball was introduced to the game), Ruth responded to the friendly confines of the Polo Grounds by hitting a record 54 home runs. The fans flocked to see him, and that season the Yankees became the first team to draw over one million customers.

On April 18, 1923, when the Yankees opened their new ballpark some 74,000 people showed up, and Ruth reacted by hitting a home run in his first time at bat. That year he hit .393 and led the Yankees to their third straight A.L. pennant and first world championship.

In his 22-year career "the Sultan of Swat" rewrote the record books time and time again. He led the American League in home runs 12 times and averaged 50 home runs a year from 1926 through '31.

Ruth's playing abilities and his exuberant, larger than life personality made him the biggest draw in baseball and the highest-paid player of his time.

The "Bambino" single-handedly changed baseball forever, by bringing on the era of the slugger, and is still considered to be the greatest player of all time.

Ruth, George Herman "The Bambino" or "The Sultan Of Swat"
BL/TL, 6'2", 215 lbs. Deb: 7/11/14

YEAR	TM/L	G	AB	R	H	2B	3B	HR	RBI	BB	SO	AVG
1914	Bos-AL	5	10	1	2	1	0	0	2	0	4	.200
1915	Bos-AL	42	92	16	29	10	1	4	21	9	23	.315
1916	Bos-AL	67	136	18	37	5	3	3	15	10	23	.272
1917	Bos-AL	52	123	14	40	6	3	2	12	12	18	.325
1918	Bos-AL	95	317	50	95	26	11	11	66	57	58	.300
1919	Bos-AL	130	432	103	139	34	12	29	114	101	58	.322
1920	NY-AL	142	458	158	172	36	9	54	137	148	80	.376
1921	NY-AL	152	540	177	204	44	16	59	171	144	81	.378
1922	NY-AL	110	406	94	128	24	8	35	99	84	80	.315
1923	NY-AL	152	522	151	205	45	13	41	131	170	93	.393
1924	NY-AL	153	529	143	200	39	7	46	121	142	81	.378
1925	NY-AL	98	359	61	104	12	2	25	66	59	68	.290
1926	NY-AL	152	495	139	184	30	5	47	146	144	76	.372
1927	NY-AL	151	540	158	192	29	8	60	164	138	89	.356
1928	NY-AL	154	536	163	173	29	8	54	142	135	87	.323
1929	NY-AL	135	499	121	172	26	6	46	154	72	60	.345
1930	NY-AL	145	518	150	186	28	9	49	153	136	61	.359
1931	NY-AL	145	534	149	199	31	3	46	163	128	51	.373
1932	NY-AL	133	457	120	156	13	5	41	137	130	62	.341
1933	NY-AL~	137	459	97	138	21	3	34	103	114	90	.301
1934	NY-AL~	125	365	78	105	17	4	22	84	103	63	.288
1935	Bos-NL	28	72	13	13	0	0	6	12	20	24	.181
Total	22	2,503	8,399	2,174	2,873	506	136	714	2,213	2,056	1,330	.342

YEAR	TM/L	W	L	PCT	G	IP	H	HR	BB	SO	ERA
1914	Bos-AL	2	1	.667	4	23	21	1	7	3	3.91
1915	Bos-AL	18	8	.692	32	217.2	166	3	85	112	2.44
1916	Bos-AL	23	12	.657	44	323.2	230	0	118	170	1.75
1917	Bos-AL	24	13	.649	41	326.1	244	2	108	128	2.01
1918	Bos-AL	13	7	.650	20	166.1	125	1	49	40	2.22
1919	Bos-AL	9	5	.643	17	133.1	148	2	58	30	2.97
1920	NY-AL	1	0	1.000	1	4	3	0	2	0	4.50
1921	NY-AL	2	0	1.000	2	9	14	1	9	2	9.00
1930	NY-AL	1	0	1.000	1	9	11	0	2	3	3.00
1933	NY-AL	1	0	1.000	1	9	12	0	3	0	5.00
Total	10	94	46	.671	163	1,221.1	974	10	441	488	2.28

Ernie Shore

Pitcher (Ernest Grady Shore)
Born: March 24, 1891, East Bend, North Carolina
Died: September 24, 1980, Winston-Salem, North Carolina

Ernie Shore pitched in the major leagues for seven seasons in the early part of the twentieth century and the big righthander had a rather unremarkable career except for one event that took place in 1917: That year he was credited with the only perfect game in baseball history thrown by a relief pitcher.

Shore was with the Boston Red Sox at the time. The Ace of Boston's pitching staff was none other than Babe Ruth, and although the Babe never pitched a no-hitter himself, he nevertheless inadvertently helped Shore pitch his perfect game.

On June 23, 1917, Ruth started in a game against the Washington Nationals. After the first batter, Ray Morgan, walked on a full count, an incensed Ruth charged umpire Brick Owens and slugged him on the jaw. The Babe was promptly banished from the game.

Shore was rushed in from the bullpen and, after Morgan was thrown out on an attempted steal, Shore proceeded to retire the next 26 batters in a row, giving Boston a 3-0 victory. Shore was credited with a perfect game.

Shore, Ernest Grady
BR/TR, 6'4", 220 lbs. Deb: 6/20/12

YEAR	TM/L	W	L	PCT	G	IP	H	HR	BB	SO	ERA
1912	NY-NL	0	0	—	1	1	8	1	1	1	27.00
1914	Bos-AL	10	5	.667	20	139.2	103	1	34	51	2.00
1915	Bos-AL	19	8	.704	38	247	207	3	66	102	1.64
1916	Bos-AL	16	10	.615	38	225.2	221	1	49	62	2.63
1917	Bos-AL	13	10	.565	29	226.2	201	1	55	57	2.22
1919	NY-AL	5	8	.385	20	95	105	4	44	24	4.17
1920	NY-AL	2	2	.500	14	44.1	61	1	21	12	4.87
Total	7	65	43	.602	160	979.1	906	12	270	309	2.47

Fred Snodgrass

Outfielder (Frederick Carlisle Snodgrass)
Born: October 19, 1887, Ventura, California
Died: April 5, 1974, Ventura, California

Fred Snodgrass, who played nine rather unremarkable seasons in the big leagues, is best remembered for one unfortunate incident which occurred in the 1912 World Series. His name will forever live in baseball infamy for making the famous "$30,000 muff."

The New York Giants were trying to hold on to a 2-1 lead over the Boston Red Sox in the bottom of the tenth inning of the final game of the Series, when Snodgrass, who played in the outfield for the Giants, dropped a routine fly ball which opened the door for the Red Sox to make a comeback and win the championship.

It didn't matter that Snodgrass made a brilliant catch on the next batter, or that Giants manager John McGraw stood by his beleaguered player afterwards and even gave him a raise in pay for the next season; Snodgrass will always be best remembered for one regrettable incident which eventually cost him and his teammates $30,000 (which was the difference between the winning and losing shares).

Snodgrass, Frederick Carlisle "Snow"
BR/TR, 5'11.5", 175 lbs. Deb: 6/4/08

YEAR	TM/L	G	AB	R	H	2B	3B	HR	RBI	BB	SO	AVG
1908	NY-NL	6	4	2	1	0	0	0	1	0	—	.250
1909	NY-NL	28	70	10	21	5	0	1	6	7	—	.300
1910	NY-NL	123	396	69	127	22	8	2	44	71	52	.321
1911	NY-NL	151	534	83	157	27	10	1	77	72	59	.294
1912	NY-NL	146	535	91	144	24	9	3	69	70	65	.269
1913	NY-NL	141	457	65	133	21	6	3	49	53	44	.291
1914	NY-NL	113	392	54	103	20	4	0	44	37	43	.263
1915	NY-NL	103	252	36	49	9	0	0	20	35	33	.194
	Bos-NL	23	79	10	22	2	0	0	9	7	9	.278
Yr		126	331	46	71	11	0	0	29	42	42	.215
1916	Bos-NL	112	382	33	95	13	5	1	32	34	54	.249
Total	9	946	3,101	453	852	143	42	11	351	386	—	.275

Lou "Chief" Sockalexis

Outfielder (Louis M. Sockalexis)
Born: October 24, 1871, Old Town, Maine
Died: December 24, 1913, Burlington, Maine

Though he never got to play for them, Lou "Chief" Sockalexis was nevertheless the first Cleveland Indian. Sockalexis was a Penobscot Indian from Maine who, in one spectacular season with the N.L.'s Cleveland Spiders in 1897, captured the hearts and minds of Cleveland's baseball fans.

Sockalexis had been a college baseball star, first at Holy Cross and then Notre Dame, from which he had been expelled when he was involved in a drunken disturbance at a local brothel.

Cleveland signed him in 1897 and he was an instant success. His ability to handle major league pitching (he hit .338 that year), combined with his tremendous throwing arm and spectacular play in right field, made him a great favorite of the fans, who would let out war whoops whenever he came up to the plate. He is believed to be the first American Indian to play major league ball.

But his love for strong drink did him in. In July he injured his leg while reportedly jumping out of a second-story window at a local bordello. He managed to play only a few more games that season, and made only brief appearances in 1898 and 1899. He eventually left the game, became a drifter and died of alcoholism in 1913.

But his memory lived on in Cleveland. He left such a strong impression with the Cleveland fans that when a local newspaper held a contest in 1915 to find a new nickname for the Cleveland American League team, the readers voted to rename it the Indians in his honor.

Sockalexis, Louis M.
BL/TR, 5'11", 185 lbs.Deb: 4/22/1897

YEAR	TM/L	G	AB	R	H	2B	3B	HR	RBI	BB	SO	AVG
1897	Cle-NL	66	278	43	94	9	8	3	42	18	—	.338
1898	Cle-NL	21	67	11	15	2	0	0	10	1	—	.224
1899	Cle-NL	7	22	0	6	1	0	0	3	1	—	.273
Total	3		94	367	54	115	12	8	3	55	20	—	.313

Al Spalding

Pitcher - Executive - Owner (Albert Goodwill Spalding)
Born: September 2, 1850, Byron, Illinois
Died: September 9, 1915, San Diego, California

It could be said of Al Spalding, that, he never met an opportunity to make money out of baseball that he didn't like. Born in Byron, Illinois, in 1850, Albert Goodwill Spalding grew up to become a star pitcher in baseball's first professional league, the National Association. From 1871 to 1875, pitching for the Boston Red Stockings he won 207 games and lost only 56 — an average of 41 wins per season.

When the National League came into being in 1876, Spalding initially managed the Chicago club, went on to become an executive with the team and then eventually owner of the franchise. He was one of baseball's great entrepreneurs. In 1876, along with his brother and brother-in-law, he established the firm of A.G. Spalding and Brothers which started out as a sporting goods store in Chicago and then evolved into a major manufacturer of sporting goods.

Spalding had no qualms about using his influence as a baseball executive to promote his business (among other things, he gave the National League free baseballs, and even paid them a dollar for each dozen they used, in return for the league designating his ball as the "official" ball of the league. This, of course, helped to create a great demand for Spalding baseballs by the public.

He also became the publisher of the *Official League Book* which carried league rules, and additionally he published *Spalding's Official Base-Ball Guide*, an annual collection of team and individual records known to feature articles which pushed Spalding's viewpoint on many baseball issues and which helped to sell massive amounts of Spalding sporting equipment.

As a baseball executive he helped to work out the territorial scheme that kept clubs from competing with each other for the same fans, and was instrumental in breaking up the Player's Brotherhood, which had called for the first players' strike in 1890.

Al Spalding organized the great world baseball tour of 1888-89, where he took his Chicago club and players from other teams on a tour around the world in order to promote the great American game of baseball. On the six-month junket they visited such places as Australia, Ceylon, Egypt, Italy, France and Britain. They played some 42 games before an estimated 200,000 people, and the game itself generally received mixed reviews. After witnessing a baseball exhibition at London's Kensington Oval, Britain's Prince of Wales stated that baseball was "an excellent game," although he considered cricket to be "superior."

Spalding partially retired from baseball in 1901, when he moved to California, joined a religious cult and eventually made an unsuccessful run for U.S. Senate.

Spalding also helped to create and promote the ridiculous Doubleday Myth. In 1905, acting on his own authority, Spalding put together a commission to investigate the origin of baseball. He remained behind the scenes, pulling all the strings, and two years later this commission came to the remarkable conclusion that a deceased Civil War hero by the name of Abner Doubleday had invented baseball, when in fact Doubleday had never, in his whole life, had anything whatsoever to do with the game.

Spalding died in Point Loma, California, in 1915. He was inducted into the National Baseball Hall of Fame in 1939.

Spalding, Albert Goodwill
BR/TR, 6'1", 170 lbs. Deb: 5/5/1871

YEAR	TM/L	G	AB	R	H	2B	3B	HR	RBI	BB	SO	AVG
1876	Chi-NL	66	292	54	91	14	2	0	44	6	3	.312
1877	Chi-NL	60	254	29	65	7	6	0	35	3	16	.256
1878	Chi-NL	1	4	0	2	0	0	0	0	0	0	.500
Total	3	127	550	83	158	21	8	0	79	9	19	.287

YEAR	TM/L	W	L	PCT	G	IP	H	HR	BB	SO	ERA
1871	Bos-n	19	10	.655	31	257.1	333	2	38	—	3.36
1872	Bos-n	38	8	.826	48	404.2	412	0	27	27	1.98
1873	Bos-n	41	14	.745	60	497.2	643	5	28	—	2.46
1874	Bos-n	52	16	.765	71	616.1	753	1	23	11.3	2.35
1875	Bos-n	55	5	.917	72	575	571	1	14	9.2	1.52
Total	5 n	205	53	.795	282	2,351	2,712	9	130		2.22
1876	Chi-N	47	12	.797	61	528.2	542	6	26	39	1.75
1877	Chi-N	1	0	1.000	4	11	17	0	0	—	3.27
Total	2	48	12	.800	65	539.2	559	6	26	41	1.78

Tris Speaker

Outfielder - Manager (Tristram E. Speaker)
Born: April 4, 1888, Hubbard, Texas
Died: December 8, 1958, Lake Whitney, Texas

In his first year as a full-time player with the Boston Red Sox in 1909, Tris Speaker hit .309. It was the first of 18 times that he would hit better than .300 in his 22-year career. Furthermore, Speaker topped the .380 mark three times, including a league-leading .386 in 1916, and his .344 lifetime batting average ranks him fifth on the all-time list. His career record of 792 doubles has never been equalled.

But as good a hitter as he was, he was also known for his defensive play. From 1910 to 1915 he led Boston's legendary outfield, which included Duffy Lewis and Harry Hooper. Speaker made 161 of their record 455 assists. He was famous for playing a shallow centerfield to catch potential hits, yet had a great knack to race back for a ball, very few of which, ever went over his head. His 488 outfield assists is an all-time record.

Speaker helped the Red Sox win two world championships during this period, but when the Red Sox tried to cut his $18,000 salary in half in 1916 (to redress the inflated salaries the team had been paying to prevent defections to the now defunct Federal League) Speaker balked, and the Red Sox ended up trading him to Cleveland.

After several years in the Indians outfield he was appointed player-manager of the club in 1919, and led them to a world championship in 1920. Speaker continued to pilot the club until 1926 when he was forced to resign under some very peculiar circumstances. It was alleged that he, along with Detroit player-manager Ty Cobb, had conspired to fix a game between the Indians and Tigers back in 1919. Though the allegation was never proven, Commissioner Landis felt it best that both clubs make the two superstars free agents. Both men were eventually absolved of the charge.

Speaker signed on with Washington for the next season, but his salary

was too much for the club to handle and they were forced to let him go. He ended up with Philadelphia in 1928 and retired at the end of the season.

Tris Speaker was inducted into the National Baseball Hall of Fame in 1937.

Speaker, Tristram E. "The Grey Eagle"
BL/TL, 5'11.5", 193 lbs. Deb: 9/14/07

YEAR	TM/L	G	AB	R	H	2B	3B	HR	RBI	BB	SO	AVG
1907	Bos-AL	7	19	0	3	0	0	0	1	1	—	.158
1908	Bos-AL	31	48	12	26	2	2	0	9	4	—	.288
1909	Bos-AL	143	544	73	168	26	13	7	77	38	—	.309
1910	Bos-AL	141	538	92	183	20	14	7	65	52	—	.340
1911	Bos-AL	141	500	88	167	34	13	8	70	59	—	.334
1912	Bos-AL	153	580	136	222	53	12	10	90	82	—	.383
1913	Bos-AL	141	520	94	189	35	22	3	71	65	22	.363
1914	Bos-AL	158	571	101	193	46	18	4	90	77	25	.338
1915	Bos-AL	150	547	108	176	25	12	0	69	81	14	.322
1916	Cle-AL	151	546	102	211	41	8	2	79	82	20	.386
1917	Cle-AL	142	523	90	184	42	11	2	60	67	14	.352
1918	Cle-AL	127	471	73	150	33	11	0	61	64	9	.318
1919	Cle-AL	134	494	83	146	38	12	2	63	73	12	.296
1920	Cle-AL	150	552	137	214	50	11	8	107	97	13	.388
1921	Cle-AL	132	506	107	183	52	14	3	75	68	12	.362
1922	Cle-AL	131	426	85	161	48	8	11	71	77	11	.378
1923	Cle-AL	150	574	133	218	59	11	17	130	93	15	.380
1924	Cle-AL	135	486	94	167	36	9	9	65	72	13	.344
1925	Cle-AL	117	429	79	167	35	5	12	87	70	12	.389
1926	Cle-AL	150	539	96	164	52	8	7	86	94	15	.304
1927	Was-AL	141	523	71	171	43	6	2	73	55	8	.327
1928	Phi-AL	64	191	28	51	22	2	3	30	10	5	.267
Total 22		2,789	10,197	1,882	3,514	792	222	117	1,529	1,381	INC	.345

Adonis Terry

Pitcher (William H. Terry)
Born: August 7, 1864, Westfield, Massachusetts
Died: February 24, 1915, Milwaukee, Wisconsin

Adonis Terry, who was given his nickname because of his good looks, spent 14 years pitching in the big leagues in the late 1800's. He also had a potent bat and played over 200 games in the outfield.

Terry, who had four 20 win seasons in his career, is best known for the two no-hitters he threw while with the A.A.'s Brooklyn Trolley Dodgers. On July 24, 1886, he no-hit the St. Louis Browns 1-0. Two years later, on May 27, 1888, the handsome hurler pitched a 4-0 no-no against the Louisville Colonels.

Terry, William H.
BR/TR, 5'11.5", 168 lbs. Deb: 5/1/1884

YEAR	TM/L	G	AB	R	H	2B	3B	HR	RBI	BB	SO	AVG
1884	Bro-AA	68	240	16	56	10	3	0	—	8	—	.233
1885	Bro-AA	71	264	23	45	1	3	1	—	10	—	.170
1886	Bro-AA	75	299	34	71	8	9	2	—	10	—	.237
1887	Bro-AA	86	352	56	103	6	10	3	—	16	—	.293
1888	Bro-AA	30	115	13	29	6	0	0	8	5	—	.252
1889	Bro-AA	49	160	29	48	6	6	2	26	14	14	.300
1890	Bro-NL	99	363	63	101	17	9	4	59	40	34	.278
1891	Bro-NL	30	91	10	19	7	1	0	6	9	26	.209
1892	Bal-NL	1	4	0	0	0	0	0	0	0	1	.000
	Pit-NL	31	100	10	16	0	4	2	11	10	11	.160
Yr		32	104	10	16	0	4	2	11	10	12	.154
1893	Pit-NL	26	71	9	18	4	3	0	11	3	11	.254
1894	Pit-NL	1	0	0	0	0	0	0	0	0	0	—
	Chi-NL	30	95	19	33	4	2	0	17	11	12	.347
Yr		31	95	19	33	4	2	0	17	11	12	.347
1895	Chi-NL	40	137	18	30	3	2	1	10	2	17	.219
1896	Chi-NL	30	99	14	26	4	2	0	15	8	12	.263
1897	Chi-NL	1	3	1	0	0	0	0	0	0	—	.000
Total	14	668	2,393	315	595	76	54	15	INC	146	INC	.249

Sam Thompson

Outfielder (Samuel Luther Thompson)
Born: March 5, 1860, Danville, Indiana
Died: November 7, 1922, Detroit, Michigan

Big Sam Thompson was a great home run hitter in an baseball era when home runs weren't appreciated. He began his 15-year major league career with the N.L.'s Detroit Wolverines in 1885, and two years later helped the club win a pennant and world championship while leading the league with 203 hits, 23 homers and a .372 batting average.

Though Thompson led the N.L. in RBI and homers two times each, and hit better than .300 nine times, the highlight of his career came in 1894 when, while playing for Philadelphia, he hit .404 and was part of the only outfield in major league history to hit over .400 combined. That year, left fielder Ed Delahanty hit .400, center fielder Billy Hamilton compiled a .399 average and reserve fielder Tuck Turner hit .416. Unfortunately, the club, which was rather poor in pitching, only managed a fourth-place finish.

Thompson's final great year was 1895 when he hit .392, and led the N.L. with 18 homers and 165 RBI. A back injury forced him out of the game in 1898. When Thompson finally retired after a brief comeback attempt in 1906, his career total of 128 home runs was a major league record that stood until Babe Ruth broke it in 1921.

Sam Thompson was inducted into the National Baseball Hall of Fame in 1974.

Thompson, Samuel Luther "Big Sam"
BL/TL, 6'2", 207 lbs. Deb: 7/2/1885 H

YEAR	TM/L	G	AB	R	H	2B	3B	HR	RBI	BB	SO	AVG
1885	Det-NL	63	254	58	77	11	9	7	44	16	22	.303
1886	Det-NL	122	503	101	156	18	13	8	89	35	31	.310
1887	Det-NL	127	545	118	203	29	23	11	166	32	19	.372
1888	Det-NL	56	238	51	67	10	8	6	40	23	10	.282
1889	Phi-NL	128	533	103	158	36	4	20	111	36	22	.296
1890	Phi-NL	132	549	116	172	41	9	4	102	42	29	.313
1891	Phi-NL	133	554	108	163	23	10	7	90	52	20	.294
1892	Phi-NL	153	609	109	186	28	11	9	104	59	19	.305
1893	Phi-NL	131	600	130	222	37	13	11	126	50	17	.370
1894	Phi-NL	102	458	115	185	29	27	13	141	40	13	.404
1895	Phi-NL	119	538	131	211	45	21	18	165	31	11	.392
1896	Phi-NL	119	517	103	154	28	7	12	100	28	13	.298
1897	Phi-NL	3	13	2	3	0	1	0	3	1	—	.231
1898	Phi-NL	14	63	14	22	5	3	1	15	4	—	.349
1906	Det-AL	8	31	4	7	0	1	0	3	1	—	.226
Total	15	1,410	6,005	1,263	1,986	340	160	127	1,299	450	INC	.331

Joe Tinker

Infielder - Manager (Joseph Bert Tinker)
Born: July 27, 1880, Muscotah, Kansas
Died: July 27, 1948, Orlando, Florida

Joe Tinker played shortstop in the Chicago Cubs' famed Tinker-to-Evers-to-Chance double-play combination of the early 1900's. This slick fielding infield helped the Cubs win three straight N.L. pennants starting in 1906. Ironically, double-plays were not recorded until 1919, so there are no statistics on how many the legendary trio, who were immortalized in a poem written in 1910 by baseball writer Franklin P. Adams, actually made.

During his 15-year career Tinker, who was no great shakes with the bat (he was a lifetime .264 hitter) led the N.L. in fielding average four times.

In a famous incident in 1905, before an exhibition game in Bedford, Indiana, Tinker and Evers got into an argument over a cab ride to the park, and ultimately ended up engaging in fisticuffs on the field. The pair did not speak to each other for the next 33 years.

After the 1912 season, when Evers was appointed manager of the Cubs, Tinker demanded to be traded and was sent to Cincinnati where he became player-manager of the Reds. A disagreement with the management caused him to jump to the newly formed Federal League in 1914. He managed the Chicago Whales to a second-place finish in 1914 and a first-place finish in 1915. After the Fed folded, Tinker returned to the Cubs, and managed the club for the 1916 season. The Cubs finished fifth, 26 ½ games behind first-place Brooklyn, and he was let go at the end of the season.

In 1946, the trio of Evers, Tinker and Chance were inducted into the National Baseball Hall of Fame.

Tinker, Joseph Bert
BR/TR, 5'9", 175 lbs. Deb: 4/17/02

YEAR	TM/L	G	AB	R	H	2B	3B	HR	RBI	BB	SO	AVG
1902	Chi-NL	133	501	54	137	19	5	2	54	26	—	.273
1903	Chi-NL	124	460	67	134	21	7	2	70	37	—	.291
1904	Chi-NL	141	488	55	108	12	13	3	41	29	—	.221
1905	Chi-NL	149	547	70	135	18	8	2	66	34	—	.247
1906	Chi-NL	148	523	75	122	18	4	1	64	43	—	.233
1907	Chi-NL	117	402	36	89	11	3	1	36	25	—	.221
1908	Chi-NL	157	548	67	146	22	14	6	68	32	—	.266
1909	Chi-NL	143	516	56	132	26	11	4	57	17	—	.256
1910	Chi-NL	133	473	48	136	25	9	3	69	24	35	.288
1911	Chi-NL	144	536	61	149	24	12	4	69	39	31	.278
1912	Chi-NL	142	550	80	155	24	7	0	75	38	21	.282
1913	Cin-NL	110	382	47	121	20	13	1	57	20	26	.317
1914	Chi-F	126	438	50	112	21	7	2	46	38	30	.256
1915	Chi-F	31	67	7	18	2	1	0	9	13	5	.269
1916	Chi-NL	7	10	0	1	0	0	0	1	1	1	.100
Total	15	1,805	6,441	773	1,695	263	114	31	782	416	INC	.263

Chris Von der Ahe

Owner - Manager (Christian Frederick Wilhelm Von der Ahe)
Born: November 7, 1851
Died: June 7, 1913

The foremost team in the American Association during the 1880's was the St. Louis Browns, who won four straight Association championships between 1885 and 1888. They were owned by the flamboyant Chris Von der Ahe, a German immigrant who was the proprietor of a beer garden in St. Louis. He had originally gotten into baseball because he saw it as a great opportunity to sell beer. At the St. Louis ball park, Von der Ahe's vendors prowled the stands at every game peddling steins of the golden liquid to the thirsty crowd.

Von der Ahe, who was basically ignorant about baseball itself, was nevertheless constantly interfering with the running of the club, much to the chagrin of field manager Charles Commiskey.

Major league baseball has had a long history of colorful team owners, and Chris Von der Ahe was the very first. Such characters as George Steinbrenner, Marge Shott, Charles O. Finley, Bill Veeck and the like, have just been carrying on a tradition that was undoubtedly started by Von der Ahe.

In *Baseball, The Early Years*, Harold Seymour says that "Von der Ahe himself could have played in vaudeville. He was a heavy-set man whose face featured a great bulbous nose and a full mustache. He wore loud clothes, spent money liberally, and liked to exclaim 'Nothing is too goot for my poys!'" and when "Der Boss President" was at the ballpark he "made the players nervous, watching their every move with field glasses, running around the stands blowing a whistle at them, or storming into the dressing room swearing at players whose errors lost the game."

Seymour tells of an incident when Von der Ahe supposedly boasted to a delegation of visitors that he had the biggest baseball diamond in the world. When Commiskey took him aside and whispered that all diamonds were the same size, Von der Ahe promptly retreated and simply claimed that he owned the the biggest infield!

Von der Ahe would ceremoniously take each day's game receipts to the bank in a wheelbarrow, flanked by armed guards, and once he allowed himself to be arrested at the ballpark after he defied a Missouri law which prohibited baseball on Sunday.

After the 1887 season, Von der Ahe, who was inspired by Chicago's sale of "King" Kelly and John Clarkson to Boston for the then-astronomical amount of $10,000 each, decided to fatten his own purse, so he promptly decimated his team by selling his top two pitchers, Robert Lee Caruthers and Dave Foutz, along with his number one catcher "Doc" Bushong to Brooklyn for $10,000, and then peddling star outfielder Curt Welch and his only shortstop Bill Gleason to Philadelphia for $5,000.

Unbelievably, Commiskey, starting from almost scratch, was able to recruit enough new players to put together a team for the following year that was was good enough to win the pennant.

The Browns finished in second place in each of the following three years, and when the American Association folded at the end of the 1891 season the club was absorbed by the National League. This proved to be a disaster for Von der Ahe.

Charles Commiskey left the club for Cincinnati in 1882 and Von der Ahe appointed himself as manager. The club descended to the N.L. basement and stayed there for most of the rest of the decade. After two unsuccessful years as a manager Von der Ahe then hired a succession of skippers for the club (he changed managers 12 times between 1895 and 1897) but to no avail; the Browns just couldn't make it in the N.L.

In an attempt to attract fans Von der Ahe installed a carousel and carnival rides in his outfield, and held horse races, band concerts, and boxing matches in the park. He called his new endeavour the "Coney Island of the West."

In 1888 the park burned down, his wife sued him for divorce after catching him with one of his many mistresses, his son took him to court over a property matter, and he himself ended up in a Pittsburgh jail, after the owner of the Pirates had him kidnapped by private detectives and brought to Pennsylvania in a dispute over a seven-year-old debt.

To make matters worse, Von der Ahe tried to sell his debt-ridden club, but he couldn't even do that because a Missouri court had appointed a receiver to dispose of the team. Von der Ahe left baseball forever, but the club survived and eventually became the St. Louis Cardinals.

Rube Waddell

Pitcher (George Edward Waddell)
Born: October 13, 1876, Bradford, Pennsylvania
Died: April 1, 1914, San Antonia, Texas

Rube Waddell was the premier southpaw of the American League in the first decade of the twentieth century, and he was also one of the most colorful and eccentric characters to ever play the game of baseball.

After spending the period from 1897 to 1901 bouncing back and forth between the N.L. and the minor leagues, and running afoul of every manager he played for, Waddell finally caught on in the big leagues in 1902 when he joined Connie Mack's Philadelphia Athletics. That year he went 24-7 (the first of four straight 20 win seasons), and led the A.L. in strikeouts for the first of six straight seasons.

In 1904 Waddell struck out 349 batters, a major league record that stood until 1965 when it was broken by Sandy Koufax. His best season was in 1905 when he led the league with 26 wins, 287 strikeouts and a 1.48 ERA. He had a blazing fastball that compared favorably with that of Walter Johnson.

Waddell, always a fan favorite, was known to indulge in some rather odd behavior, both on, and off the field. Sometimes during exhibition games he would wave his teammates off the field and then strike out the side. And once during a regulation game (when he was required to have nine men on the field) he had his outfielders come in close and sit down on the grass and then proceeded to strike out the side.

Waddell drank heavily, seemed to spend every cent he made, was married three times and went to jail quite often for missing alimony payments, rocked team busses, wrestled alligators in Florida during the winter and held up the start of games he was scheduled to pitch while he played marbles with children outside the park.

He suffered an injury to his left shoulder while engaging in horseplay with teammate Andy Coakley in 1905 and was never quite the same pitcher again. This caused him to become increasingly unstable and violent, so much so that several teammates refused to show up for spring training in 1908 unless Mack got rid of him. So he was shipped off to the St. Louis Browns where he spent the next two and a half seasons. After the Browns released him in 1910, Waddell bounced around the minor leagues for several years.

In 1912 he became sort of a hero when he stood in deep icy water and piled sand bags on the embankments to help save the town of Hickman, Kentucky, from a flood. But the incident affected his health. He ended up in a sanitarium the following year and then died of tuberculosis in 1914 at the age of 37.

Rube Waddell was inducted into the National Baseball Hall of Fame in 1946.

Waddell, George Edward
BR/TL, 6'1.5", 196 lbs. Deb: 9/8/1897

YEAR	TM/L	W	L	PCT	G	IP	H	HR	BB	SO	ERA
1897	Lou-NL	0	1	.000	2	14	17	0	6	5	3.21
1899	Lou-NL	7	2	.778	10	79	69	4	14	44	3.08
1900	Pit-NL	8	13	.381	29	208.2	176	3	55	130	2.37
1901	Pit-NL	0	2	.000	2	7.2	10	0	9	4	9.39
	Chi-NL	14	14	.500	29	243.2	39	5	66	168	2.81
	Yr	14	16	.467	31	251.1	249	5	75	172	3.01
1902	Phi-AL	24	7	.774	33	276.1	224	7	64	210	2.05
1903	Phi-AL	21	16	.568	39	324	274	3	85	302	2.44
1904	Phi-AL	25	19	.568	46	383	307	5	91	349	1.62
1905	Phi-AL	27	10	.730	46	328.2	231	5	90	287	1.48
1906	Phi-AL	15	17	.469	43	272.2	221	1	92	196	2.21
1907	Phi-AL	19	13	.594	44	284.2	234	2	73	232	2.15
1908	StL-AL	19	14	.576	43	285.2	223	0	90	232	1.89
1909	StL-AL	11	14	.440	31	220.1	204	1	57	141	2.37
1910	StL-AL	3	1	.750	10	33	31	1	11	16	3.55
Total	13	193	143	.574	407	2,961.1	2,460	37	803	2,316	2.16

Honus Wagner

Infielder (John Peter Wagner)
Born: February 24, 1874, Mansfield, Pennsylvania
Died: December 6, 1955, Carnegie, Pennsylvania

The bowlegged, barrel-chested, long-limbed Wagner is still considered by baseball experts to have been the finest shortstop to have ever played the game. He had large hands and when he fielded grounders he also scooped up big chunks of dirt which would usually accompany the ball on the throw to first.

Wagner started his major league career in 1887 with the N.L.'s Louisville Colonels where he played various positions in both the infield and outfield. Wagner hit .338 that year, the first of 17 straight seasons in which he hit .300 or better. After the 1899 season the Louisville franchise was discontinued and Wagner was transferred to the Pittsburgh Pirates. At Pittsburgh in 1900 he hit .381 and won the first of his eight N.L. batting titles. In his 21-year career he would also lead the league in stolen bases five times, doubles eight times, and triples three times.

In 1903 Wagner finally became a full-time shortstop and won his second batting championship. The Pirates won the pennant that year and played Boston in the first modern-day World Series. Wagner only batted .222 in the eight-game Series, which was won by Boston. His only other World Series appearance was in 1909 when the Pirates faced the Detroit Tigers and the brash young Ty Cobb. In the second game Cobb taunted Wagner by calling him a "krauthead," so when Cobb came sliding into second base with his spikes up, Wagner cut his lip with a hard tag across the mouth. Cobb had to get three stitches, and from then on gave Wagner his everlasting respect.

Wagner was a model of good sportsmanship and clean living. His disdain for smoking caused him to object to a baseball card issued by Piedmont Cigarettes in 1910 that had his portrait on it. The card was withdrawn from the market and subsequently became the most prized baseball picture of all time. In 1990 hockey star Wayne Gretzky paid $451,000 for one copy of it.

In 1917, his final year as a player, Wagner was made manager of the Pirates. After four losses and one victory he decided he didn't like the job and quit. He came back to the Pirates as a coach in 1933 and stayed on in that capacity until 1951.

Honus Wagner was inducted into the National Baseball Hall of Fame in 1936.

Wagner, John Peter "The Flying Dutchman"
BR/TR, 5'11", 200 lbs. Deb: 7/19/1897

YEAR	TM/L	G	AB	R	H	2B	3B	HR	RBI	BB	SO	AVG
1897	Lou-NL	61	237	37	80	17	4	2	39	15	—	.338
1898	Lou-NL	151	588	80	176	29	3	10	105	31	—	.299
1899	Lou-NL	147	571	98	192	43	13	7	113	40	—	.336
1900	Pit-NL	135	527	107	201	45	22	4	100	41	—	.381
1901	Pit-NL	141	536	100	196	37	11	6	126	53	—	.353
1902	Pit-NL	137	538	105	177	30	16	3	91	43	—	.329
1903	Pit-NL	129	512	97	182	30	19	5	101	44	—	.355
1904	Pit-NL	132	490	97	171	44	14	4	75	59	—	.349
1905	Pit-NL	147	548	114	199	32	14	6	101	54	—	.363
1906	Pit-NL	142	516	103	175	38	9	2	71	58	—	.339
1907	Pit-NL	142	515	98	180	38	14	6	82	46	—	.350
1908	Pit-NL	151	568	100	201	39	19	10	109	54	—	.354
1909	Pit-NL	137	495	92	168	39	10	5	100	66	—	.339
1910	Pit-NL	150	556	90	178	34	8	4	81	59	47	.320
1911	Pit-NL	130	473	87	158	23	16	9	89	67	34	.334
1912	Pit-NL	145	558	91	181	35	20	7	102	59	38	.324
1913	Pit-NL	114	413	51	124	18	4	3	56	26	40	.300
1914	Pit-NL	150	552	60	139	15	9	1	50	51	51	.252
1915	Pit-NL	151	566	68	155	32	17	6	78	39	64	.274
1916	Pit-NL	123	432	45	124	15	9	1	39	34	36	.287
1917	Pit-NL	74	230	15	61	7	1	0	24	24	17	.265
Total	21	2,787	10,441	1,735	3,418	640	252	101	1,732	963	INC	.327

Fleet Walker

Catcher (Moses Fleetwood Walker)
Born: October 7, 1856, Mount Pleasant, Ohio
Died: May 11, 1924, Cleveland, Ohio

Who was the first black player in major league history? Jackie Robinson? No. In 1884 when the Toledo Blue Stockings moved up from the minor Northwestern League into the American Association, they brought Moses Fleetwood Walker, their regular catcher, with them.

Walker, who had faced racial prejudice throughout his minor league career, was generally well received in the Association cities, the exception being Louisville where he was hissed at on the field and attacked by a fan in the street after a game. He also had to face prejudice from his own teammates. Toledo's ace pitcher Tony Mulane later stated that Walker "was the best catcher I ever worked with, but I disliked a Negro and whenever I had to pitch to him I used to pitch anything I wanted without looking at his signals."

Walker played 42 games for the Blue Stockings that year, posting a .263 batting average. His brother Welday briefly joined him on the team and played five games in the outfield. A shoulder injury forced the team to release Fleet Walker in September. He spent the next five seasons in the minors, where he teamed up with pitching star George Stovey to form the first black battery in organized baseball for the International League's Newark Little Giants.

An incident in 1887, when Chicago White Stockings manager Cap Anson refused to allow his team to take the field against these two black players in an exhibition game, indirectly led to major league baseball adopting its infamous "color bar," which prohibited black players from competing at a major league level, a policy that lasted until 1947 when Jackie Robinson put on a Brooklyn Dodger uniform.

Walker was a well-educated man. He attended Oberlin College and the University of Michigan and in later life wrote a book entitled *Our Home Colony* which advocated black emigration to Africa as the best response to American racial intolerance.

Walker, Moses Fleetwood
BR/TR, 159 lbs. Deb: 5/1/1884 F

YEAR	TM/L	G	AB	R	H	2B	3B	HR	RBI	BB	SO	AVG
1884	Tol-AA	42	152	23	40	2	3	0	8	—	—	.263

Bobby Wallace

Infielder - Manager - Umpire (Roderick John Wallace)
Born: November 4, 1873, Pittsburgh, Pennsylvania
Died: November 3, 1960, Torrance, California

Bobby Wallace began his 25-year major league career as a pitcher with the N.L.'s Cleveland Spiders in 1894 and compiled a 24-22 record in three seasons. He moved over to third base in 1897 where he hit .335, and drove in 112 runs, both career highs. When the Cleveland franchise was moved to St. Louis in 1899 he moved to shortstop and remained at that position for the next 14 years.

Wallace, who only hit above .300 twice in his career, was considered to be one of the best shortstops in baseball due to his fielding skills, a category in which he often led the league. In fact, it was his defensive abilities that prompted the crosstown Browns to lure him away from the Cardinals in 1902 with a $32,000, five-year, no-trade contract — making him the highest-paid player in baseball at the time.

Wallace managed the Browns during the 1910 and 1911 seasons, compiling a dreadful 57-134 record and was grateful when he was relieved of the job so he could go back to playing full-time.

After injuries had forced him out of his regular job at shortstop, he interrupted his playing career in 1915 and 1916 to do a stint as an American League umpire. Wallace found umpiring not to his liking and returned to the Browns as a back-up for John Lavan, the man who had replaced him as shortstop. He finished up his playing days in 1918 with the Cardinals at the age of 44.

Later in life, he coached for the Cincinnati Reds briefly in 1927 and then spent the next 33 years scouting for the club.

Bobby Wallace was inducted into the National Baseball Hall of Fame in 1953.

Wallace, Roderick John
BR/TR, 5'8", 170 lbs. Deb: 9/15/1894

YEAR	TM/L	G	AB	R	H	2B	3B	HR	RBI	BB	SO	AVG
1894	Cle-NL	4	13	0	2	1	0	0	1	0	1	.154
1895	Cle-NL	30	98	16	21	2	3	0	10	6	17	.214
1896	Cle-NL	45	149	19	35	6	3	1	17	11	21	.235
1897	Cle-NL	130	516	99	173	33	21	4	112	48	—	.335
1898	Cle-NL	154	593	81	160	25	13	3	99	63	—	.270
1899	StL-NL	151	577	91	170	28	14	12	108	54	—	.295
1900	StL-NL	126	485	72	130	25	9	4	70	40	—	.268
1901	StL-NL	134	556	69	179	34	15	2	91	20	—	.322
1902	StL-AL	133	495	71	142	32	9	1	63	45	—	.287
1903	StL-AL	135	519	63	127	21	7	1	54	28	—	.245
1904	StL-AL	139	550	57	150	29	4	2	69	42	—	.273
1905	StL-AL	156	587	67	159	25	9	1	59	45	—	.271
1906	StL-AL	139	476	64	123	21	7	2	67	58	—	.258
1907	StL-AL	147	538	56	138	20	7	0	70	54	—	.257
1908	StL-AL	137	487	59	123	24	4	1	60	52	—	.253
1909	StL-AL	116	403	36	96	12	2	0	35	38	—	.238
1910	StL-AL	138	508	47	131	19	7	0	37	49	—	.258
1911	StL-AL	125	410	35	95	12	2	0	31	46	—	.232
1912	StL-AL	100	323	39	78	14	5	0	31	43	—	.241
1913	StL-AL	55	147	11	31	5	0	0	21	14	16	.211
1914	StL-AL	26	73	3	16	2	1	0	5	5	13	.219
1915	StL-AL	9	13	1	3	0	1	0	4	5	0	.231
1916	StL-AL	14	18	0	5	0	0	0	1	2	1	.278
1917	StL-NL	8	10	0	1	0	0	0	2	0	1	.100
1918	StL-NL	32	98	3	15	1	0	0	4	6	9	.153
Total	25	2,383	8,642	1,059	2,303	391	143	34	1,121	774	INC	.266

YEAR	TM/L	W	L	PCT	G	IP	H	HR	BB	SO	ERA
1894	Cle-NL	2	1	.667	4	26	28	1	20	10	5.19
1895	Cle-NL	12	14	.462	30	228.2	271	3	87	63	4.09
1896	Cle-NL	10	7	.588	22	145.1	167	2	49	46	3.34
1902	StL-AL	0	0	—	1	2	3	0	0	1	0.00
Total	4	24	22	.522	57	402	469	6	156	120	3.87

Ed Walsh

Pitcher (Edward Augustine Walsh)
Born: May 14, 1881, Plains, Pennsylvania
Died: May 26, 1959, Pompano Beach, Florida

Spitballer Ed Walsh was the pitching ace of the "Hitless Wonder" Chicago White Sox club of the early 1900's. Walsh had learned the pitch from roommate Elmer Stricklett when he first joined the club in 1904, but he didn't use it in a game until 1906, when he felt he had mastered it. That year he posted a 17-13 record, led the league in shutouts (10) and was the main reason why the White Sox won their first A.L. pennant and then went on to defeat the Cubs in the World Series.

The following year he went 24-18 and led the league in innings pitched (422) and ERA (1.60). But his finest year was in 1908 when workhorse Ed appeared in 66 of his club's 156 games and set a modern record of 464 innings pitched. He led the league in strikeouts with 269 while walking only 56, and his 40 wins that year are the most by a pitcher in the twentieth century. During a pressure-packed, three-way pennant race that fall, Walsh pitched a four hitter to Cleveland on October 2, only to lose 1-0 to Addie Joss, who just happened to throw a perfect game that day.

In 1909 Walsh's arm began to give out and he threw only half as many innings, posting a 15-11 record. He still retained his effectiveness with a 1.41 ERA and a league-leading eight shutouts.

Walsh bounced back during the next three seasons. He led the league with a 1.27 ERA in 1910, and then won 27 games in both 1911 and '12 while leading the league in innings pitched in both years as well. He threw the only no-hitter of his career on August 27, 1911, a 5-0 victory over Boston.

In 1913 he pitched less than 100 games and by 1916 his arm was completely dead. The White Sox released him at the end of the season. He tried to make a comeback with the Boston Braves in 1917 but failed. In 1922 Walsh worked as an umpire in the American League, but when that didn't work out, he went back to the White Sox and spent the next several years as a coach with the club.

Ed Walsh was inducted into the National Baseball Hall of Fame in 1946.

Walsh, Edward Augustine "Big Ed"
BR/TR, 6'1", 193 lbs. Deb: 5/7/04

YEAR	TM/L	W	L	PCT	G	IP	H	HR	BB	SO	ERA
1904	Chi-AL	6	3	.667	18	110.2	90	1	32	57	2.60
1905	Chi-AL	8	3	.727	22	136.2	121	0	29	71	2.17
1906	Chi-AL1	7	13	.567	41	278.1	215	1	58	171	1.88
1907	Chi-AL	24	18	.571	56	422.1	341	3	87	206	1.60
1908	Chi-AL	40	15	.727	66	464	343	2	56	269	1.42
1909	Chi-AL	15	11	.577	31	230.1	166	0	50	127	1.41
1910	Chi-AL	18	20	.474	45	369.2	242	5	61	258	1.27
1911	Chi-AL	27	18	.600	56	368.2	327	4	72	255	2.22
1912	Chi-AL	27	17	.614	62	393	332	6	94	254	2.15
1913	Chi-AL	8	3	.727	16	97.2	91	1	39	34	2.58
1914	Chi-AL	2	3	.400	8	44.2	33	0	20	15	2.82
1915	Chi-AL	3	0	1.000	3	27	19	0	7	12	1.33
1916	Chi-AL	0	1	.000	2	3.1	4	0	3	3	2.70
1917	Bos-NL	0	1	.000	4	18	22	0	9	4	3.50
Total	14	195	126	.607	430	2,964.1	2,346	23	617	1,736	1.82

John Montgomery Ward

Pitcher - Infielder
Born: March 3, 1860, Bellefonte, Pennsylvania
Died: March 4, 1925, Augusta, Georgia

John Montgomery Ward began his amazing career in baseball as a pitcher with the N.L.'s Providence Grays in 1878. As a 18-year-old rookie he pitched a four-hit shutout against Indianapolis in his first start, and then hurled a two-hit shutout against the same team two days later. That season he quickly established himself as the team's best pitcher when he compiled a 22-13 record and led the league with a 1.51 ERA.

The following season Ward won 47 games, led the league in strikeouts with 239 and helped the Grays win their first N.L. pennant. In 1880 he posted a 40-24 record and, on June 17 of that year, pitched the second perfect game in N.L. history, a 5-0 victory over Buffalo and Pud Galvin.

But it wasn't long before his pitching arm gave out and, after the 1882 season, Providence traded him to New York where he switched positions and soon established himself as one of the best shortstops in baseball. He was a solid hitter and a excellent basestealer (in 1887 he led the league with 111 steals). Ward helped the Giants win N.L. pennants in 1888 and '89.

In 1885 Ward, who had obtained a law degree by studying at night at Columbia Law College, became president of baseball's first labor organization, the National Brotherhood of Base Ball Players. The organization was born out of player frustration with limited salaries, unjust fines and the reserve clause (which virtually bound a player to the same team for life).

After a number of clashes with major league brass over the next several years, Ward led the Brotherhood in open revolution at the end of the 1889 season, and this resulted in the formation of the Players League in 1890. Over 100 major league players jumped to new league. Ward became manager and part owner of the Brooklyn entry. He also played shortstop for the club.

When the Players League folded at the end of the year, Ward went back to the N.L. He managed and played for the Brooklyn team in 1891 and '92 and then rejoined the Giants in '93 as shortstop and manager. Ward led the Giants to a second-place finish in 1894, which was followed by a four-game sweep of the first place Baltimore Orioles in the first Temple Cup series.

After that season, Ward, who was only 34 at the time, left baseball to pursue a profitable law career. He returned to baseball twice: as president of the Boston Braves in 1911, and as business manager of the Federal League's Brooklyn Tip-Tops in 1914.

John Montgomery Ward was inducted into the National Baseball Hall of Fame in 1964.

Ward, John Montgomery
BL/TR, 5'9", 165 lbs. Deb: 7/15/1878

YEAR	TM/L	G	AB	R	H	2B	3B	HR	RBI	BB	SO	AVG
1878	Pro-NL	37	138	14	27	5	4	1	15	2	13	.196
1879	Pro-NL	83	364	71	104	9	4	2	41	7	14	.286
1880	Pro-NL	86	356	53	81	12	2	0	27	6	16	.228
1881	Pro-NL	85	357	56	87	18	6	0	53	5	10	.244
1882	Pro-NL	83	355	58	87	10	3	1	39	13	22	.245
1883	NY-NL	88	380	76	97	18	7	7	54	8	25	.255
1884	NY-NL	113	482	98	122	11	8	2	51	28	47	.253
1885	NY-NL	111	446	72	101	8	9	0	37	17	39	.226
1886	NY-NL	122	491	82	134	17	5	2	81	19	46	.273
1887	NY-NL	129	545	114	184	16	5	1	53	29	12	.338
1888	NY-NL	122	510	70	128	14	5	2	49	9	13	.251
1889	NY-NL	114	479	87	143	13	4	1	67	27	7	.299
1890	Bro-PL	128	561	134	189	15	12	4	60	51	22	.337
1891	Bro-NL	105	441	85	122	13	5	0	39	36	10	.277
1892	Bro-NL	148	614	109	163	13	3	1	47	82	19	.265
1893	NY-NL	135	588	129	193	27	9	2	77	47	5	.328
1894	NY-NL	136	540	100	143	12	5	0	77	34	6	.265
Total	17	1,825	7,647	1,408	2,105	231	96	26	867	420	326	.275

Mickey Welch

Pitcher (Michael Francis Welch)
Born: July 4, 1859, Brooklyn, New York
Died: July 30, 1941, Concord, New Hampshire

E. W. BOGARDUS,   349 SIXTH AVE, N. Y.

Mickey Welch began his 13-year major league career with the N.L.'s Troy Trojans in 1880 and posted a 34-30 record that year. He and Tim Keefe teamed up to become co-aces of the club's pitching staff for most of the next decade. The diminutive Welch, who stood 5'8" and weighed 160 lbs., had a good curveball, a change of pace and a screwball (a pitch it is believed he invented).

On July 4, 1881, the durable righthander pitched two complete game victories over Buffalo on the same day. He posted a 21-18 record that year, the second of nine 20 or more win seasons that he would record in his career, seven of them in a row.

In 1883 the franchise was moved to New York City and Welch had the honor of pitching the first game his club played at the original Polo Grounds, which was located at Fifth Avenue and 110th St. The next season the club's name was changed from the Gothams to the Giants. Welch struck out the first nine batters he faced in a game against Cleveland on August 28, 1884, a major league record that still stands. Also that year, Welch pitched 557 innings, won 39 games, completed 62 of 65 starts and had a career high 345 strikeouts.

His finest year came in 1885 when he won 17 consecutive games, threw seven shutouts, struck out 256 batters and posted a 44-11 record and a 1.66 ERA. In 1888 he helped pitch the Giants to their first N.L. pennant with a 26-19 record. He split two decisions in that year's version of the World Series, in which the Giants beat the St. Louis Browns six games out of ten.

The Giants repeated as N.L. champions the following year, with Welch posting a 27-12 record. He lost his only decision in the World Series, but the Giants nevertheless beat the Brooklyn Bridegrooms six games to three.

Welch spent three more years with the Giants and retired from baseball in 1892 with 307 wins under his belt, to become baseball's third 300 game winner.

When asked the secret of his pitching success, "Smiling Mickey" always attributed it to drinking beer. He even wrote a little poem on the subject:

Pure elixir of malt and hops
Beats all the drugs and all the drops

Mickey Welch was inducted into the National Baseball Hall of Fame in 1973.

Welch, Michael Francis "Smiling Mickey"
BR/TR, 5'8", 160 lbs. Deb: 5/1/1880

YEAR	TM/L	W	L	PCT	G	IP	H	HR	BB	SO	ERA
1880	Tro-NL	34	30	.531	65	574	575	7	80	123	2.54
1881	Tro-NL	21	18	.538	40	368	371	7	78	104	2.67
1882	Tro-NL	14	16	.467	33	281	334	7	62	53	3.46
1883	NY-NL	25	23	.521	54	426	431	11	66	144	2.73
1884	NY-NL	39	21	.650	65	557.1	528	12	146	345	2.50
1885	NY-NL	44	11	.800	56	492	372	4	131	258	1.66
1886	NY-NL	33	22	.600	59	500	514	13	163	272	2.99
1887	NY-NL	22	15	.595	40	346	339	7	91	115	3.36
1888	NY-NL	26	19	.578	47	425.1	328	12	108	167	1.93
1889	NY-NL	27	12	.692	45	375	340	14	149	125	3.02
1890	NY-NL	17	14	.548	37	292.1	268	5	122	97	2.99
1891	NY-NL	5	9	.357	22	160	176	7	97	46	4.27
1892	NY-NL	0	0	—	1	5	11	0	4	1	14.40
Total	13	307	210	.594	564	4,802	4,587	106	1,297	1,850	2.71

Deacon White

Catcher - Infielder (James Laurie White)
Born: December 7, 1847, Canton, New York
Died: July 7, 1939, Aurora, Illinois

When Deacon White stepped up to the plate for the Cleveland Forest Citys on May 4, 1871, he was the first batter in the first game ever played in the first professional baseball league, (the National Association) and he got a double, to give him the first hit. White played in the N.A. for all of the five seasons that it existed, the last three with Harry Wright's powerful Boston Red Stockings club. At Boston, catcher White joined pitcher Al Spalding, first baseman Cal McVey and second baseman Ross Barnes to form baseball's first Big Four.

The defection of the Big Four to Chicago in 1876 was one of the reasons why the N.A. folded and the National League began. It was also a main reason why Chicago won the first N.L. pennant that year. White returned to Boston the following season to help that city's new N.L. club win the 1877 pennant, and he led the league with a .387 batting average.

He moved on to Cincinnati in 1878 and teamed up with his pitcher-brother Will to form baseball's first sibling battery. In 1881 he and Will joined the Buffalo Bisons, and Deacon, along with first baseman Dan Brouthers, second baseman Hardy Richardson and shortstop Jack Rowe, formed baseball's second Big Four.

Deacon, who got his nickname because he was in fact, a nondrinking, nonsmoking, bible-toting church official, was the best barehanded catcher of his time. He was one of the first catchers to move up and play direct-ly behind the batter, and is credited with inventing the chest protector for catchers in the early 1880's.

When the Buffalo franchise folded at the end of the 1885 season the Big Four were sent to the Detroit Wolverines, where they joined future Hall of Famers Ned Hanlon and Big Sam Thompson to give the Detroit club its one and only N.L. pennant in 1887. That autumn the Wolverines went on to wallop Chris Von der Ahe's St. Louis Browns ten games to five in baseball's longest World Series, which was played in ten different cities.

In 1890 White went back to play in Buffalo, this time as part owner of the Players League franchise. When the league, and the team, folded at the end of the year, White, who had spent the last 20 years playing pro-fessional baseball, retired at the age of 42.

White, James Laurie
BL/TR, 5'11", 175 lbs. Deb: 5/4/1871

YEAR	TM/L	G	AB	R	H	2B	3B	HR	RBI	BB	SO	AVG
1871	Cle-NA	29	146	40	47	6	5	1	21	4	1	.322
1872	Cle-NA	22	108	21	37	3	2	0	22	4	1	.343
1873	Bos-NA	60	310	79	121	20	8	0	64	0	2	.390
1874	Bos-NA	70	350	75	106	4	7	3	—	4	—	.303
1875	Bos-NA	80	372	77	136	20	4	1	—	2	—	.366
Total	5 n	261	1,286	292	447	53	26	5	INC	14	INC	.348
1876	Chi-NL	66	303	66	104	18	1	1	60	7	3	.343
1877	Bos-NL	59	266	51	103	14	11	2	49	8	3	.387
1878	Cin-NL	61	258	41	81	4	1	0	29	10	5	.314
1879	Cin-NL	78	333	55	110	16	6	1	52	6	9	.330
1880	Cin-NL	35	141	21	42	4	2	0	7	9	7	.298
1881	Buf-NL	78	319	58	99	24	4	0	53	9	8	.310
1882	Buf-NL	83	337	51	95	17	0	1	33	15	16	.282
1883	Buf-NL	94	391	62	114	14	5	0	47	23	18	.292
1884	Buf-NL	110	452	82	147	16	11	5	74	32	13	.325
1885	Buf-NL	98	404	54	118	6	6	0	57	12	11	.292
1886	Det-NL	124	491	65	142	19	5	1	76	31	35	.289
1887	Det-NL	111	449	71	136	20	11	3	75	26	15	.303
1888	Det-NL	125	527	75	157	22	5	4	71	21	24	.298
1889	Pit-NL	55	225	35	57	10	1	0	26	16	18	.253
1890	Buf-PL	122	439	62	114	13	4	0	47	67	30	.260
Total	15	1,299	5,335	849	1,619	217	73	18	756	292	215	.303

George Wright

Infielder
Born: January 28, 1847, Yonkers, New York
Died: August 21, 1937, Boston, Massachusetts

Seventeen-year-old George Wright played his first game of organized baseball in 1864 when he joined the Gotham Club of New York. During the next few years he played shortstop for such early "amateur" clubs as the Philadelphia Olympics, the Union Club of Morrisania, N.Y., and the Washington Nationals. By 1868 George had established a reputation as the best shortstop in baseball and was named to the nation's first all-star team by writer Henry Chadwick.

In 1869, when his brother Harry formed the the first truly professional team, the Cincinnati Red Stockings, George joined the club for a salary of $1,400, which was the highest on the team. The Red Stockings barnstormed all across the country that year, and carried a 79-game undefeated streak into the middle of the following summer.

When the Red Stockings broke up at the end of the year, the Wright brothers went to Boston to form a new entry in baseball's first professional league, the National Association. The club, which was called the Boston Red Stockings, won the N.A. pennant four out of the five years that the league existed. The team was so dominant that in 1875, the league's last year, they had a record of 71-8. Harry was the manager and George played shortstop. George hit .412 in 1871 and then hit better than .300 during the next four seasons.

When the National League was formed in 1876, Harry's club became part of the new venture. George was the first batter in National League history. He led off in the League opener at Philadelphia on April 22, and grounded out. Although Boston only managed a fourth-place finish that year, they then went on to win N.L. pennants in both 1877 and '78, giving Harry and George six championship teams in seven years.

In 1879 George left the Boston club to play for and manage the Providence Grays. In a hotly contested pennant race, George piloted the Grays to a first-place finish, beating out Harry's club by five games.

George retired from playing in 1882 to form his own sporting goods company. He reemerged in 1884 as president of the Boston Reds of the Union Association. Among his other achievements, George is said to be the first person to play a game of golf in the United States. Later in life he was named to (but never actually served on) the Mills Commission, which came up with the ridiculous story that Abner Doubleday invented baseball.

George Wright was inducted into the National Baseball Hall of Fame in 1937.

Wright, George
BR/TR, 5'9.5", 150 lbs. Deb: 5/5/1871

YEAR	TM/L	G	AB	R	H	2B	3B	HR	RBI	BB	SO	AVG
1876	Bos-NL	70	335	72	100	18	6	1	34	8	9	.299
1877	Bos-NL	61	290	58	80	15	1	0	35	9	15	.276
1878	Bos-NL	59	267	35	60	5	1	0	12	6	22	.225
1879	Pro-NL	85	388	79	107	15	10	1	42	13	20	.276
1880	Bos-NL	1	4	2	1	0	0	0	0	0	0	.250
1881	Bos-NL	7	25	4	5	0	0	0	0	3	1	.200
1882	Pro-NL	46	185	14	30	1	2	0	9	4	—	36	.162
Total	7	329	1,494	264	383	54	20	2	132	43	103	.256

YEAR	TM/L	W	L	PCT	G	IP	H	HR	BB	SO	ERA
1875	Bos-NA	0	1	.000	2	4	5	0	0	11.3	.263
1876	Bos-NL	0	0	—	1	1	1	0	0	9.0	0.00

Harry Wright

Outfielder - Manager (William Henry Wright)
Born: January 10, 1835, Sheffield, England
Died: October 3, 1895, Atlantic City, New Jersey

English-born Harry Wright, a professional cricket player and a jeweler by trade, joined the Knickerbocker Base Ball Club in 1858 as an outfielder. He had developed a love of this new game that the Knickerbockers had invented by watching them play at Elysian Fields in Hoboken. Harry, who excelled in organization and instruction, soon abandoned cricket and devoted most of his time to baseball. In 1867 he formed the Cincinnati Red Stockings Base Ball Club. It started out as an amateur team, but he soon turned it into the first openly professional baseball club.

Harry hired top players from all over the country, including his younger brother George who was an all-star shortstop in New Jersey. The Red Stockings barnstormed all across the country that year, and had a 79-game undefeated streak going when they were finally defeated by the Brooklyn Atlantics the following summer.

When the Cincinnati team broke up at the end of the year, Harry packed up the bright red stockings that the team had worn and moved to Boston where he formed the Boston Red Stockings. In 1871 the club became part of baseball's first professional league, the National Association. With Harry as manager and George playing shortstop, the powerful Red Stockings won the N.A. pennant four out of the five years that the league existed.

Following the 1874 season Harry, and his star pitcher Al Spalding, embarked on a baseball tour of England, where they demonstrated this new American sport and engaged in the odd game of cricket.

When the N.A. folded after the 1875 season and was replaced by the National League, Nathaniel T. Apollonio was awarded the Boston franchise. Harry was named manager and George remained with him as shortstop.

The Boston Red Caps, as they were called, only managed a fourth-place finish in the league's initial season, but they then went on to win N.L. pennants in both 1877 and '78, giving Harry and George six championship teams in seven years.

Harry Wright was the first manager to employ coach's signals. Though he never berated his players and seldom argued with umpires, he nevertheless became so proficient at heckling opponents that the league considered adopting a rule in 1877 that would prohibit managers from sitting on the bench, just so they could get rid of him.

Wright left Boston in 1882 to manage the Providence Grays for a couple of seasons and then began a 10-year stint with Philadelphia. In the city of brotherly love, the closest he came to another pennant was a second-place finish in 1887. Harry retired in 1893 after managing professional baseball clubs for 23 years. The league created the position of chief of umpires for him, and he served in this post until his death in 1895.

Harry Wright was inducted into the National Baseball Hall of Fame in 1953.

Wright, William Henry
BR/TR, 5'9.5", 157 lbs. Deb: 5/5/1871

YEAR	TM/L	G	AB	R	H	2B	3B	HR	RBI	BB	SO	AVG
1871	Bos-NA	31	147	42	44	5	2	0	26	13	2	.299
1872	Bos-NA	48	208	39	54	6	0	0	22	9	2	.260
1873	Bos-NA	58	266	57	67	8	3	2	33	10	3	.252
1874	Bos-NA	40	184	44	56	9	2	2		4		.304
1875	Bos-NA	1	4	1	1	0	0	0		0		.250
Total	5 NA	178	809	183	222	28	7	4	81	36	7	.274
1876	Bos-NL	1	3	0	0	0	0	0	0	0	1	.000
1877	Bos-NL	1	4	0	0	0	0	0	0	0	1	.000
Total	2	2	7	0	0	0	0	0	0	0	2	.000

Cy Young

Pitcher (Denton True Young)
Born: March 29, 1867, Gilmore, Ohio
Died: November 4, 1955, Newcomerstown, Ohio

He is the winningest pitcher in baseball history, and each year the best pitcher in both the American and National leagues receives an award in his honor. Denton True "Cy" Young holds the major league record for most wins (511), most losses (316), most starts (815), most complete games (749), most innings pitched (7,354) — over a 22-year career in which he averaged 23 wins per season.

The strapping 6'2", 210 lb. farm boy from Gilmore, Ohio, got his nickname while pitching for Canton in the Tri-State league in 1890, his first professional season. One day, some of his pregame pitches splintered an outfield fence causing someone to remark, "It looks like a cyclone hit the fence," so they started calling him Cyclone, which was later shortened to Cy.

Later on that year the National League's Cleveland Spiders bought his contract. In Young's first full major league season (1891) he won 27 games and, while usually pitching after two days' rest and frequently after one (which was how they did it in those days), he won 20 or more games per year in his next eight consecutive seasons.

In 1883 Young won 36 games and lost only 12, giving him a league-leading .750 winning percentage. His ERA was 1.93. In the 1895 season he led the Spiders to victory over Baltimore in the post-season Temple Cup series, allowing the Orioles only seven runs in the three complete game victories that he pitched, as Cleveland took the best of seven series four games to one.

He pitched his first of three no-hitters in 1897 (a 6-0 victory over Cincinnati). After playing the 1899 and 1900 seasons for St. Louis (for the league maximum salary of $2,400 per year), the 33-year-old Young jumped to Boston in the brand new American League in 1901 (for $3,000 per year) and led the league in wins in its first three seasons with 33, 32 and 28 victories.

In 1903 Young's two wins helped Boston defeat Pittsburgh (5 games to 3) in the first modern-day World Series. In 1904 his perfect game 3-0 victory over Philadelphia is considered by many to be the finest game of his career. He threw his third no-hitter in 1908 (defeating New York 8-0).

Cy Young was inducted into the Baseball Hall of Fame in 1937.

Young, Denton True
BR/TR, 6'2", 210 lbs. Deb: 8/6/1890

YEAR	TM/L	W	L	PCT	G	IP	H	HR	BB	SO	ERA
1890	Cle-NL	9	7	.563	17	147.2	145	6	30	39	3.47
1891	Cle-NL	27	22	.551	55	423.2	431	4	140	147	2.85
1892	Cle-NL	36	12	.750	53	453	363	8	118	168	1.93
1893	Cle-NL	34	16	.680	53	422.2	442	10	103	102	3.36
1894	Cle-NL	26	21	.553	52	408.2	488	19	106	108	3.94
1895	Cle-NL	35	10	.778	47	369.2	363	10	75	121	3.26
1896	Cle-NL	28	15	.651	51	414.1	477	7	62	140	3.24
1897	Cle-NL	21	19	.525	46	333.2	391	7	49	88	3.80
1898	Cle-NL	25	13	.658	46	377.2	387	6	41	101	2.53
1899	StL-NL	26	16	.619	44	369.1	368	10	44	111	2.58
1900	StL-NL	19	19	.500	41	321.1	337	7	36	115	3.00
1901	Bos-AL	33	10	.767	43	371.1	324	6	37	158	1.62
1902	Bos-AL	32	11	.744	45	384.2	350	6	53	160	2.15
1903	Bos-AL	28	9	.757	40	341.2	294	6	37	176	2.08
1904	Bos-AL	26	16	.619	43	380	327	6	29	200	1.97
1905	Bos-AL	18	19	.486	38	320.2	248	3	30	210	1.82
1906	Bos-AL	13	21	.382	39	287.2	288	3	25	140	3.19
1907	Bos-AL	21	15	.583	43	343.1	286	3	51	147	1.99
1908	Bos-AL	21	11	.656	36	299	230	1	37	150	1.26
1909	Cle-AL	19	15	.559	35	295	267	4	59	109	2.26
1910	Cle-AL	7	10	.412	21	163.1	149	0	27	58	2.53
1911	Cle-AL	3	4	.429	7	46.1	54	2	13	20	3.88
	Bos-NL	4	5	.444	11	80	83	4	15	35	3.71
Total	22	511	316	.618	906	7,354.2	7,092	138	1,217	2,803	2.63

Team Histories

Altoona Mountain Citys

Union Association - 1884
Record 6-19

The Mountain Citys were only around for the first month of the Union Association's one year of existence. Altoona, Pennsylvania, with a population of 25,000 in 1884, was the smallest city in major league history. After opening the season in Cincinnati and losing their first 11 games on the road, the under-funded Mountain Citys came home to find that they were averaging a mere 1,000 fans per game. Soon, the club owners could not meet the payroll and the team folded on May 29. League president Henry V. Lucas promptly moved the franchise to Kansas City.

Baltimore Monumentals

Union Association - 1884
Record 58 - 47

Despite the best of intentions, a third-place finish and a winning record, the Monumentals were not able to compete with the American Association's Baltimore Orioles for fans in 1884. The Monumentals and the Union Association folded at the end of the year.

Baltimore Orioles

American Association - 1882 - 1891, Record - 490-601

National League - 1892 - 1899, Record - 644-447

American League - 1901 - 1902, Record - 118-153

The original Baltimore Orioles were charter members of the American Association when it was founded in 1882. In its 10 years in the A.A. the club usually floundered in the league's basement, never finishing better than third. The Orioles actually dropped out of the Association in 1890 after a dispute with league management. They played in the minor Atlantic Association for half a season and then rejoined the A.A. when the Brooklyn Gladiators folded in late August.

When the A.A. went out of business after the 1891 season, the Orioles were absorbed by the National League. In 1892, their first season in the N.L., they finished dead last. Towards the end of the season Ned Hanlon was hired to manage the club, and under his guidance the Orioles became the pre-eminent baseball club of the 1890's.

The legendary Orioles featured such future Hall of Famers as third baseman John McGraw, shortstop Hugh Jennings and outfielders Joe Kelly and Wee Willie "Hit 'em where they ain't" Keeler.

The Orioles played in four straight Temple Cup World Series from 1894 to 1897. Renowned for the "Old Oriole Spirit" which impelled men to ignore injuries and keep on playing, the feisty Orioles made baseball into a real team sport, specializing in in relays and cut-offs — and pioneering the hit and run. They were known as baseball's first "greatest team of all time."

At the end of the 1899 season the National League decided to cut back to eight clubs. The Baltimore Orioles were one of the four teams that were dropped. But two years later, when the American League was formed, the Orioles were reborn. The first manager of the A.L. Orioles was John McGraw who had a brand-new, 8,500-seat, steel and concrete ballpark constructed for the club on the site of the old A.A. ballpark. The Orioles raided the N.L. for such players as catcher Roger Bresnahan, outfielder Cy Seymour and pitcher Joe McGinnity.

But the A.L. Orioles were not a success, either on the field or financially, and the club only lasted for two years. They finished the 1901 season in fifth place and then ended the 1902 season dead last, some 34 games behind the Philadelphia A's.

The franchise was then moved to New York City for the 1903 season where it would become known as the Highlanders, and later the Yankees.

1899 Baltimore Orioles

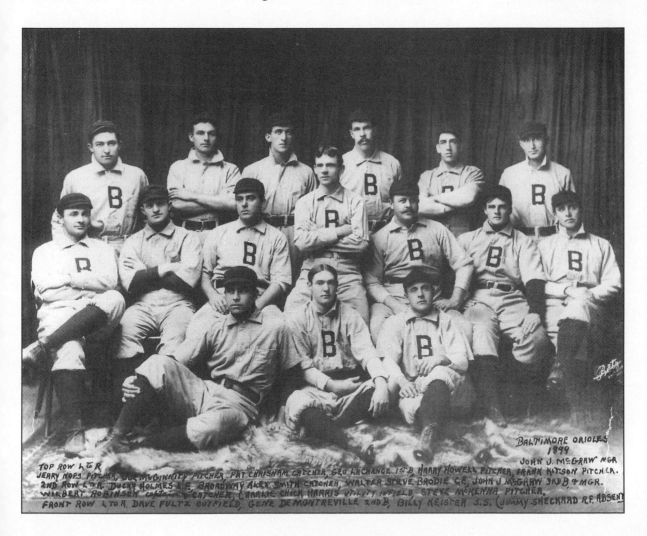

BALTIMORE ORIOLES
1899
JOHN J. McGRAW MGR

TOP ROW L TO R
JERRY NOPS PITCHER, JOE McGINNITY PITCHER, PAT CRISHAM CATCHER, GEO LACHANCE 1st B, HARRY HOWELL PITCHER, FRANK KITSON PITCHER.
2ND ROW L TO R DUCKY HOLMES L.F. BROADWAY ALEX SMITH CATCHER, WALTER STEVE BRODIE C.F. JOHN J. McGRAW 3RD B & MGR.
WILBERT ROBINSON CAPTAIN & CATCHER, CHARLIE CHICK HARRIS UTILITY INFIELD STEVE McKENNA PITCHER,
FRONT ROW L TO R. DAVE FULTZ OUTFIELD, GENE DEMONTREVILLE 2ND B, BILLY KEISTER S.S. (JIMMY SHECKARD R.F. ABSENT)

Baltimore Terrapins

Federal League - 1914 - 1915
Record - 131-177

When the Terrapins began play in the Federal League in 1914 they drew 28,000 fans into their brand-new stadium on opening day and beat the Buffalo Blues 3-2. The club, behind the pitching of Jack Quinn (26-14) and George Suggs (24-14), then went on to notch a 84-70 record that season and finish third in the standings, and the club owners made a profit of $9,000.

Things were different the next season though; the pitching fell apart and the hitting was almost non-existent (the club had the highest ERA and the lowest batting average in the league). The Terrapins finished in last place, 40 games behind league-leading Chicago, and lost $75,000. Both the club and the league folded at the end of the year.

Boston National League Franchise

Nicknamed: Red Caps (1876-82), Beaneaters (1883-1906),
Doves (1907-10), Rustlers (1911), Braves (1912-52)
Record (1876-1919) - 2873 - 2795

On April 22, 1876, the Boston Red Caps won the first National League game ever played, defeating the Philadelphia Athletics 6-5 at Philadelphia. The Red Caps were a continuation of the Boston Red Stocking franchise that so totally dominated the recently departed National Association (from 1871-75 the club had a 205-50 record and won four out of five N.A. pennants).

After finishing in fourth place, some 15 games behind Chicago in the league's first year, the club rebounded to win two straight N.L. pennants in '77 and '78, behind the pitching of Tommy Bond, who won 40 games in both seasons.

When shortstop George Wright and outfielder Jim O'Rourke defected to the Providence Grays after the '78 season ended, Boston owner Arthur Soden was inspired to invent the infamous reserve clause, which virtually bound a player to the same team for life. It was first instituted in 1880 and soon became a standard part of all N.L. player contracts.

In the 1880's the club won one pennant (in '83) and finished second twice. In 1887 the Beaneaters shocked the baseball world by acquiring superstar slugger Mike "King" Kelly from Chicago for an unprecedented $10,000. Though he never won a pennant for the club, the colorful Kelly became the most popular player in the franchise's history. The hard-drinking Irishman, who was as famous for his off-the-field antics as he was for his baseball

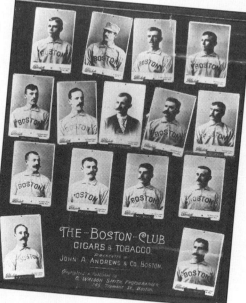

1889 Boston Beaneaters

1908 Boston Doves

achievements, only played for the club for three years before jumping to the ill-fated Players League in 1890.

The 1890's were the most successful decade in the franchise's history. The club won five pennants during this period, mainly due to the outstanding pitching of Kid Nichols and Jack Stivetts, the booming bats of outfielders Hugh Duffy and Tommy McCarthey and the managerial genius of Frank Selee.

The club then went into a tailspin in the first two decades of the twentieth century, managing to come in first only once. That occasion was in 1914 when they were dubbed the "Miracle Braves" after staging one of the most incredible comebacks in baseball history. After finding themselves in last place, some 15 games behind the Giants at the start of July, the Braves then won 52 of their last 66 games to catapult themselves into first place on September 8 and walk off with the pennant at the end of the season.

1914 Boston Braves

Boston Red Sox

American League - 1901 - Present
Record (1901-1919) - 1548 - 1258

1903 Boston Red Sox

When the Boston Red Sox started out in 1901 as one of the original franchises in the brand-new American League they were called the Somersets, in honor of team owner Charles Somers. At various times during the next few years, the club would be known as the Puritans, Pilgrims, Plymouth Rocks and Americans. It wasn't until 1907 that Red Sox was finally adopted for the team nickname.

Among the National League players that jumped over to the Somersets in their first season were two future Hall of Famers: pitcher Cy Young and infielder Jimmy Collins, who departed the crosstown rival Beaneaters to manage the new club. After finishing second in 1901 and third in 1902, the club won the A.L. pennant in 1903 and then went on to win the first

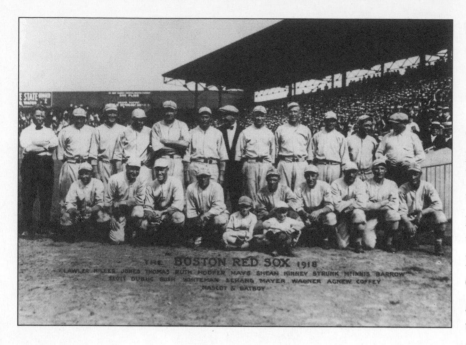

THE BOSTON RED SOX 1918

1918 Boston Red Sox

modern-day World Series, defeating the Pittsburgh Pirates five games to three in a best of nine affair.

The Red Sox would eventually win five more pennants and four more World championships in their first two decades of play. The 1912 series, in which they edged John McGraw's Giants and Christy Mathewson four games to three (with one tie), is said to be one of the most exciting series ever played. This was the series in which Giants outfielder Fred Snodgrass committed the famous "$30,000 muff," dropping a routine fly ball in the tenth inning of the final game to help turn a narrow Giant lead into a Boston world championship.

In 1914 the Red Sox signed a young pitcher by the name of Babe Ruth. He soon blossomed into one of the best hurlers in the league, but his ability to handle the bat soon caught the Red Sox management's eye and they gradually moved him into the outfield. In 1918 Ruth's 66 RBI was third best in the league, and when he walloped a league-leading 29 homers the following season his career as a pitcher was over.

After the 1919 season, cash-strapped Boston owner Harry Frazee sold Ruth to the Yankees for $100,000 and a $300,000 mortgage on Fenway Park ... and the rest, as they say, is history. While Ruth was helping to create a Yankee dynasty in New York, the Red Sox embarked on a 15-year journey into baseball oblivion, never playing above .500 or finishing better than fifth until 1934.

Boston Reds

Union Association - 1884, Record 58-51

Players League - 1890, Record 81-48

American Association - 1891, Record 93-42

In the 1880's and '90's Boston had three baseball clubs named the Reds, and each one only lasted for one season. The first Reds played in the ill-fated Union Association in 1884, its only year of existence. Despite finishing the season with a winning record, the club ended up in fourth place, some 34 games behind the pennant-winning St. Louis Maroons. The next Reds came along in 1890 as part of another league that only lasted one year, the Players League.

King Kelly, Boston's most popular player of the era and baseball's first superstar, jumped to the Reds from the Beaneaters, and managed the club

1890 Boston Players League

to the Players League's only pennant. Kelly hit .326 and played shortstop, catcher and the outfield. The defection of Kelly and other top players of the day gave the league instant credibility. Joining Kelly on the Reds were fellow future Hall of Famers first baseman Dan Brouthers (who hit .300) and pitcher Charles "Old Hoss" Radbourn (who went 27-12). Towards the end of the season Kelly was offered $10,000 by Al Spalding to return to the N.L. Kelly reluctantly turned the offer down, only to see the Players League fold a short while later.

When the P.L. collapsed the Reds were transferred to the American Association by club owner Charles A. Prince for the 1891 season. The A.A. Reds weren't able to hold on to Kelly, but did keep Brouthers (who led the A.A. with a .350 batting average) and added right fielder Hugh Duffy (who hit .336). The Reds won the 1891 A.A. pennant by 8.5 games, but couldn't compete at the box office with the N.L.'s Beaneaters, who managed to get Kelly back near the end of the season. When the A.A. amalgamated with the N.L. at the end of the year, the Reds were dissolved.

Brooklyn Dodgers

National League - 1890 - 1957

Record (1890-1919) - 2067 - 2240

1890 Brooklyn Ball Club

When the Brooklyn Bridegrooms transferred from the American Association to the National League in 1890, they managed to keep almost all of their players, even though most N.L. teams suffered mass defections to the Players League that year. This was mainly due to the fact that club owner Charles Byrne paid the highest salaries in the major leagues.

The Bridegrooms won the N.L. pennant that year and went on to meet Louisville in a World Series that was called off due to bad weather and poor attendance after both clubs had won three games and tied one.

The Bridegrooms did not win another pennant until 1899 when Baltimore owners Harry Von der Horst and Ned Hanlon bought half interest in the club and moved such Oriole stars as Hughie Jennings, Joe Kelly,

Wee Willie Keeler, Jim Hughes and Doc McJames into the Brooklyn line-up. They also changed the name of the club to the Superbas.

During the following winter the N.L. dropped four of its clubs including Baltimore, causing even more Orioles to migrate to the Superbas, pitcher Joe "Iron Man" McGinnity among them. Once again Brooklyn won the pennant. They then went on to win their first world championship, defeating Pittsburgh three games to one in the Chronicle-Telegraph Cup Series.

The club spent most of the next decade and a half in the second division and didn't win another pennant until 1916. During this period Charles Ebbets, who had risen from a ticket seller to become president and owner of the club, had renamed the team the Dodgers (in 1911 in honor of the original Trolley Dodger franchise) and built them a brand new stadium to play in, the legendary Ebbets Field, which opened in 1913.

In 1914 the club went through another name change when they were renamed the Robins in honor of manager Wilbert Robinson, who was a great favorite of the fans (the club would keep this nickname until Robinson retired in 1931, and then they became the Dodgers once again).

After their 1916 pennant win the club met Boston in a World Series in which they lost to the Red Sox four games to one. The Robins won their next pennant in 1920, and lost that World Series to the Indians five games to two. Brooklyn would not win another pennant for more than 20 years.

1916 Brooklyn Dodgers

308

Brooklyn Gladiators

American Association - 1890
Record 26 - 73

The Brooklyn Gladiators were a rag-tag group of nobodies that was hastily thrown together to combat the defection of the Bridegrooms to the National League. The club (which didn't even play its home games in Brooklyn — they played in two different parks in Queens) had a hard time competing with the Bridegrooms and the Brooklyn Wonders of the Players League for fans. The Gladiators didn't even finish out the season. The club was disbanded on August 25 and the franchise was moved to Baltimore, where it became the Orioles.

Brooklyn Hartfords

National League - 1877

Record 31 - 27

In 1877, the National League's second year of existence, Hartford Dark Blues owner Morgan G. Bulkeley became the first N.L. owner to shift a franchise from one city to another when he moved his club to Brooklyn. Although the team had done well on the field in Hartford (with a 47-21 record) they hadn't fared well at the box office.

Unfortunately they didn't do much better when they got to Brooklyn. Despite a winning record, the Hartfords of Brooklyn (as they were known) weren't able to replace the recently departed New York Mutuals in the hearts and minds of local baseball fans. Bulkeley lost $2,500 on the venture and disbanded the club at the end of the year.

Brooklyn Tip-Tops

Federal League - 1914 - 1915
Record 147-159

Brooklyn Tip-Tops owner Robert B. Ward built a brand new steel and concrete stadium for his club to play in when the Federal League season opened in 1914. Although 15,000 fans showed up at Washington Park for opening day, the Tip-Tops could not compete with the cross-town rival Dodgers and suffered from poor attendance for most of the season.

In 1914 John Montgomery Ward (no relation) was the club's business manager, and former Baltimore and Brooklyn great Wee Willie Keeler served as a coach. The club was unable to put any big-name stars on the field. Their best two players were right fielder Steve Evans, who hit .348, and pitcher Tom Seaton, who went 25-13. After being in contention for most of the season, the Tip-Tops finished up in fifth place.

The club, which was named after Ward's Tip-Top bakeries, did not improve in the 1915 season, either on the field or at the box office, finishing in seventh place and folding, along with the rest of league, at the end of the season. Robert Ward, who had lost more than $800,000 on the venture, died of a heart attack that October. It is believed that it was the strain of running the club that put him under.

Brooklyn Trolley Dodgers

American Association - 1884 - 1889
Record 410 - 354

Ever wonder how the Los Angeles Dodgers got that strange nickname of theirs? Well, today's L.A Dodgers of the National League originally started out as the American Association's Brooklyn Trolley Dodgers in 1884. At the time Brooklyn was actually a city (the third largest in the country with a population of 600,000) and its citizens were often referred to as "trolley dodgers" because they apparently spent a lot of time jumping out of the way of the numerous trolleys that seemingly ran everywhere in the hustling, bustling metropolis.

After finishing no better than third place in their first four years of existence, Trolley Dodger owner Charles Byrne hired Bill McGunnigle to manage the club at the end of the 1887 season, and then purchased the entire New York Metropolitan franchise just so he could grab the best players for his lineup. Byrne then bought all-star pitchers Bob Caruthers and Dave Foutz from St. Louis for an earth-shattering $10,000. The result was a second-place finish in '88 and a N.L. pennant in '89. (The club then lost the 1889 version of the World Series to the New York Giants six games to three.)

The following season the franchise, which was now known as the Bridegrooms (because several players had recently married) was moved to the National League. This franchise would go through several more name changes over the years before finally ending up as the Dodgers. (For the continuing adventures of this club see: Brooklyn Dodgers.)

Brooklyn Wonders

Players League - 1890
Record 76 - 56

John Montgomery Ward, who had been instrumental in founding the Brotherhood of Professional Base Ball Players, helped to lead the great rebellion of 1890, which resulted in the formation of the Players League. Ward became manager and part owner of the Brooklyn entry in the new venture.

Joining Ward on the Wonders (who were named after a local bread company) were such American Association stars as first baseman Dave Orr (who hit .337 and drove in 124 runs), second baseman Lou Bierbaur (who hit .306 and drove in 99 runs) and Gus Weyhing (who went 30-16). Ward, who played shortstop for the club, hit .337 and stole 63 bases. Though the Wonders did well on the field (finishing second, six-and-a-half games behind Boston) they only averaged 1,200 fans per game. The club, and the league, folded at the end of the year.

Buffalo Bisons

National League - 1879 - 1885, Record 314-333

Players League - 1890, Record 36-96

1878 Buffalo Bisons

In the 1800's Buffalo had two major league clubs named the Bisons. The first Bisons spent seven seasons in the National League starting in 1879. Though great things were expected of them, the club never managed to finish better than third. The Bisons' pitching ace was Hall of Famer Jim "Pud" Galvin who went 37-27 in his rookie season of 1879, then won 20 or more games for the club during each of the next five seasons. He eventually became baseball's first 300 game winner.

Their offence was led by another future Hall of Famer — first baseman Dan Brouthers, who won N.L. batting championships with the Bisons in 1882 and 1883. His .342 lifetime batting average is the highest for a first baseman in the history of the game. With the Bisons, he teamed up with outfielders Hardie Richardson and Deacon White, and catcher Jack Rowe to form the "Big Four" of the National League.

Unfortunately the Bisons were never able to put enough spectators in the stands to be a success. The club lost money almost every season of its existence. On September 17, 1885, the Bisons management sold the entire team to the Detroit Wolverines for $7,000. The Bisons were allowed to finish out the final three weeks of the season before officially folding.

White and Rowe came back to Buffalo in 1890 as player-investors in the Players League Bisons. Catcher Connie Mack and outfielder Dummy Hoy

1890 Buffalo Bisons

also played for, and sunk money into, the new venture. With Rowe as manager, the club won their first four games and then plummeted to last place by mid-May, and stayed there for the rest of the season. Despite playing in a refurbished Olympic Park, the Bisons averaged fewer than 1,000 fans per game and folded at the end of the season, along with the league.

Buffalo Blues

Federal League - 1914 - 1915
Record 154-149

Even though they constructed a brand new 20,000-seat stadium for the Buffalo fans, and snared flashy first baseman "Prince" Hal Chase from the Chicago White Sox, the Federal League's Buffalo Blues had a difficult time competing with the minor International League's Bisons, who had already established themselves in the small Buffalo market.

Despite a winning record and a respectable fourth-place finish the Buffeds (as they were called in their first season) only averaged 2,400 fans per game in 1914. And although they lowered their ticket prices for their second season, the turnout was even smaller. The club wound up declaring bankruptcy, some $90,000 in debt, soon after the League folded at the end of the season.

1915 Buffalo Feds

Chicago Browns

Union Association - 1884
Record 33-35

The Chicago Browns weren't even able to finish out their one and only season in the Windy City. They found that trying to compete against the powerful and popular White Stockings for Chicago baseball fans was an impossible task. The Browns had not been successful at luring name players away from N.L. or A.A. clubs, and fielded a very mediocre team.

By mid-August Browns owner A.H. Henderson had lost $15,000 on the ill-fated venture, so he pulled the plug and moved the franchise to Pittsburgh.

Chicago Pirates

Players League - 1890
Record - 75-62

The Chicago Pirates were one of the more successful Players League franchises. They were able to compete against the N.L.'s White Stockings (and outdraw them by 50%) due to the fact that they had recruited most of the White Stockings regular players, including second baseman Fred Pfeffer and future Hall of Famer Hugh Duffy. The Pirates also pirated several players away from the A.A.'s St. Louis Browns, including player-manager Charles Commiskey and outfielder Tip O'Neill.

The Pirates were a contender for most of the season, but finally finished up in fourth place, 10 games behind Boston. Pitcher Mark Baldwin led the league in wins with 34, and the entire outfield of O'Neill, Duffy and Jimmy Ryan batted over .300.

After the league folded at the end of the season Pirates owner John Addison was able to sell the whole team to Al Spalding of the White Stockings for $33,000.

Chicago Whales

Federal League 1914 - 1915
Record: 173-133

1914 Chicago Whales

Both on the field and off the field, the Chicago Whales were the most successful franchise in the Federal League's two-year existence as a major league. In 1914 team owner Charles Weeghman built a brand new, state-of-the-art stadium for his new club to play in, and that year they led the F.L. in attendance, outdrawing the N.L.'s Cubs.

The Whales, under manager Joe Tinker (a Chicago favorite, formerly part of the Cubs' legendary Tinker-to-Evers-to-Chance double-play combination of the early 1900's), finished second, only 1.5 games behind Indianapolis in the 1914 season, and then, in 1915, beat out St. Louis by one percentage point to finish first.

When the Federal League folded after the 1915 season, Weeghman bought the Cubs and moved them into Weeghman Park, and they've been there ever since (it was renamed Wrigley Field in 1926).

Chicago White Sox

American League - 1901 - Present
Record (1901-1919) - 1542 - 1267

When Charles Commiskey moved his minor Western League St. Paul franchise into Chicago in 1901, Chicago's N.L. club let him have the use of a decaying stadium called Brotherhood Park under one condition — Commiskey's team could not identify itself as a Chicago club! Commiskey agreed to this provision and then got around it by calling his club the White Stockings. The N.L. club had long since stopped using this nickname, yet everyone knew it was a name that belonged to Chicago.

It was all part of a move to upgrade the Western League (renamed the American League) to major league status. That year the White Stockings won the first A.L. pennant behind the pitching of manager Clark Griffith, who won 24 games for the club. In 1904 the club became known as the White Sox when the *Chicago Tribune* shortened their name for headline writing purposes.

The White Sox won their next pennant in 1906 mainly due to the pitching rotation of Spitballer "Big Ed" Walsh (17-13 and a league leading ten shutouts), Doc White (18-6 and a league leading 1.52 ERA), Frank Owen (22-13) and Nick Altrock (20-13). The team's batting average was a measly .230, which was why they became known as "the Hitless Wonders." Although the White Sox only hit .198 in the World Series, they nevertheless outscored the Cubs in total runs 22-18 and defeated their crosstown rivals four games to two.

The following season the White Sox slipped down to third place, and didn't win another pennant until 1917. That year pitcher Eddie Cicotte (28-12 and a league leading 1.53 ERA) helped lead them to their most successful season ever. The White Sox finished up with a 100-54 record, which gave them a .649 winning percentage, the best in club history.

In 1919 the White Sox won another American League pennant. They finished with a 88-52 record and were 5-1 favorites to beat the Cincinnati Reds in the World Series.

But even before the Series began there were rumors swirling about that the "fix" was in. And when Cincinnati took the best of nine series 5 games to 3, it didn't sit well with a lot of baseball fans. One year later a Chicago Grand Jury blew the whole thing wide open, naming eight Chicago players as having conspired with gamblers to throw the series.

As it turned out, Chicago's poorly paid players (owner Charles Commiskey was one of the stingiest men in baseball) were easy pickings for the gamblers who had offered the eight teammates $100,000 (but actually only paid them $10,000) to lose the series.

The most famous conspirator was outfielder "Shoeless Joe" Jackson, an illiterate farm boy from South Carolina, whose lifetime batting average of

1919 Chicago White Sox

.356 and outstanding running and fielding abilities would have eventually put him in the Hall of Fame, if it hadn't been for this tragedy.

Rocked by the scandal, major league baseball appointed its first commissioner, a stern, no-nonsense federal judge by the name of Kenesaw Mountain Landis, to try and restore the game's reputation for integrity.

Landis ruled baseball with an iron fist, and even though the eight players were acquitted in a conspiracy trial (after some of the transcripts of their testimony mysteriously disappeared from court files) Landis nevertheless banned them all from baseball for life.

Chicago White Stockings
Colts - Orphans - Cubs

National League - 1876 - Present
Record (1876-1919) - 3261 - 2419

The Chicago White Stockings were one of the founding members of National League when it was formed on 1876, and the club has been in business ever since, going through several name changes before finally winding up as the Cubs in 1902.

Chicago owner William Hulbert turned his club into a powerhouse when he persuaded Boston's "Big Four" — Ross Barnes, Deacon White, Cal McVey and Al Spalding — to leave the N.A.'s Boston Red Stockings after the 1875 season and join his club when the new league started in 1876. He also grabbed future Hall of Famer Adrian "Cap" Anson from the Philadelphia Athletics. The result was a first-place finish for the White Stockings with pitcher-manager Spalding getting 47 of the club's 52 victories.

Spalding suffered an arm injury the following season and had to leave the mound for first base. As a result the club plummeted to a fifth-place finish. Spalding retired as a player after the next season so he could devote his time to his young sporting goods firm.

Anson took over as manager in 1879 and led the club to five N.L. pennants and four second-place finishes in the next 13 years. The White Stockings were the N.L.'s pre-eminent team in the

1885 Chicago Team

1. Ryan.
2. Williamson.
3. Farrell.
4. Pfeffer.
5. The Mascot.

Jos. Hall, Photo., Brooklyn, N.Y.

6. Capt. Anson.
7. Van Haltren.
8. Borchers.
9. Burns.
10. Daly.

CHICAGO BALL CLUB, 1888.

Chicago Ball Club, 1888

1880's. Besides Anson, the club featured such outstanding players as superstar Mike "King" Kelly and pitchers Larry Corcoran and John Clarkson. In 1882 Al Spalding came back to the White Stockings as the club's president, and served in that capacity until 1891.

Spalding turned the baseball world upside-down when he sold Kelly to Boston after the '86 season and Clarkson to the same club a year later, for $10,000 each.

After losing most of their key players to the Players League in 1890, the club bounced back in '91 and spent most of the year in first place, only to have the pennant snatched away from them in late September by Boston.

The team finished no better than 14 games out during the rest of the 1890's, an era when they were called the "Colts" due to a youth movement on the club, and then named the "Orphans" when Cap Anson was fired as manager in 1898 after 19 years on the job.

The Cubs returned to their championship form in the 1900's, winning four pennants during the first decade of the century behind the pitching of Three Finger Brown and the stalwart defense of legendary double-play combination Joe Tinker, Johnny Evers and Frank Chance.

In 1916 the club got a new owner and a new ballpark. Charles Weeghman bought the club and moved it into the park he had built for his now-defunct Chicago Whales of the Federal League, and the Cubs have been in Wrigley Field ever since. In the war-shortened season of 1918 they won their only pennant of the decade, finishing 10.5 games ahead of the Giants. The White Stockings-Colts-Orphans-Cubs are the oldest continuous running franchise in major league history.

Cincinnati Outlaw Reds

Union Association - 1884
Record 69 - 36

The Outlaw Reds were a wild and woolly bunch that competed with the A.A.'s Reds for Cincinnati's baseball customers in a rather relentless, cut-throat fashion, as their parks were located only three blocks from each other. Before games hawkers from both clubs filled the streets, attempting to shanghai fans to one park or the other.

The Outlaw Reds, who were mainly composed of a rowdy collection of players recruited from the ranks of various N.L. and A.A. teams, were managed by Dan O'Leary. O'Leary, who liked to take his players out drinking nightly and was known to bet on his team's games, was fired 35 games into the season and replaced by second baseman Sam Crane.

In August the Outlaws pulled another raid on the N.L. and grabbed shortstop Jack Glasscock, catcher Fatty Briody and pitcher Jim McCormick from Cleveland. Glasscock hit .419 in 38 games and Briody batted .337 in 22 games. McCormick went 21-3 for the club and was one of three 20 game winners on the Outlaw Reds staff that season. Nevertheless the club fell short of the pennant by 21 games, finishing up in second place. The Outlaw Reds of course, along with the rest of the league, vanished at the end of the season.

Cincinnati Porkers

American Association - 1891

Record 43 - 57

When the Players League folded, a bunch of veterans who could find no other place to play followed aging superstar King Kelly to Cincinnati to join him on the new club he had been hired to manage. The Porkers had been created to challenge the Reds, who had just jumped from the American Association to the National League.

Chris Von der Ahe, the colorful owner of the St. Louis Browns, was a majority owner of the Porkers and naturally spent a good deal of time meddling in the club's operation. The Porkers played their home games in suburban Pendleton, a place that could only be reached by a one-hour steamboat ride from Cincinnati.

It's a wonder that the Porkers, who were probably best known for all the eating, drinking and brawling they did, managed to win as many games as they did. The club finally went broke in August and was replaced by Milwaukee in the Association.

Cincinnati Reds

National League - 1876 - 1880, Record - 125 - 217

American Association - 1882 - 1889, Record - 549 - 396

National League - 1890 - Present, Record (1890-1919) - 2151 - 2187

The first incarnation of the Cincinnati Reds were charter members of the National League when the circuit was formed in 1876. Club owner Josiah Keck, a local meat-packing magnate, formed the club in an attempt to capitalize on the tradition of the legendary undefeated Red Stocking club of 1869-70, the first avowedly professional team. Unfortunately this club was horrendous, racking up a 9-56 record and finishing in last place some 42.5 games behind Chicago that year.

In its five years of existence the money-losing franchise went through several ownership changes. The best season this team ever had was in 1878 when manager Cal McVey piloted the team to a respectable second-place

1882 Cincinnati Reds

finish. In 1880 the Reds slid back into the league basement, and the franchise folded at the end of the season when they were booted out of the league for selling beer at home games and leasing their park to teams that played on Sunday.

In 1882 the second edition of the Reds took the brand new American Association by storm, capturing the first A.A. pennant with a 55-25 record (and a .688 winning percentage that is still a Reds club record). The team managed to put together six

winning seasons and two second-place finishes in the next seven years, before moving to the National League in 1890.

The Reds floundered in mediocrity for the next 28 years, managing to finish no better than third during this period. In 1919 the Reds won their first N.L. pennant behind the pitching of Slim Salle (21-7), Hod Eller (20-19) and Dutch Ruether (19-7), all of whom had career seasons. The Reds then went on to defeat the Chicago White Sox in the World Series, but the victory was tainted, as it was later revealed that eight members of the White Sox had conspired with gamblers to throw the series.

1892 Cincinnati Reds

Cleveland Blues

National League - 1879 - 1884
Record 249 - 299
American Association - 1887 - 1888
Record - 89 - 174

The first edition of the Blues started out in the National League as the Cleveland Forest Citys in 1879, but when the club changed their flashy checkered uniforms for a more conservative solid navy blue model in 1882, they also changed their nickname.

After a sixth-place finish in their first season, the club improved their lineup by adding second baseman Fred Dunlap, shortstop Jack Glasscock and outfielder Ned Hanlon to their ranks. This resulted in a third-place finish in 1880. Manager-pitcher Jim McCormick notched a career-high 45 wins that year. It was the club's best finish ever.

After finishing no better than sixth during the next two seasons, the Blues were in first place in 1883 when McCormick suffered a season-ending arm injury after winning 23 games, and the club ended up in fourth place.

The following year the Blues were hit hard by defections to the Union Association. McCormick, Dunlap, Glasscock and catcher Fatty Briody all jumped to the upstart league. Attendance plummeted in Cleveland and the franchise folded at the end of the season.

The next version of the Blues sprang to life in 1887 and spent two dreadful years in the American Association. The team was mainly composed of rookies and castoffs from other clubs, and after a last-place finish in '87 they managed to climb all the way up to sixth place in '88, finishing some 40.5 games behind first-place St. Louis. At the end of the season club owner Frank De Hass Robison saw a chance to move his club into the more lucrative National League and he took it. (For the continuing adventures of this franchise, see Cleveland Spiders.)

Cleveland Indians

American League - 1901 - Present
Record (1901-1919) - 1439 - 1379

The Cleveland Indians actually started out as a minor league club. In 1900 Ban Johnson's Western League moved their Grand Rapids franchise into Cleveland, which had no professional ball club at the time (the N.L.'s Cleveland Spiders had folded at the end of the 1899 season). When the 1901 season began, the Western League changed its name to the American League and declared itself to be a major league, and the Indians (who were called the Blues at the time) instantly became a big league club.

The team finished in seventh place in its first A.L. season. The next year the club (which was now called the Bronchos) climbed up to fifth place (with a .507 winning percentage) after acquiring superstar second baseman Nap Lajoie, outfielder Elmer Flick and pitchers Bill Bernhard and Addie Joss.

After Lajoie led the club to a third-place finish the following season he was appointed manager. Lajoie was so popular with the Cleveland fans that they changed the nickname of the club to the Naps in his honor.

The Naps were a moderately successful club over the next several years. In 1908, after engaging in an exciting end-of-season pennant battle (during which Addie Joss pitched a perfect game), the Naps finished up in second place, a half a game behind Detroit. They did not finish this high in the standings again until 1918.

In 1915, after Lajoie left the club, they were renamed the Indians in honor of Lou Sockalexis, an American Indian who had played for the N.L.'s Cleveland Spiders in the late 1890's and made a lasting impression on Cleveland fans.

After acquiring future Hall of Famer Tris Speaker and pitchers Jim Bagby and Stan Coveleski in 1916, the Indians jumped from sixth to a third-place finish in 1917. Two close second-place finishes followed in 1918 and '19, then finally, in 1920, the Indians won their first pennant, beating out Chicago by two games in the last week of play. (Cleveland would not win another pennant until 1948.) The Indians went on to defeat Brooklyn in the 1920 World Series five games to two.

1908 Cleveland Baseball Club

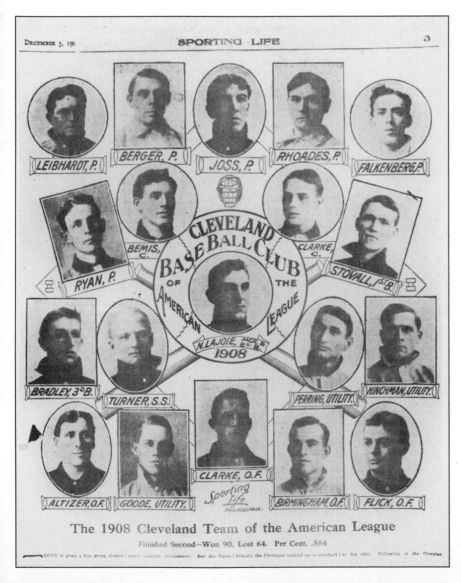

The 1908 Cleveland Team of the American League

Finished Second—Won 90, Lost 64. Per Cent. .584

Cleveland Infants

Players League - 1890
Record - 55 - 75

Cleveland streetcar line operator Albert L. Johnson was the principal backer for the Cleveland Players League franchise. He assembled a club of league jumpers consisting of many of the N.L.'s Cleveland Spiders regular players, plus a young Ed Delahanty from the N.L.'s Philadelphia Phillies and superstar Pete Browning from the A.A.'s Louisville Colonials.

The Infants wallowed in seventh place for most of the season, and although they outdrew the Spiders at the box office that year, Johnson nevertheless lost over $300,000 on the venture when the club and the league vanished at the end of the season.

Cleveland Spiders

National League - 1889 - 1899
Record - 738 - 764

The Cleveland Spiders have the distinction of being, in their last year of operation, the worst team in the history of major league baseball. The club was born in 1889 when owner Frank De Has Robison moved his Cleveland Blues into the National League from the American Association and renamed them the Spiders.

They finished in the bottom half of the league in their first three years of operation, but the arrival of a rookie pitcher by the name of Cy Young and an outfielder by the name of Jesse Burkett in 1891 soon turned things around.

Under the leadership of manager Patsy Tebeau, the Spiders developed

a reputation as the rowdiest, most intimidating team in baseball, next to the Baltimore Orioles. They finished second to the Orioles in 1895 and 1896 and played them in the post-season Temple Cup series both years. (The Spiders won the first series four games to one, and lost the second series in four straight games.)

Burkett hit .356 in his eight seasons with the Spiders. (He batted over .400 two seasons in a row — 1895 and '96). Young won 241 games in nine years with the club. He led the league in wins in '95 (35) and strike-outs in '96 (140) and threw a no-hitter against Cincinnati in 1897.

In 1897 the Spiders acquired an American Indian by the name of Lou Sockalexis. In one glorious season he thrilled the Cleveland fans with his tremendous hitting and fielding abilities. Sockalexis hit over .400, until he injured his foot in July and was never the same afterwards. He finished the year with a .338 average and then made brief appearances in '88 and '89 before finally leaving baseball. (But the fans loved him so much that, 18 years later, they renamed their American League franchise "The Cleveland Indians" in his honor.)

In early 1899 Robison purchased the St. Louis Browns, and then promptly moved all his best players (including future Hall of Famers Young, Burkett and Bobby Wallace) from Cleveland to the St. Louis club in exchange for a bunch of nobodies.

As a result, the 1899 Spiders racked up the worst single-season record in major league history. That year the Spiders won a total of 20 games and lost 134, finishing 84 games behind first-place Brooklyn. Six times the Spiders lost 11 or more straight games, and once they went 24 games without a win.

The Spiders played 113 of their 154 games on the road that year, and it was probably just as well, because in the 41 games they played at home they drew a grand total of 6,088 spectators, or an average of 148.5 fans per game! Needless to say, the hapless Spiders folded at the end of the season.

Columbus Colts

American Association - 1883 - 1884

Record - 101 - 104

American Association - 1889 - 1891

Record - 200 - 209

Columbus, Ohio, was an American Association city on two separate occasions. The Columbus Colts (who, at various times were also known as the Senators, Buckeyes and Solons) were created in 1883 when the A.A. expanded from six to eight teams after a successful first season.

After finishing sixth in their first year, the Colts rocketed up to second place in 1884 behind the pitching of Frank Mountain (23-17) and rookie Ed Morris (34-13).

In the interim the A.A. had expanded again and was now in 12 cities. This turned out to be a financial disaster, so at the end of the year the Association decided to cut back to eight clubs, and Columbus, being one of the smallest cities in the Association, was bounced out of the league.

Columbus re-entered the American Association in 1899 as a replacement for Cleveland which had defected to the National League. They went from a sixth-place finish in 1889, to a second-place finish in 1890 mainly due to the hitting of outfielder Speed Johnson (.346) and catcher Jack O'Connor (.324), and the pitching of Hank Gastright (30-14). The club had a succession of three managers that year.

In the following season, which turned out to be their last, the club finished in fifth place. When the National League absorbed the A.A. at the end of the season, Columbus was not included in the new 12 team N.L.

Detroit Tigers

American League - 1901 - Present
Record (1901-1919) - 1473 - 1336

The Detroit Tigers were charter members of the American League when it raised itself to major league status in 1901. The club spent most of its first six seasons in the second division, but when they acquired a high-powered new manager by the name of Hughie Jennings in 1907, things changed drastically.

That year, Jennings managed the Tigers to the first of three straight American League pennants. He eventually spent 14 seasons piloting the club. Jennings would direct the team from the third-base coaching box, and was famous for cheering them on with his piercing cry of "Ee-yah!"

On the field, the Tigers were sparked by a young outfielder by the name of Ty Cobb. In 1907, Cobb's first full big league season, he led the league in batting (.350), hits (212), RBI (119) and stolen bases (49). He followed this with 21 straight years of hitting .320 or better, during which he won 11 more batting titles. The "Georgia Peach" topped the .400 mark three times during his 24 seasons with the Tigers.

During their three-year pennant streak, the Tigers unfortunately didn't do well in the post season, losing each World Series.

There were no more pennants during the Cobb era. In 1910 the Tigers finished up in third place. During the following decade, the best they could do was two second-place finishes. Jennings left the club in 1920 and Cobb took the helm for the next six years. He managed to pilot them to a second-place finish in 1923, but the Tigers didn't win their next pennant until 1934, and finally won their first world championship in 1935.

1907 Detroit Tigers

Detroit Wolverines

National League - 1881 - 1888
Record - 426 - 437

When the Cincinnati Reds were booted out of the National League following the the 1880 season they were replaced in the league by the Detroit Wolverines.

In their first five seasons the Wolverines never finished higher than fourth, but things turned around when the Wolverines purchased the entire Buffalo Bisons team for $7,000 at the end of the 1885 season. Among the players they acquired from Buffalo were baseball's "Big Four:" infielder Dan Brouthers, outfielders Hardy Richardson and Jack Rowe and catcher Deacon White.

In 1886 the "Big Four" along with slugger Sam Thompson and pitcher Lady Baldwin (with 42 wins) led the Wolverines to a 87-36 record and a second-place finish.

The following season the Wolverines won their one and only the pennant with a 79-45 record. They then took on the A.A's St. Louis Browns in a 15-game roadshow version of the World Series which was played in 10 different cities. The Wolverines trounced the Browns 10 games to five in the series.

In 1888 the Wolverines slipped down to fifth place, the fans lost interest, the club lost money and management sold off some of the best players. This resulted in the demise of the franchise at the end of the season.

1880s Detroit Baseball Team

Hartford Dark Blues

National League - 1876

Record - 47 - 21

The Hartford Dark Blues were charter members of the National League when it was formed in 1876. The club, which was carried over from the National Association, was owned by Hartford insurance magnate Morgan G. Bulkeley. Bulkeley was also appointed the National League's first president, and served in that capacity for the 1876 season.

The Dark Blues, behind the bat of right fielder Dick Higham (.327) and the pitching of Tommy Bond (31-13) and alleged curveball inventor Candy Cummings (16-8), managed a third-place finish that year.

But they did poorly at the box office, and at the end of the season the club was shifted to Brooklyn, becoming the first franchise in N.L. history to change locations.

Indianapolis Blues

National League - 1878
Record - 24 - 36
American Association - 1884
Record - 29 - 78

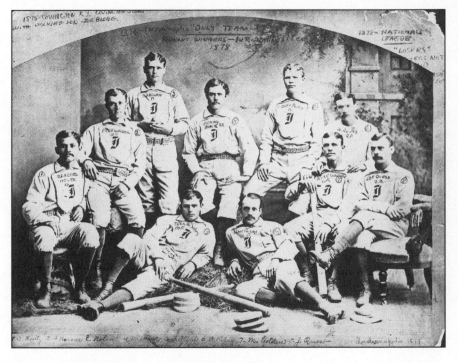

The first edition of the Indianapolis Blues (also known as the Hoosiers) was one of three clubs admitted to the National League in 1878 to fill the gap when Brooklyn, Louisville and St. Louis dropped out. The Blues, which had thrived as an independent club the previous season, proved incapable of attracting enough paying customers to make it in the N.L., and after a dismal fifth-place finish, they folded at the end of the season.

The second version of the Indianapolis Blues was one of four new teams created by the American Association in 1884 solely for the purpose of keeping as many players as possible out of the clutches of the newly formed Union Association.

The team, which was composed of a bunch of rookies and castoffs from other clubs, did poorly at the box office and finished eleventh in the 12-team Association. When the U.A. threat was over at the end of the season, the A.A. reverted back to eight clubs and the Blues were dropped from the league.

Indianapolis Hoosiers

National League - 1887 - 1889

Record - 146 - 249

Federal League - 1914

Record - 88 - 65

The first edition of the Indianapolis Hoosiers was created in 1887 to replace the St. Louis Maroons in the National League. Despite having such outstanding players on their roster as shortstop Jack Glasscock and pitchers Larry Corcoran and Amos Russie (1899 only), the Hoosiers never managed to finish higher than seventh in an eight-team league. After three years of existence, the club was disbanded at the end of the 1899 season as part of the N.L.'s plan to strengthen itself in anticipation of the forthcoming battle with the Players League.

The second version of the Indianapolis Hoosiers was created when the Federal League came along in 1914. Despite their first-place finish, no one in Indianapolis took the Federal League, or the Hoosiers seriously, and the club suffered from poor attendance. As a result, the franchise was moved to Newark, N.J., for the 1915 season. The 1914 Hoosiers have the distinction of being the only club in major league history to win a pennant in its only year of existence.

Kansas City Blues

American Association - 1888 - 1889
Record - 98 - 171

The Kansas City Blues replaced the New York Metropolitans in the American Association in 1888. It was Kansas City's third major league team in five years, and this one was also a failure.

The Blues suffered from a lack of on-field talent. Their best hitter (Jumbo Davis) could only manage a .267 average, and their best pitcher (Henry Porter, 18-37) led the Association in losses. The club went through three different managers in its first season and finished in last place.

The following season the Blues improved slightly and managed to finish in seventh place. The club never was a hit at the box office, and at the end of the year, with the impending Players League war coming on, the Blues resigned from the A.A. and joined the minor Western League.

Kansas City Cowboys

National League - 1886

Record - 30 - 91

The Kansas City Cowboys were a last-minute addition to the National League at the start on the 1886 season. The club, which was a hurriedly assembled bunch of rookies and has-beens, was known throughout the league for its unruly players and fans. Other teams, and league umpires, would dread the thought of a visit to Kansas City.

The Cowboys finished the year in seventh place, some 58.5 games out. Poor attendance for most of the season caused the club to be disbanded at the end of the year.

Kansas City Packers

Federal League - 1914 - 1915
Record - 148 - 156

The Kansas City Packers were basically a run-of-the-mill club located in a market too small to support a major league franchise. They were only able to persuade one star player from the two established major leagues to jump to their club when the league began in 1914. That was George Stoval of the A.L.'s St. Louis Browns, who also managed the Packers to a sixth-place finish in their first year.

The club improved somewhat in 1915 and was embroiled in a five-way battle for first place for most of the season. They were actually in first place in mid-August, but had dropped to fifth by the end of the month and finally finished fourth. The money-losing club vanished, along with the rest of the league, at the end of the year.

Kansas City Unions

Union Association - 1884
Record - 16 - 63

When the Altoona Mountain Citys folded early in the season, Union League president Henry V. Lucas moved the franchise to Kansas City, and the Kansas City Unions were born in early June. Only two players from the Mountain Citys made the trip, so a team was hastily assembled from a bunch of unknowns and local amateurs.

One of the provisions in their agreement with the league prohibited the new club from being eligible to win the U.A. pennant that year, but there was little danger of that, as the team proceeded to rack up a rather sorry 16-63 record. The Unions were nevertheless good at the box office in Kansas City, and the team made a $7,000 profit that season. But the club, along with the league, folded at the end of the year.

Louisville Colonels

American Association - 1882 - 1891

Record - 575 - 638

National League - 1892 - 1899

Record - 419 - 683

The Louisville Colonels (who were also called the Eclipse and Cyclones at various times) were one of only two teams that played in all 10 seasons of the major league American Association (St. Louis was the other). They finished third in their first season behind the bat of rookie Pete Browning who hit .378 (and won the first of three batting crowns), and the pitching of Tony Mulane, who went 30-24.

After slipping down to fifth in 1883, they ended up in third again in '84 thanks to the pitching of Guy Hecker, who won 52 of the club's 68 victories. For the next six seasons the Colonels were a bunch of also-rans. In

1888 Louisville Colonels

1899 they went through four managers and ended up in last place. But the following season they turned things completely around and won their one and only pennant behind the bat of William "Chicken" Wolf (.363) and the pitching of Scott Straton (34-14) and Red Ehret (25-14). When the A.A. folded at the end of the 1891 season the Colonels were one of four clubs taken into the N.L.

In the National League the Colonels were a disaster, both financially and on the field. They started out under a cloud of bankruptcy and went through several changes of ownership during their eight years in the league. The club never had a winning season, or managed to finish higher than ninth during this period. They finished in the basement three straight seasons from 1894 to '96. When the league cut back from twelve to eight teams after the 1899 season, Louisville was merged with the Pittsburgh Pirates.

1898 Louisville Colonels

Louisville Grays

National League - 1876 - 1877
Record - 65 - 61

The Louisville Grays, who were charter members of the National League, were also participants in the N.L.'s first great scandal. In their first season the Grays fielded a run-of-the-mill club that managed to finish in fifth place. Their best player was pitcher Jim Devlin, who posted a 30-35 record and hit .315, which was tops on the club.

In the following season of 1877 a much improved Louisville club was in first place in mid-August when they suddenly collapsed, losing seven suspicious games to rivals Boston and Hartford. Boston eventually won the pennant, and the Grays finished second. It was later discovered that Devlin, along with three other Louisville players, George Hall, Al Nichols and Bill Craver, had conspired with gamblers to throw enough games to make it possible for Boston to win the pennant.

William Hulbert, who had just taken over as N.L. president, banned the four players from baseball for life. The Grays, who were not able to find adequate replacements for the four players, dropped out of the league before the start of the next season.

Milwaukee Brewers

American Association - 1891

Record - 21 - 15

American League - 1901

Record - 48 -89

The original Milwaukee Brewers' brief sojourn in the American Association began in mid-August of 1881 when they moved up from the minor Western League to replace the defunct Cincinnati Porkers. By the end of the season the Brewers had racked up a 21-15 record, made a profit for the club's owners, and were looking forward to another season in the big leagues.

But it was not to be; when the National League absorbed the A.A. at the end of the season, Milwaukee was not included in the new 12-team N.L., and the Brewers went back to the Western League in 1882.

The club spent the next nine years in the Western League, then in 1901, when the Western League raised itself to major league status after changing its name to the American League, the Milwaukee Brewers were in the big leagues once again.

Unfortunately, the season turned out to be a disaster. After manager Connie Mack had left the Brewers for Philadelphia before the season started, future Hall of Famer Hugh Duffy was hired to manage the team, but the club's owners would not spend any money to attract new players. The Brewers finished the season in last place, some 35.5 games behind first-place Chicago, and did not draw enough paying customers to keep them in business for another year. The following season the franchise was transferred to St. Louis where it became the Browns.

Milwaukee Grays

National League - 1878

Record - 15 - 45

Union Association - 1884

Record - 8 - 4

The Milwaukee Grays (also known as the Cream Citys) joined the National League in 1878, and barely made it through the season. On the field their performance was abysmal (they led the league with 376 errors and were plagued with injuries all season) and attendance was poor. The club, which almost went broke several times during the season, was finally dissolved in December with several players still waiting for their paychecks.

The next version of the Grays spent most of the 1884 season in the minor Northwestern League before they were brought in to the Union Association in September to replace the Wilmington Quicksteps. The Grays played a grand total of 12-games in the U.A. before the season ended.

Their 8-4 record gave them a .667 won-lost percentage, which happens to be the best in major league history. When the U.A. folded at end of the year the Grays returned to the minor leagues, this time to the Western Association.

New York Giants

National League - 1883 - 1957
Record (1883-1919) - 2,926 - 2,218

1884 New York Gothams

The New York Giants started out in the National League in 1879 as the Troy (NY) Trojans. When the Trojans folded at the end of the 1882 season, the franchise was moved to the Big Apple. The club was called the Gothams in its first two New York seasons. Legend has it that one day in 1884 manager James Mutrie walked out onto the field, opened his arms wide and cried out for all to hear, "These are my big fellows ... these are my Giants." And as a result, the following season the the team was renamed the Giants.

After finishing no better than fourth in its first two seasons, the club seemed to come to life in 1885 after acquiring pitcher Timothy Keefe. That year, led by the pitching of Keefe and Mickey Welch (they had a combined 76 wins) and the hitting of Hall of Fame first baseman Roger Conner (a league leading 169 hits and .371 batting average), the Giants finished out the season in second place, only two games behind Chicago.

But it took the Giants until 1888 to win their first N.L. pennant (finishing nine games ahead of Chicago), they then went on to defeat the A.A.'s St. Louis Browns six games to four in the World Series. The Giants won their second pennant the following season, and this time they polished off the Brooklyn Bridegrooms six games to three in post-season play.

The Giants didn't win another pennant until 1904. It was John McGraw's second full season at the helm, and he guided them to a 106-47 record, the best in club history. McGraw then refused to face Boston in a World Series because he felt the champions of the upstart American League were not worthy opponents.

The Giants repeated as pennant winners the following season behind the pitching of Christy Mathewson (31-9 and a 1.28 ERA) and the bat of "Turkey Mike" Donlin (.356). This time the Giants agreed to participate in the World Series. They defeated Connie Mack's Philadelphia Athletics four games to one, with Mathewson throwing three shutouts.

The Giants didn't win their next pennant until 1911, although they came close in 1908, when they narrowly lost out in late September due to the famous "Merkle's Boner" incident when infielder Fred Merkle failed to touch second base in a crucial game. The 1911 pennant was the first of three first-place finishes in a row for the Giants, but they lost all three World Series.

Their next pennant came in 1917, but once again they lost the Annual Fall Classic, this time to the Chicago White Sox four games to two. Three straight years of second-place finishes followed before McGraw steered them to four straight pennants from 1921-24. The Giants won ten pennants in the 29 years John McGraw spent piloting the club.

1888 New York Giants

1894 New York Giants

New York Metropolitans

American Association - 1883 - 1887
Record - 270 - 309

The New York Metropolitans, who had started out as a minor league club in 1880, were admitted to the American Association in 1883 when it expanded from six to eight clubs. They were owned by John B. Day who, at the same time, also owned the National League's New York Giants. From 1883 to 1885 the Mets and the Giants both shared the original Polo Grounds, playing their home games in separate fields located side-by-side.

In their first A.A. season, the Mets racked up a 54-42 record and finished fourth behind the pitching of future Hall of Famer Tim Keefe who went 41-27, and completed 68 games in 68 starts. In 1884 Keefe and the club's other starter, Jack Lynch, both had 37 wins each, and first baseman Dave Orr hit .354 as the Mets breezed to a first-place finish. That October they took on the N.L. champion Providence Grays in the first World Series ever held. Providence won the series in three straight games.

The Metropolitans slid down to seventh place the following season. In 1886, after going through a change of ownership, the club began playing their home games on Staten Island. Two more seventh-place finishes and poor attendance caused the club to be disbanded after the 1887 season. The franchise was then moved to Kansas City.

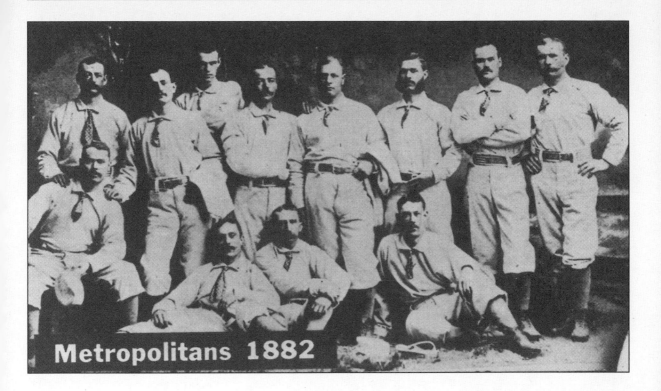

Metropolitans 1882

New York Mutuals

National League - 1876
Record - 21 - 35

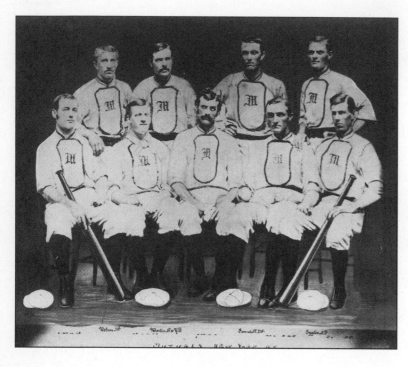

The New York Mutuals were originally formed in 1857 as an amateur club. In 1871 they became charter members of baseball's first professional league, the National Association. The Mutuals remained in the N.A. for all five years of its existence, and when it was replaced by the National League in 1876, they joined the new circuit.

Over the years the Mutuals had developed a notorious reputation for "hippodroming" or fixing games, and even though William Hulbert had created the N.L. to clean up baseball, he nevertheless admitted the Mutuals to the league because he felt it necessary to have a franchise in the New York City area.

But the Mutuals only lasted in the National League for one season. At the end of the year they, along with the Philadelphia Athletics, were thrown out of the league for failing to make their final western road trips at the end of the season. (Neither city was admitted back into the league until 1883.)

Newark Peppers

Federal League - 1915
Record - 80 - 72

In 1915 the Federal League, which already had a club operating in Brooklyn, decided to plant another team in the New York City area by moving the 1914 pennant-winning Indianapolis Hoosier club into Newark, N.J.

A brand new 20,000-seat stadium was built in neighboring Harrison for the

NEWARK FEDERAL LEAGUE TEAM - 1915

Newark's 1915 Federal League Team - Top Row (left to right): Phillips, MGR; Billiard, P; Mullin, P; Campbell, OF; Kaiser, OF; Rooney, 1B; Dolan, 1B; Rariden, C; *Middle Row:* Falkenberg, 2B; Vandergrift, 2B; Scheer, OF; Kaiserling, P; Roush, OF; Booe, OF; Harter, P; *Bottom Row:* Warren, C; Mosely, P; Kauff, OF; Textor, C; Esmond, SS; LaPorte, 2B; McKechnie, 3B.

Peppers to play in. The club had a lineup almost identical to the previous season's Hoosiers. They remained competitive for most of the season, thanks to the bats of outfielders Vin Campbell (.310) and Edd Roush (.298) and the pitching of Ed Reulbach (20-10). But after a disastrous eight-game losing streak in September the Peppers finished up the season in fifth place.

The Newark Peppers were the only major league baseball team New Jersey ever had and they, along with the league, vanished after the season was over.

New York Players League Giants

Players League - 1890
Record - 74 - 57

In 1890, the great players' revolt was on, and nearly the whole roster of the National League New York Giant club followed the lead of team captain Buck Ewing and defected to the Players League version of the Giants.

Club backers Edwin A. McAlpin and Edward Talcott constructed a brand new version of the Polo Grounds at Coogan's Bluff in Manhattan for the P.L. Giants to play in. Sparked by the pitching of Hank O'Day (22-13), and the hitting of first baseman Roger Connor (14 homers, .349 batting average, 103 RBI), outfielder Jim O'Rourke (9 homers, .360 batting average, 115 RBI) and Ewing himself (who hit .338), the P.L. Giants came in third at the end of the season.

When the league folded at end of the year, McCalpin and Talcott found they had lost about $8,000 on the venture. Most of the players returned to the N.L. Giants for the following season.

New York Yankees

American League - 1903 - Present
Record (1903-1919) - 1221 - 1298

The New York Yankees started out as the Baltimore Orioles in 1901. The franchise was moved to New York City in 1903 and the team became known as the Highlanders due to the high elevation of the land where their northern Manhattan stadium was located.

The club wasn't called the Yankees until 1913 when they left Hilltop Park and moved into the Polo Grounds. The Yankees shared that facility with the Giants until 1923, and then moved into Yankee Stadium.

After a fourth-place finish in their first season, the 1904 Highlanders managed to finish a close second, some 1.5 games behind Chicago, mainly due to the pitching of Jack Chesbro who recorded 41 wins that year, a twentieth-century record. After another second-place finish in 1906, the club plummeted to last place in 1908, losing a club-record 103 games. It would be another 12 years until the franchise was a serious pennant contender once again.

A change of ownership in 1914 led to a major

1909 New York Yankees

rebuilding campaign. The following year the Yankees acquired pitcher Bob Shawkey from the Philadelphia A's, and his 24 wins in 1916 helped the Yankees record their first winning season in six years.

In 1918 they picked up outfielder Duffy Lewis and pitchers Ernie Shore and Dutch Leonard from the Red Sox but only managed a fourth-place finish. That season the Yankees would go over to Harrison Park near Newark, N.J., to play their Sunday home games, as Sunday baseball wasn't legalized in New York until the following year.

In 1919 the club acquired temperamental submarine baller Carl Mays from Boston in mid-season. His nine wins combined with 20 from Shawkey gave the Yankees a third-place finish that year, their best in eight seasons. That winter the Yankees, on the recommendation of manager Miller Huggins, purchased a pitcher-turned-hitter by the name of Babe Ruth from the Red Sox for a record $125,000 cash and a $300,000 mortgage on Fenway Park.

In 1920 (the year that a livelier ball was introduced to the game) the Babe responded to the friendly confines of the Polo Grounds by hitting a record 54 home runs. The fans flocked to see him and that season the Yankees became the first team to draw over one million customers. A Yankee dynasty had begun.

Philadelphia Athletics

National League - 1876, Record - 14 - 45

American Association - 1882 - 1891, Record - 633 - 564

American League - 1901 - 1954, Record (1901-1919) - 1444 - 1342

The Philadelphia Athletics, who were originally organized as an amateur club in 1860, were one of only three clubs to play all five seasons of baseball's first pro league, the National Association. When the N.A. was replaced by the National League in 1876, the A's were carried over by the new league. On April 22, 1876, Philadelphia hosted the first National League game ever played, which they lost to Boston by the score of 6-5.

That season the club did poorly at the box office and ended up in seventh place, some 34.5 games behind first place Chicago. When the year was over the Athletics were thrown out of the league for failing to make the final western road trip of the season.

1888 Philadelphia Athletics

The city of Philadelphia then went without a major league baseball team until 1882 when the next version of the Athletics became charter members of the American Association. After a second-place finish in their first season, the A's took home the A.A. pennant in 1883, behind the pitching of Bobby Mathews (30-13) and the bat of Harry Stovey who led the league in homers (14), doubles (31) and runs (110).

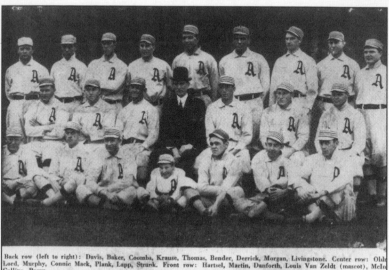

Back row (left to right): Davis, Baker, Coombs, Krause, Thomas, Bender, Derrick, Morgan, Livingstone. Center row: Oldr Lord, Murphy, Connie Mack, Plank, Lapp, Strunk. Front row: Hartsel, Martin, Danforth, Louis Van Zeldt (mascot), McIn Collins, Barry.

1911 Philadelphia A's

After plummeting to seventh place the following season, the Athletics never managed to finish higher than third during the rest of the decade. The club, which suffered heavy financial losses in the Players League war of 1890, folded in 1891 when the N.L. took over the American Association.

The third version of the Philadelphia Athletics was created in 1901 when the fledgling American League moved into town. A.L. president Ban Johnson chose Connie Mack to manage the A's and made him quarter owner of the club. Mack, who spent the next 50 years as manager of the Athletics, put together a club that won six pennants and had two close second-place finishes in the next 14 years. The club, at various times, featured such future Hall of Famers as pitchers Rube Waddel, Eddie Plank and Chief Bender and sluggers Napoleon Lajoie (the first year only), Eddie Collins and Frank Baker. The Athletics also managed to win three World Series during this period.

In 1915, unable to compete with Federal League salaries, Mack dismantled his championship club. The Athletics sank to last place and remained there for seven years. They did not win another pennant until 1929.

Philadelphia Keystones

Union Association - 1884
Record - 21 - 46

Soon after the Union Association's one and only season got underway in 1884, the Philadelphia Keystones found that they just couldn't compete with the two major league clubs already established in Philadelphia. The Keystones suffered huge financial losses and folded in early August after losing twice as many games as they had won. They were immediately replaced in the U.A. by the Wilmington Quicksteps.

Philadelphia Phillies

National League - 1883 - Present
Record - (1883-1919) - 2604 - 2523

In 1883, six years after the Philadelphia Athletics had been thrown out of the National League, the Phillies were organized to bring the city of brotherly love back into the N.L. In their first season the hastily assembled club, which was composed of nobodies and castoffs from other teams, finished in last place with a 17-81 record, some 46 games out of first.

Baseball legend Harry Wright was brought in to manage the club in 1884, and he soon turned the Phillies into a respectable operation. In 1885 they had their first winning season, and in 1887 the club finished second — just 3.5 games behind Detroit. Wright spent 11 years with the club.

In the early 1890's the Phillies fielded an outfield of three future Hall of Famers — Ed Delahanty, Billy Hamilton and Sam Thompson. In 1894, these three, along with utility outfielder Tuck Turner, became the only outfield in major league history to hit over .400 combined (that year the team hit .349, which is still a major league record).

In the late 1890's and early part of the twentieth century the Phillies usually managed to finish in the upper division. They had two second-place finishes in 1901 and 1913 before finally winning their first pennant in 1915. That year their pitching ace Grover Cleveland Alexander led the league in wins (31), shutouts (12), strikeouts (241) and ERA (1.22). The Phillies lost the World Series to the Boston Red Sox four games to one.

Two more 30 win seasons by Alexander gave the Phillies two second-place finishes in 1916 an 1917. That winter Philadelphia's money-hungry owner William F. Baker sold Alexander, along with catcher Bill Killefer, to the Cubs for $60,000. The club then went into a tailspin that lasted for over three decades. The Phillies didn't win another pennant until 1950, and didn't win a World Series until 1980.

Philadelphia Quakers

Players League - 1890
Record - 68 - 63

Although a number of players from both local major league clubs, the N.L. Phillies and the A.A. Athletics, jumped over to the Quakers in the great players' revolt of 1890, the Quakers failed to attract much of a following in Philadelphia. They did poorly at the box office and barely made it through the season. In spite of a winning record, the club finished out the year in fifth place. After the season was over, the Quakers, and the league, were out of business.

Pittsburgh Alleghenys

American Association - 1882 - 1886
Record - 239 - 296

The Pittsburgh Alleghenys were charter members of the American Association when it was formed in 1882. Club owner Denny McKnight was appointed president of the new league. After going through their first four seasons in a rather lackluster fashion the Alleghenys purchased future Hall of Fame pitcher Pud Galvin from Buffalo in 1885, and his 29 wins in 1886 sparked the Alleghenys to a second-place finish.

After McKnight was unceremoniously dumped from the A.A. presidency in 1886, the Alleghenys were given the opportunity to join the National League. In 1887 they became the first club to leave the A.A. for the senior circuit. (For the further adventures of the Pittsburgh Alleghenys, see Pittsburgh Pirates.)

1885 Allegheny Club

Pittsburgh Burghers

Players League - 1890
Record - 60 - 68

When the Pittsburgh Burghers were formed during the great players' revolt of 1890, nearly the whole roster of the Pittsburgh National League club joined manager Ned Hanlon in defecting to the new Players League club.

The Burghers had a lackluster season, in which they finished in sixth place and averaged fewer than 2,000 fans per game. When the league folded at the end of the season most of the players went back to the N.L. club, and the two franchises merged and became known as the Pittsburgh Pirates.

Pittsburgh Pirates

National League - 1887 - Present
Record (1887-1919) - 2505 - 2220

1911 Pittsburgh Pirates

The Pittsburgh Pirates were known as the Alleghenys when they jumped from the American Association to the National League in 1887. They kept that name until 1890 when they were called the Innocents for one season. In 1891 they finally became known as the Pirates due to the aggressive and somewhat questionable manner in which the club recruited players following the demise of the Players League.

After finishing in the second division in their first three years in the N.L., the franchise had its worst season of all time in 1890. That year most of the club's regular players jumped to the rival Pittsburgh Burghers of the Players League, and the Innocents finished in the basement, some 66.5 games out of first, with a 23-113 record.

After retrieving many of their players when the P.L. folded, the Pirates nevertheless ended up in last place again the following season. The club eventually managed to claw its way up to a second-place finish in 1893 behind the pitching of Frank Killen who led the league with 34 wins that year.

But the Pirates ended up in the second division again for the next six seasons. In 1900 the defunct Louisville Colonials were merged with the Pirates, bringing such all-stars as Honus Wagner, Fred Clarke, Chief Zimmer and Deacon Phillipe to the club. Under the guidance of player-manager Clarke, a dynasty was created that would last for the next decade. From 1900 to 1909 the Pirates won four pennants and came in second four times.

The Pirates won three straight N.L. pennants from 1901 to 1903. In 1903 they faced Boston in the first modern-day World Series, which Boston won five games to three. The Pirates' next pennant came in 1909. They then faced Ty Cobb and the Detroit Tigers in the World Series and beat the Tigers four games to three to win their first world championship.

It was the end of an era though; the Pirates spent the next decade as also-rans — their best finish was second place in 1912. The club didn't win another pennant until 1925.

Pittsburgh Rebels

Federal League - 1914 - 1915
Record - 150 - 153

After a seventh-place finish in their first year the Pittsburgh Rebels (who got their nickname from their manager Rebel Oakes) turned things around in the 1915 season. Sparked by two newly acquired players, first baseman Ed Konetchy (.314) and pitcher Frank Allan (23-13), the Rebels climbed into first place in late August, only to lose the pennant by a half a game in the final week of the season. The club, along with the league, folded at the end of the year.

Pittsburgh Stogies

Union Association - 1884
Record - 7 - 11

Halfway through the Union Association's one and only year of existence, the Chicago Browns were forced to relocate due to financial difficulties. They moved to Pittsburgh in mid-August and became the Stogies. But the franchise didn't do any better in Pittsburgh than it did in Chicago and the club was dissolved in less than a month. The St. Paul Saints of the Northwestern League were then recruited by the U.A. to play out the rest of Pittsburgh's schedule.

Providence Grays

National League - 1878 - 1885
Record - 438 - 278

The Providence Grays were one of the great teams of baseball's early era. The Grays joined the National League in 1878, and in their eight years of existence only had one losing season, their last. In their first season the Grays managed a third-place finish mainly due to the hitting of outfielder Paul Hines who led the league with a .358 batting average, and the pitching of an 18-year-old rookie by the name of John Montgomery Ward who went 22-13.

The following season the Grays hired legendary shortstop George Wright as player-manager and he piloted the club to their first pennant. Also contributing to the club's success were Hines, who once again led the league in hitting with a .357 average; recently acquired outfielder "Orator" Jim O'Rourke, who hit .348; and Ward, who went 47-19.

During the next four seasons the Grays finished second three times. In 1884 they had their greatest season ever. The club compiled a 84-28 record and won their second pennant, behind the pitching of Charles "Old Hoss" Radbourn who won 60 games that season, an all-time major league record. The Grays then went on to face the A.A. champion New York Metropolitans in the very first World Series ever played. The Grays took the best of five affair in three straight games. Radbourn won all three contests.

In 1885 the Grays sunk to a fourth-place finish and home attendance, which never had been very good to begin with, suffered as a result. This caused the club to be dissolved at the end of the season.

Richmond Virginias

American Association - 1884

Record - 12 - 30

When the Washington Nationals folded in August, 1884 the American Association called upon the Richmond Virginias, who had been playing in the Eastern League, to finish out the rest of the Nationals' schedule. The Virginias were definitely not up to the challenge, as their 12-30 record will attest. (Washington-Richmond had a combined 24-81 record.) When the A.A. cut back from 12 to eight clubs for the next season, Richmond was dropped.

Rochester Hop Bitters

American Association - 1890
Record - 63 - 63

Rochester was one of three smaller cities that were admitted to the American Association in 1890 (the others were Syracuse and Toledo). The A.A. Hop Bitters were basically the same club that had finished third in the International Association the season before. In their one and only season in the A.A. the club managed to put together a .500 fifth-place finish.

The highlight of the Hop Bitters' season came on September 15 when Cannonball Titcomb pitched a 7-0 no-hitter against Syracuse. It was the only no-no thrown in the majors that year. But Rochester did not prove to be a major league city and the A.A. dropped the club at the end of the year. The following season the Hop Bitters returned to the minor league from which they had come.

St. Louis Browns

National League - 1876 - 1877, Record - 73 - 51

American Association - 1882 - 1891, Record - 782 - 433

American League - 1902 - 1953, Record - (1902-1919) - 1148 - 1524

The St. Louis Brown Stockings (as they were originally called) were charter members of the National League when it was formed in 1876. In its first season the club finished in second place due to the bats of outfielder Lip Pike (.323), catcher John Clapp (.305) and infielder Joe Battin (.300), and the pitching of George Washington Bradley, who went 45-19 and, on July 15, threw the first no-hitter in National League history, a 2-0 win over Hartford.

The club finished in fourth place the next season, which would be its last in the N.L. Following a major dispute with league brass, club president John Lucas removed his club from the league at the end of the year.

The next version of the St. Louis Browns came along in 1881 as an independent club. When the American Association was formed the following year the Browns became charter members and went on to become the most successful franchise in the A.A.'s 10-year history, winning four straight pennants and one world championship from 1885-88, and coming in second four times.

The Browns were owned by Chris Von der Ahe, a flamboyant German immigrant who ran a beer garden in St. Louis. He had originally gotten into baseball so he could sell his beer at the ball park. The club was run by manager and first baseman Charles Commiskey, who had revolutionized the way first base was played by playing off the bag.

During their pennant-winning years the club was led by slugger Tip O'Neill, whose best year was 1887 when he hit .435 (he was originally credited with a .492 batting average as walks were counted as hits for that one season), and pitchers Bob Caruthers, who won 40 games in '85 and then followed up with seasons of 30 and 29 wins, and Dave Foutz, who

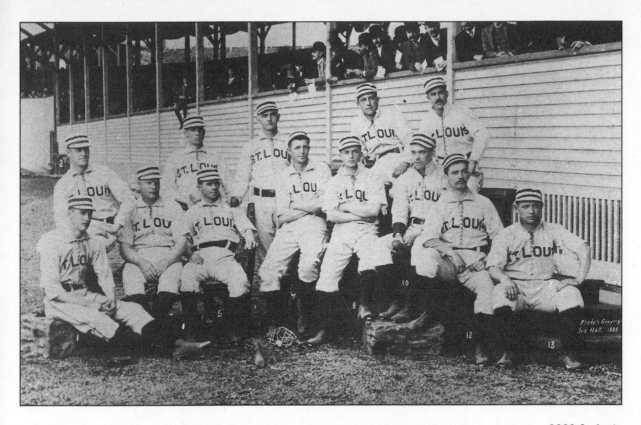

1888 St. Louis

won 33 games in '85, then followed up with seasons of 41 and 24 wins.

After the '87 season Von der Ahe sold Caruthers and Foutz to Brooklyn after acquiring pitcher Silver King, who went 34-11 that year. In 1888 King (who racked up a 45-21 record and led the league with a 1.64 ERA) combined with Nat Hudson (25-10) to give the Browns one more pennant.

The club went into a decline the following season, but still managed to finish in second place, only two games behind Brooklyn. Two more second-place finishes followed in 1890 and '91. When the 1891 season ended the A.A. was absorbed by the National League and the Browns moved into the senior circuit where they would eventually change their name to the St. Louis Cardinals. (For the continuing adventures of this club, see St. Louis Cardinals.)

The American League version of the St. Louis Browns started out as the Milwaukee Brewers in 1901. After finishing in the A.L. basement, the franchise was moved to St. Louis for the 1902 season and renamed the

Browns. Before the season began the Browns raided the rival N.L. Cardinals for two future Hall of Famers — Jesse Burkett and Bobby Wallace — and also grabbed their three best pitchers. The result was a second-place finish that season.

Unfortunately this was the best finish the club would have for the next 20 years as the Browns sunk to sixth place the following season and stayed mostly in the second division for the next four decades. They did not win a pennant until 1944. (In 1954 the Browns became the modern day Baltimore Orioles.)

1908 St. Louis Browns

St. Louis Cardinals

National League - 1892 - Present
Record - (1892-1919) - 1632 - 2425

When the American Association was absorbed by the National League after the 1891 season the St. Louis Browns became part of a new reorganized N.L. Manager Charles Commiskey, who had just guided the club to three straight second-place finishes in the A.A., left the club for Cincinnati, and owner Chris Von der Ahe appointed himself manager for the 1892 season.

The result was a disaster, as the Browns nose-dived to an eleventh-place finish in the split season of 1892 and then spent the next decade in or near the league cellar. The club, which went through numerous managerial changes in the 1890's, finished in last place, some 63.5 games out of first in 1897, and followed this by losing a club-record 111 games in 1898, once more finishing in last place, another 63.5 games out.

Von der Ahe finally went bankrupt in 1899, and the club was taken over by Frank and Stanley Robison, who also controlled the Cleveland Spiders. They transferred all the best players from the Spiders, including three future Hall of Famers — Cy Young, Bobby Wallace and Jesse Burkett, to St. Louis. This resulted in a fifth-place finish in 1899. The club was called the Perfectos for that one season, and then it was finally renamed the Cardinals in 1900.

The Cardinals managed to rise as high as fourth place in 1901, but in 1902 (after Young, Wallace and Burkett had all deserted the club for the upstart American League) the Cardinals descended into the second division for the next dozen years. In 1914 manager Miller Huggins guided the club to a third-place finish. In 1915 rookie Rogers Hornsby joined the team; he would go on to win six batting titles while with the Cards. In 1917 the club managed another third-place finish, but third was as high as the Cardinals would go until 1925 when they finally won their first N.L. pennant.

St. Louis Maroons

Union Association - 1884

Record - 94 - 19

National League - 1885 - 1886

Record - 79 - 151

The St. Louis Maroons were owned by Henry V. Lucas, the founder and president of the upstart Union Association, which attempted to become a third major league in 1884. Lucas spared no expense when he raided the A.A. and N.L. to stock up his club with players. The result was a team that outclassed the rest of the Union Association, as the Maroons racked up a 94-19 record, and cruised to a first-place finish some 21 games ahead of second-place Cincinnati.

The Maroons were sparked by infielder Fred Dunlap, whose .412 batting average and 13 homers were tops in the league, and pitchers Billy Taylor, who abandoned the Maroons in mid-season to go back to the A.A. after posting a 24-7 record for the Maroons, and Charlie Sweeney, who posted a 25-14 record after leaving the N.L.'s Providence Grays to take Taylor's place on the Maroons.

When the Union Association folded at the end of the season, the Maroons were the only U.A. club to survive, and in 1885 they were admitted to the National League. But the Maroons found the going to be rough in the N.L as the club went through two losing seasons, finishing in last place in '85 and sixth in '86. They were unable to compete with the crosstown-rival Browns at the box office, and the club folded after the 1886 season.

St. Louis Terriers

Federal League - 1914 - 1915
Record - 149 -156

After a last-place finish in 1914 the Terriers bolstered their lineup by stealing future Hall of Fame pitcher Eddie Plank from the A.A.'s Philadelphia Athletics, and infielder Charlie Deal from the N.L.'s Boston Braves.

In 1915 Plank and fellow starters Dave Davenport and Doc Crandall all had 20 win seasons, and Deal batted .323 as the Terriers rebounded to end the season in second place with a 87-67 record, only one percentage point behind Chicago, in the closest pennant race in major league history.

The Terriers, and the league, folded at the end of the 1915 season.

St. Paul Saints

Union Association - 1884
Record - 2 - 6

In September of 1884 the St. Paul Saints (who were also known as the White Caps) had just finished a season in the minor Northwestern League when the Union Association called upon them to play the remaining games of the Pittsburgh Stogies.

The Saints played a total of nine games in the U.A. (two wins, six losses, and one tie) to make them the shortest-lived franchise in major league history, and all the games were played on the road, which makes the Saints the only big-league club to never have played a home game.

When the season was over, the Union Association went out of business.

Syracuse Stars

National League - 1879

Record - 22 - 48

American Association - 1890

Record - 55 - 72

The Syracuse Stars had been very successful franchise in the minor International Association when they moved up to the National League in 1879, along with the Buffalo Bisons.

The N.L.'s insistence on a 50-cent admission fee proved to be fatal for the Stars, as it turned out that the local fans would just not pay that kind of money to watch a losing team. The club was $2,500 in debt when it folded in early September with two weeks still remaining on the schedule.

In 1890 the American Association, facing defections of whole clubs to the Players League, recruited three smaller cities (Syracuse, Rochester and Toledo) to help fill in the holes. The Stars, who managed to finish sixth in an eight-team league, were then dropped from the A.A. (along with Rochester and Toledo) after the season was over and the Players League had been eliminated.

Toledo Blue Stockings

American Association - 1884

Record - 46 - 58

The Toledo Blue Stockings, who had won the minor Northwestern League pennant in 1883, were admitted to the American Association for the 1884 season. Despite the addition of pitcher Tony Mullane (35-25) to the lineup, the Blue Stockings finished a dismal eighth in a 12-team league. When the A.A. cut down to eight clubs for the next season, Toledo was dropped from the circuit.

The Blue Stockings made history when they defied baseball's unofficial color bar by including major league baseball's first black player, catcher Moses Fleetwood Walker, in their lineup. Fleet's brother Welday also played briefly for the club. After Walker was released by Toledo in September due to injuries, no black player was allowed to compete at a major league level again, until Jackie Robinson put on a Brooklyn Dodger uniform in 1947.

Toledo Maumees

American Association - 1890
Record - 68 - 64

In 1890 the American Association, which faced defections of whole clubs to the Players League, tried to shore up their faltering circuit by recruiting four new teams. Three of the new franchises were located in the small cities of Syracuse, Rochester and Toledo.

The Toledo Maumees, sparked by the bat of outfielder Ed Swartwood (.327) and the pitching of Egyptian Healy (22-21), had a winning season and finished a respectable fourth. But none of the three small cities proved capable of supporting a big league club. When the season (and the Players League war) ended, the Association promptly dropped Toledo and the other two clubs from the league.

Troy Trojans

National League - 1879 - 1882
Record - 134 - 191

In their four years in the National League the Troy Trojans (who were also known as the Haymakers) never had a winning season. During this period they had five future Hall of Famers on the club at various times. Pitchers Mickey Welch and Tim Keefe, and sluggers Roger Connor, Dan Brouthers and Buck Ewing were all Trojans at one time or another, yet the highest the club ever managed to finish was fourth place in 1880.

Troy, N.Y., with a population of 57,000, was definitely not a major league city. Troy had originally been granted a big league franchise as part of a successful manoeuvre by the N.L. to drive a couple of New York State minor leagues out of business. The Trojans generally averaged about 400 spectators per game, and on one occasion in 1881 only 12 paying customers showed up for a rain-soaked contest with Chicago, to set an all-time-low major league attendance record.

The club finally folded after the 1882 season and the franchise was moved to New York City, where it eventually became known as the New York Giants.

1881-1882 Troy Club

Washington Nationals

American Association - 1884
Record - 12 - 51

The A.A. version of the Washington Nationals was thrown together in haste, in an attempt to challenge the Union Association's club of the same name. The A.A. Nationals, who were composed of a bunch of nobodies, soon found that the popularity of the U.A. Nationals was too great to overcome. After compiling a horrendous 12-51 record, the A.A. Nationals folded in early August, 1884.

Washington Nationals

Union Association - 1884

Record - 47 - 65

The Washington Nationals can trace their roots back to 1859 when as an amateur club, they played in the backyard of the White House. In the 1870's the Nationals became part of baseball's first pro league, the National Association.

The Union Association version of the Nationals had been formed in 1883 as an independent club, and already had a following when they joined the U.A. for the 1884 season.

The club, which was mainly composed of local amateurs, managed to finish the season in sixth place. After the season was over and the U.A. had folded, the Nationals survived to play the next season in the minor Eastern League, then they joined the National League in 1886. (For the continuing adventures of this club, see Washington Senators.)

Washington W. & Ball Club of Union Association of 1884

Washington Senators

National League - 1886 - 1889, Record - 163 -337

American Association - 1891, Record - 43 - 92

National League - 1892 - 1899, Record - 410 - 697

American League - 1901 - 1960, Record - (1901-1919) - 1235 - 1570

The Washington club that entered the National League in 1886 was pretty much the same team that had won the previous season's Eastern League pennant, and the year before that, had played in the Union Association. The club, which was also known as the Statesmen, finished in last place, some 60 games behind first-place Chicago, in 1886. That year they acquired a young rookie catcher by the name of Connie Mack who went on to become one of baseball's best defensive catchers (before spending 50 years managing the Philadelphia A's).

The Senators managed to finish next to last in 1887, but then ended up in the basement again in '88 and '89. When 11 of their players jumped to the Players League at the end of the '89 season the club decided to fold rather than get caught up in the impending Players League war.

When the Players League war ended after the 1890 season another Senators club was installed in Washington for the 1891 season, this time as an American Association franchise. The club, which had to start from scratch, went through four managers and several dozen players that year, before ending up in last place some 50 games out of first.

When the American Association was absorbed by the National League after the 1891 season, the Senators were moved into the new 12-team N.L. in 1882. The club was owned by two entrepreneur brothers by the name of J. Earl and George Wagner, who cared more about making money than they did about putting a good team on the field. When the Wagners weren't busy trading away the club's best players for a profit, they were busy hiring and firing managers. As a result the Senators spent the next eight years wallowing in the second division of National League, never finishing higher than seventh.

When the N.L. cut down to eight clubs after the 1899 season, Washington was one of four clubs that were dropped.

When the American League declared itself a major league in 1901, a franchise was installed in Washington, and a new version of the Senators was born. After a sixth-place finish in their first season, the club added slugger Ed Delahanty to their lineup. He led the league with 43 doubles and a .376 batting average in 1902, but the Senators still finished in sixth place.

In 1903, following the untimely death of Delahanty and much squabbling among the club brass, the Senators ended up in last place. And things got worse the following season: not only did they finish in the basement once again, some 55.5 games out of first, but they lost a club-

1888 Washington Senators

record 113 games. What followed was a series of last-place and next-to-last-place finishes for the next seven years.

In 1907 the Senators signed a young fireballer by the name of Walter Johnson. Johnson would go on to win 417 games in his next 21 seasons with the Senators, and is considered by many to be the greatest pitcher of all time.

But the club did not have a winning season until Clark Griffin took over as manager in 1912. Griffin revamped the lineup with younger players and the Senators finished the season in second place with a 91-61 record. Johnson won 33 games that year, and led the league with a 1.39 ERA.

The Senators came in second again in 1913. It was Johnson's best season ever — he went 36-7, had a league-leading 1.14 ERA and struck out 243 batters while walking only 38. He also led the league with 11 shutouts.

The Senators slipped out of contention the following season, finishing up in third, some 19 games out. And, with the exception of a four games back, third-place finish in war-shortened 1918, the Senators stayed out of contention until 1924 when they finally managed to win their first pennant (and a 37-year-old Walter Johnson got to play in his first World Series).

Wilmington Quicksteps

Union Association - 1884
Record - 2 - 16

After the Wilmington Quicksteps had clinched the minor Eastern League pennant in mid-August with a 51-12 record, Union Association president Henry V. Lucas invited the club to join the U.A. as a replacement for the ailing Philadelphia Keystones.

On August 18, soon after Wilmington joined the U.A., several of their best players left for the greener pastures of the American Association and the Quicksteps were only able to compile a 2-16 record during the next month.

Poor attendance at home (they averaged about 400 fans per game) forced the club to fold in mid-September, unable to finish out the season.

Worcester Ruby Legs

National League - 1880 - 1882
Record - 90 - 159

In 1880 the Worcester Ruby Legs (also known as the Brown Stockings) moved up from the minor National Base-Ball Association to take the recently departed Syracuse Stars' spot in the National League. The highlight of the Ruby Legs' first N.L. season occurred on June 12 when their pitching ace Lee Richmond retired 27 batters in a row to record the first perfect game in major league history, a 1-0 win over the Cleveland Blues.

The Ruby Legs managed a respectable fifth-place finish that year, but then ended up in the league basement for the next two seasons. When the 1882 season was over the N.L. decided it was time to re-admit Philadelphia and New York City to the league, so they ousted their two smallest cities, Troy and Worcester, to make room for the two big cities.

Index